CF

GW00696662

5/96

50p

AUSTRIA

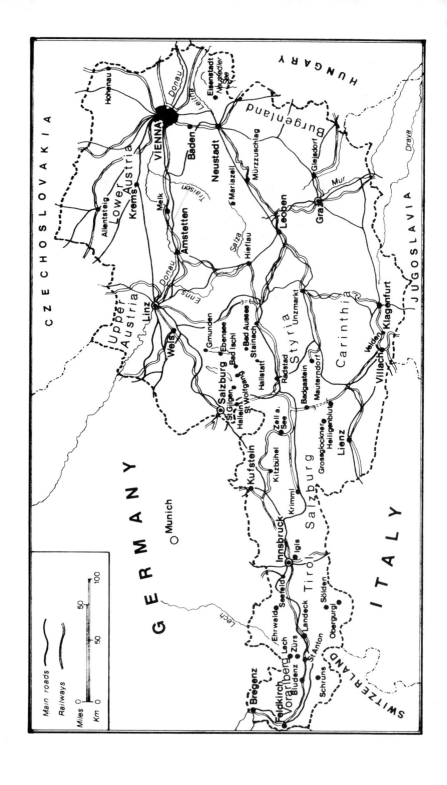

AUSTRIA

TRICIA HAYNES

B.T. BATSFORD LTD, LONDON

To Minn

ISBN 0 7134 5098 3

Typeset by Vision Typesetting, Manchester
Printed in Great Britain by
The Bath Press, Bath
for the publishers
B.T. Batsford Ltd
4 Fitzhardinge Street
London W1H 0AH

Contents

Acknowledgments

The author would like to thank the Austrian Embassy, the Austrian National Tourist Offices in London, Vienna, Salzburg and Kitzbühel, and particularly Dr Louise Oberrieder, Frau Traudl Lisey, Frau Roswitha Holz and Dr Josef Ziepl for their assistance during the research of this book. In addition she would like to thank Friederike Krammer-Hirsch, Julia Gerner and Peter Gurtler.

The author would also like to thank the following for kind permission to reproduce their photographs: the Austrian National Tourist Offices in London, Vienna, Salzburg and Kitzbühel; the Venice-Simplon Orient Express.

I

INTRODUCTION

'Land der Berge, Land am Strome' (land of mountains, land of the stream) – so runs the opening bars of Austria's national anthem. In 1918 Austria became a republic and the Austrians needed a suitable tune to symbolize their new status, so they looked for inspiration in their landscape. The poet Paula von Preradovic wrote the lyrics to Mozart's melody based on his *Brüder reicht die Hand zum Bunde*, and the anthem was warmly received by her compatriots.

Ever since the Babenbergs, the Austrians have seemed paradoxical to the rest of Europe. On the one hand they are traditionalists, on the other, avant-garde; cautious to the point of dullness, yet vociferous over issues like the 1985 energy plan to build a hydroelectric power plant in the Vienna Woods. While an Austrian will complain about paying his taxes he will cheerfully pay for the arts.

The popular conception of Austria abroad is of a country filled with people who have a propensity for music and merriment; and to substantiate the notion Austria can claim an impressive number of composers and musicians from Wolfgang Amadeus Mozart to Arnold Schoenberg. To their credit the Austrians cultivated that untranslatable cliché, Gemutlichkeit, a seemingly effortless charm which makes visitors feel at home. If Vienna is a mere two hours flying time from London can it simply be the Austrians' proverbial love of gaiety that makes their country so different, so appealing, so simple to get along in?

In a way it is. A landlocked country usually looks in on itself and whether it likes it or not, exudes a particular image. Austria, a federal state of 32,367 square miles (83,827 sq. km) (more than double the size of Switzerland) lies in southern central Europe and is surrounded by Czechoslovakia, Hungary, Yugoslavia, Italy, Germany, Switzerland and Liechtenstein. It is predominantly an Alpine country made up of nine provinces: Upper Austria, Lower Austria, Salzburg, Styria, Burgenland, Carinthia, Tirol, Vorarlberg and Vienna, where the saying is 'everyone is against everyone else'.

For centuries Austria was a melting pot for Hungarians, Czechs and Slovenes. 'Asia,' said Metternich 'begins at the Landstrasse' (the main thoroughfare of the eastern district of Vienna). Today Austria offers temporary asylum to refugees passing from one country to another and as a result its population, which at present stands at 7,500,000, an increase of 100,000 since 1971, fluctuates.

Celts were living in present-day Austria when the Romans arrived and began making their settlements along the Danube. They planted vineyards and made use of the hot springs which these days comprise the spas of Bad Gastein, Baden and Ischl. Migrations of tribes from the north soon followed. Over the succeeding centuries Austria survived the Thirty Years' War, staved off Turkish sieges, Napoleonic armies and a 640 year rule by the Habsburgs. In 1914 Archduke Franz Ferdinand was assassinated at Sarajevo, thus sparking off the First World War. It was the end of an empire and from then on Austria faced a series of crises from the murder of Chancellor Dollfuss in 1934 to the annexation of Austria by Adolf Hitler in 1938.

Through the centuries the Austrians learned to live with assassinations, murders and suicides in the Royal House of Austria from Elizabeth of Bavaria's murder in Switzerland to Crown Prince Rudolf's suicide in Mayerling. When the Nazis marched into Vienna in 1938 a yet darker shadow fell over Austria.

After the 'Anschluss' the Austrians never anticipated living happily ever after. Many fled to America, including psychoanalyst Sigmund Freud. The fact that in 1985 Austrians celebrated 40 years of the reinstatement of their once glorious republic came as something of a surprise to them, and today they still prefer to discuss rather than war. Their predilection for reasonableness, rather than action, has always been part of the Austrian psyche.

Psychological distances, as well as physical ones, separated the provinces, making the Austrians of the Tirol a different breed from those of Burgenland at the other end of the country. Austrians themselves admit it takes a foreigner to lead a rebellion, which makes it all the more astonishing that thousands of them should get so angry about the proposed hydroelectric power plant at Hainburg that they were ready to make public demonstrations.

Nor is it in any way unusual to discover as you travel through the country that Austrians in one province have a totally different view from those in another. The landscape of Austria itself varies in its nine provinces, so it is not unusual to find the Austrians themselves in disagreement over certain issues. The Viennese are criticised for being snobbish, the Salzburgers for seeming like Bavarians, the Vorarlbergers for being provincial, and so it goes on.

Austria stretches from the eastern Alps to the Danube basin, yet although it has no seaboard it has close links with Italy and Yugoslavia, its Mediterranean neighbours. It is one of Europe's most densely wooded countries with forests covering 44 per cent of the land. It is also mountainous with vast areas of gneiss and granite highlands, Alpine foothills and a range of northern Alps. Its highest mountain is the Grossglockner which reaches 12,465ft (3800m). Its mountain areas have triggered fantastic feats of engineering in highways over mountain passes (like the spiralling Grossglockner Pass from Salzburg to Carinthia) and railroads (like that of the Arlberg tunnel). East Tirol was formerly cut off, but, thanks to roadbuilders and engineers, it is now easily accessible.

Austria has its grasslands in the Pannonian lowlands where a huge colony of birds has its habitat in the reeds and marshes of Lake Neusiedler, the only steppe lake in Central Europe. Alpine meadows show a range of flowers from Edelweiss to gentianella, Alpine asters and pansies. Alpine plants grow above the upper limits of the forests and bloom through July to September. Austrian fir trees grow above 1500ft (460m). Above 4000ft (1220m), the fir gives way to Zirbe (pine trees). On the northern slopes Fichte (spruce) grows and on the limestone ranges is the Austrian black pine.

Weather

While Austria lies in a temperate zone there are still seasonal differences, with the Alpine hills getting more rain than the Pannonal region. On the whole the climate ranges from 1 °C (34 °F) in January to 18–22 °C (64–72 °F), in summer. In Vienna the summer can seem much hotter than by the lakes, and by late April is beginning to get surprisingly warm due to its southern position. While spring and early autumn can be good months for the lake regions and for touring the surrounding areas, there can be fog on occasions. The Föhn, the wind felt north of the Alps, bothers some people – they claim it has strange effects on them – but affects others not at all. Summer is an ideal time to visit the Salzkammergut, while the Tirol with its fashionable ski resorts is for the winter months, autumn and spring for museums and the opera.

Wildlife

Wildlife in Austria varies from roe deer to hare, pheasant, partridge and chamois in the upper mountain ranges. Around the lakes and marshes populations of birds thrive, while in the lakes and rivers trout, carp and pike await the keen angler.

Art and museums

Art treasures are as much a part of Austria as its landscapes, from monasteries like Melk Abbey in Lower Austria to museums such as the Imperial Treasury in Vienna which houses a wealth of antiquities from ancient manuscripts, and the eighth-century Tassilo chalice, one of the oldest in the Christian world, in Kremsmunster Abbey in Upper Austria. Add to that a plethora of architectural styles, from the likes of Fischer von Erlach to art nouveau, exponents like Otto Wagner, music contrasting from Mozart to Anton von Webern, the light-hearted ambience of the Heuriger taverns in the Vienna Woods, and you will see that Austria is a country of distractions.

Museums are a delight. Some are traditional, others unusual, like the Museum of Hairdressing at Feldkirch in the Vorarlberg. There's a cider museum in St Marienkirch in Upper Austria, and in Pernegg in Styria is a museum specialising in drugs and distilling. Skiing museums showing the start of the sport in Austria abound. There are plenty of wine museums too, but do not overlook the Museum of Crime in the Scharnstein Palace in Upper Austria.

The Danube valley

The Danube, the second longest river in Europe and the longest in Central Europe, flows through eastern Austria for only 224 miles (358km). On its banks stand the cities of Vienna and Linz, and the great Abbey of Melk. The Danube could never have been blue due to the amount of shipping it supported, but nonetheless it is a romantic river as it winds past abbeys, monasteries and vineyards. In Roman times it was a strategic route, and ever after was the route chosen by invading armies from the Turks to Napoleon's troops.

The Nibelung

The mythical Nibelung, a race of dwarfs, dwelt in the Danube valley and comprised one of Bavaria's greatest sagas. Eventually they became synonymous with the Burgundians, the enemies of the Huns. The epic is based on fifth-century legends telling of the Huns' defeat of the Burgundians' kingdom, and the final annihilation of the Nibelung. As part of her plan of revenge, which simmered for 13 years, Kriemhild, the sister of the King of Burgundy, married Attila the Hun, as the first step in her plan to wipe out the Huns, and sailed down the Danube with him.

The Danube was linked not only with the Nibelung but also gave its name to the Danube School of Painting, which flourished in the early sixteenth century and was so called because artists painted scenes of the river.

Architecture

All over Austria the differences in the domestic architecture of the nine provinces are very much apparent. The Danube Plain is noted for its farm buildings constructed around a central courtyard, while the Vorarlberg prefers the Appenzell houses found in Switzerland and the Rhineland with their apex roofs and shutters at the windows. Gabled roofs characterise the houses of the Tirol, the walls of which are often enlivened by paintings.

Town planning in Styria and Carinthia is particularly noticeable as most towns of any size are built around the Strassenplatz, a wide, rectangular street which doubles as a square, while the main square of most provincial towns have their *Pestäule* columns, erected to the victims of the plague at the end of the seventeenth century, and usually a fountain as well. Even the agricultural aspects of the provinces differ. You have only to glance at a haystack in Carinthia, or note the corn drying from the gables of the village houses in the Burgenland, to realise this. On the roadsides as you drive through the towns and villages you will notice wooden crosses, often with roofs, shrines to Our Lady, and bidstocks, tall rounded posts with roofs, sometimes decorated with paintings.

Fairs

Fairs are held in several towns throughout the year ranging from the International Spring Fair in Vienna and the Spring Fair held at the beginning of May in Graz, to agricultural and autumn fairs. Innsbruck holds a fair at the end of September. Some regions, like the Tirol, hold religious festivals and processions, such as the spring Corpus Christi. Throughout Austria 15 August is celebrated with street processions, as is the grape harvest at the end of September (or beginning of October) in wine-growing areas like the Burgenland and Lower Austria. The New Year is celebrated in winter ski resorts by masked downhill races and torchlight ski processions, while Vienna, during Fasching (the Lent Carnival) is the scene of lavish balls including the Grand Opera Ball.

National costume

Regional costumes are not just aired on fête days either, for the Austrians take pride in their national dress and never more so than in Styria where the Steirer Anzug, the grey suit with its green lapels, is virtually a uniform, while the ladies favour the dirndl. Originally each province sported its own national dress, but today's fashions tend to be a blur of regional styles. The dirndl from Salzburg, however, is still worn with a white blouse and bodice. In the Vorarlberg the fringed scarf is much in evidence, while the Linz bonnet is favoured on occasions by the older generation, but the dirndl, bodice and apron are ubiquitous at festive events. Costume museums in Innsbruck, Vienna, Salzburg and Graz illustrate the finer points of Austrian dress.

A recent survey showed no less than 81 per cent of Austrians being in favour of national dress, from leather breeches, kalmyk jackets from the Waldviertel, to loden coats. Emperor Franz Josef popularised Austria's national costume and the von Trapp family increased this popularity. While the streets of Austria's main cities will show fine examples of day-to-day traditional wear, from hunting hats to knitted stockings, at festivals embroidered blouses of the Wachau make their appearance alongside the lace aprons of the Burgenland and velvet waistcoats of Carinthia, while the men suffice with their leather knickerbockers and hunting jackets.

Traditionally, married and unmarried women could be distinguished by their dress. In the Vorarlberg married women folded their scarves in a special way, while the ladies of the Wachau sported golden bonnets (the bonnet was always associated with married women) while the ladies of Linz handed down their bonnets from one generation to the next.

You can buy Austrian national dress in the smart shops of Vienna and Salzburg – some shops specialise solely in national costume, their windows displaying a colourful splash of reds and hunting greens, enlivened by patterned, fringed shawls – but it takes an Austrian to carry off national costume with aplomb. Indeed they say it takes an Austrian face to wear a hunting hat. The wearing of national dress, and not just on special occasions, shows a sense of national pride.

Government and society

These days Austria is a parliamentary democracy, with the Nationalrat and Bundesrat forming the country's main legislative bodies. The Nationalrat, or Lower House, comprises the three chief political parties: the Austrian Socialist party, the SPÖ, Social Democrats with 80 seats; the Austrian Peoples Party, the ÖVP (Öesterreichische Volkspartei) Christian Democrats with 77 seats, and the Liberals or FPÖ (Freiheitliche Partei Österreichs) with 18 seats (finally the Green Party with 8). There is also a Communist Party founded in 1918 immediately after the proclamation of the Republic.

The Bundesrat or Upper House's representation is by province, and thus illustrates the federal aspects of Austria's system of government. Since the establishment of the Second Republic, the balance of power has been between the Socialist Party and the People's Party. The Federal government is headed by the Chancellor and his Cabinet, who administer those government affairs not handled by the President. Basic rights have been part of Austrian rule ever since the Austro-Hungarian monarchy. There is no discrimination regarding birth, sex, status, class, religion, race or language. Legislation is based on the principles contained in the United Nations Declaration of Human Rights of 1948.

Austria's armed forces provide national military defence and are pledged to assist other countries at the request of such international bodies as the International Red Cross Society. As for labour relations, Austrian employees are represented by the Austrian Trade Union Federation (ÖGB) and the Chambers of Labour and Agriculture. Membership of the Trade Union Federation is voluntary.

From 1918 Austria was plagued by strikes, with employers and employees at loggerheads. Disputes continued for nearly two decades, which accounts for today's non-strike action policies. (There were only four strikes in 1983.) No longer do opposing factions harangue each other with grievances. They simply sit down at the table and talk, with the proverbial reasonableness for which Austria is famed, until an amicable solution is arrived at. The word 'strike', which arouses such tension in other nations, has almost passed out of the Austrian's vocabulary.

What the visitor to Austria notes most, in fact, is this very reasonableness so that he begins to wonder what, if anything, does arouse passions. If a citizen is too protected surely he is likely to run the danger of becoming complacent? Life in Austria today does seem a little too overprotected, with the social services taking care of each citizen from birth to death with amazing efficiency. The average Austrian is concerned with his health, the environment, his 40 hour working week and his annual paid holiday. Working women who are expecting a child are entitled to leave of absence, two months prior to the birth of a child and two months after, during which social insurance allowance is paid. The Austrian Health Service is an excellent one with most people covered by insurance against illness and accidents. There are also private health schemes. Austria is in the vanguard of health incentives. Scattered throughout the world from the Gambia to Europe you can see in operation the SOS Children's Villages set up by Hermann Gmeiner.

Better health is the aim of most Austrians. Great advances have been made regarding the care of old people, who now have a wide range of social services to call upon, from improved intensive care, meals on wheels and home helps, enabling them to remain in their own homes instead of clinics.

Austria's standard of living is amongst the highest in the world. With the Austrian schilling closely tied to the German mark, Austria has tried to keep inflation down by keeping as many people in employment as is conceivably possible. Its economic record has been a source of envy to many of its close neighbours; but for how long can it last? Equality has long been a policy with the Austrians which has meant more and more women seeking employment. Women constitute 52 per cent of the total population and women's emancipation has long been a *fait accompli* in Austria. The law reform of 1975 implemented complete equality between husband and wife with each sharing responsibility for the family and maintaining the home. A woman need no longer take her husband's name if she chooses not to. Partnership is the operative word. Fraulein has been replaced by Frau, Doktor or equivalent title, and the male faction makes no objections.

The Austrian government's policy of neutrality has meant that Austria has become a place of asylum for many different nationalities. Since 1955 Austria has been a member of the United Nations (Austrian Kurt Waldheim, now Austrian President, was elected as the Secretary General in 1972 and remained in office until 1981) but it is not a member of the EEC. In the centre of Europe, Austria has continued as a crossroads. If at times domestic attitudes seem introverted it is largely due to Austria's inability, or the desire, to do anything at speed. The Austrians much prefer to mull over things before arriving at major decisions.

Tourism

But while reforms are taking place on the domestic front, Austria is obliged to look to tourism to stay afloat financially. Whereas mountain passes once cut off Austria from its neighbours (the Tirol is a case in point which, until the Arlberg massif was blasted to make way for the $6\frac{1}{2}$ mile (10km) tunnel in 1884, was effectively blocked off), construction of mountain passes such as the Grossglockner and the Brenner, and motorways like the Tauern highway which straddles the Alpine chain between Salzburg and Carinthia, have made access easy and opened up the Tirol to travel and tourism. The Arlberg Pass, a 6000ft (1828m) high route through the eastern Alps, was once the only crossing between Switzerland and Innsbruck. Snow often blocked the route, but with the completion of the Pass – the fastest Alpine tunnel ever – a route was opened to central Europe.

As 40 per cent of Austria is wooded, the image of the cosy Gasthaus with its friendly proprietor is still true in many mountain areas. The Austrians are noted for their easy-going friendliness, and nowhere more so than in the Alps, where hospitality is legendary. The ski slopes are an easy venue for tour operators to sell. Not only are they picturesque, but Austria has some of the best skiing to be found anywhere in the world. But, surprisingly, summer visitors almost outpace the winter sports enthusiasts.

While more visitors pour in annually, Austria has to build more hotels and pensions to accommodate them. As the ski runs grow more crowded and the queues for the lifts and cable cars longer, so new locations must be found with the result that new installations have scarred the slopes, and still the crowds go on increasing. Soon the small family Gasthaus will all but vanish except in remote mountain areas.

Not only are tourists descending on rural and urban areas, they are also buying up as much porcelain as their bags will carry. Souvenirs are another money spinner as well as ski equipment. The winter sports industry nets Austria a 40 per cent share of the ski market. The friendly image of the tourism industry spills over into Austria's towns and cities such as Vienna, where foreigners try to get their hands on tickets for the opera, and meanwhile stay in such hotels as the Sacher, where on occasion it is almost impossible to get a room.

Austrians

The Austrian, who has been variously represented as a yodeller, a Schuhplattler (pleasure seeker) and as a frivolous fellow besotted with the operettas of Franz Lehar, is, in fact, a staunch traditionalist. Austrians not only like their national costume, they wear it whenever an occasion arises. Loden coats and Tirolean hats banded by roped cords and chamois brushes are commonplace in the streets of Vienna, Linz and Innsbruck. Austrians are likely to be as traditional about behaviour and service as they are about dress and institutions. One has only to go to a Weinstube, Gasthaus or Konditorei to notice the service. Even in the most modest Keller, bar or café you will be helped on and off with your coat on arrival and departure and be greeted by 'Grüss Gott' (God's greetings). Austrians shrug if you mention the fact, exclaiming that it is quite normal. Their general attitude is one of caution coupled with scepticism. Even the youth of cities such as Vienna remain traditionalists rather than innovators. On the surface at least it appears to be *Alles in Ordnung*. And that's the way the Austrians like it.

Most of the population are German speaking. In Burgenland and Carinthia you may hear Slovene and Croat. Many Austrians are good linguists, speaking English, French and Italian. Emperor Franz Josef spoke with a distinct Viennese accent although he was purported to speak five other languages as well.

Thirty per cent of Austrians live in the five main cities of Vienna, Graz, Salzburg, Linz and Innsbruck, all of which number over 10,000 inhabitants. Industrial cities, such as Linz, have lured workers away from agricultural areas so that today only about ten per cent of the labour force is employed on the land.

Culture

During Empress Maria Theresa's reign, school reform of 1774 set up the state educational system. From that moment on there have been endless reforms. Austria has long been intellectually represented. The National Library in Vienna is one of the most important in the world and contains a fine collection of manuscripts. Monasteries and abbeys like Melk in Lower Austria, Admont in Styria and Klosterneuburg in Vienna contain priceless collections. Religious paintings and frescoes can be seen in the multitudinous churches scattered across the country. The architectural heritage of Vienna still has the ability to surprise and in some cases shock, from high baroque to art nouveau.

Austria is synonymous with music – Wolfgang Amadeus Mozart has ensured that – but it is also noted for its philosophers, among them Ludwig von Wittgenstein, psychoanalysts like Sigmund Freud and Arthur Adler, and painters such as Gustav Klimt whose work is enjoying a revival. Today the country is obliged to contend with a clutch of economic and political complexities from wine production to proposals for hydroelectric power plants.

Traditional souvenirs

Visitors (the largest percentage of foreign tourists comes from West Germany, closely followed by the Dutch, Belgians, British, French and Americans) will see none of the Austrian's domestic attitude at a superficial glance as they window shop in Vienna or gaze upon the architectural splendours of Salzburg. They are more likely to encounter the Gemütlichkeit of the average Austrian as he does business with them in his porcelain factory, or as they buy up the glassware at the Riedel factory (noted for the classical sophistication of its designs) and shop in the boutiques lining the Graben and Karntnerstrasse which sell the most famous of Austria's craft exports, the *petit point* embroidery which has an international reputation.

Each province has its own specialities from china in the Burgenland and the unusual amber coloured Bernstein (from the village of this name), a kind of jade, to Bregenz dolls in the Vorarlberg, wrought iron in Upper Austria, *petit point* embroidery – a Viennese tradition which dates back to Empress Maria Theresa's time – in Lower Austria, Mozartkugeln chocolates in distinctive hexagonal red boxes in Salzburg, linen in Styria and ceramics in Carinthia. But while the typical Austrian makes light of his industry, feigning to be a playboy, or at the very least a romantic violinist, the work gets done. Crystal chandeliers made in Austria grace the Metropolitan Opera House in New York, the Council Room in the Kremlin, and the Hilton Hotel in Paris. Vienna's own State Opera House exhibits a fine display of Austrian crystal.

As for porcelain, the Vienna Augarten range, specialising in rococo designs, finds immediate buyers. Replicas of the famous Lippizaner stallions in Augarten porcelain are highly prized and can be bought in all sizes. Noted for their remarkable craftsmanship, they have been given to Queen Elizabeth II and President Reagan. The first Augarten porcelain factory was founded in 1717. Empress Maria Theresa was so impressed by the quality she installed a workshop at Augarten. The factory went on to make the Schonbrunn service for Napoleon.

Enamel work is also popular. In Vienna alone there are 50 firms employing workers to make tapestries, handbags, jewelcases and such like in *petit point*, many of which are exported to the USA. Austrian craftsmanship is good and reliable, for despite the fact that Austrians claim to prefer artistic pursuits to industrial hard work, they still know how to produce a well made product.

Antiques are a great speciality of Austria. Most visitors to Vienna will head for the Dorotheum, originally founded as a pawnbroker's, and today a famous auction room and mecca for collectors. Today the Dorotheum auction rooms have branches in Graz, Innsbruck, Salzburg, Linz, Klagenfurt and Wiener Neustadt. If you don't buy every souvenir from alpenstocks to rucksacks, lederhosen, hunting hats and porcelain, at airports you will find Wildlife Appeal drops where you can deposit any remaining schillings before leaving

Austria. Austrians are keen conservationists, enamoured of their parks and green spaces as well as wildlife.

Travel

Austrian Airlines and British Airways operate regular flights from London to Vienna. The individual traveller may take an airticket to a major city like Vienna, Salzburg and Innsbruck. Dan Air operates a three times weekly service by Britain's new BAe 146 jet from Gatwick to Innsbruck. Package tour operators offer comprehensive packages to the Carinthian lakes, lasting seven or fourteen days, which will probably cost not much more than a regular return air ticket from London to Vienna. Winter sports operators arrange a variety of package holidays to ski resorts, some of which include ski passes. Charter flight deals operated by companies such as Pegasus, from London to Vienna and Salzburg, can be obtained considerably cheaper than regular scheduled flights. No advance purchase is necessary as flights depend on seat availability. You may well find yourself flying Austrian Airlines on a charter price ticket if you approach the right charter company. Several such companies have extended their European operations to include Vienna and Salzburg, so it is wisest to get the latest update from travel agencies.

There are other ways of reaching Austria, such as package coach holidays. You can reach Innsbruck directly from London by Europabus. By car you can arrive in Austria by autobahn from Germany and Switzerland. Once in Austria the tollroads, and sometimes breathtaking Alpine motorways such as the Tauern highway which climbs over the Alps, make towns and winter resorts easily accessible. Most ski resorts can be reached by bus or train from main airports. Ski areas like Kitzbühel are so close to Bavaria – a mere 80 miles (130km) from Munich – that many day skiers arrive to swell the already crowded resort.

As distance is no problem in Austria and because trains actually run on time, most travellers use the rail network to get from city to city or into the Alps for ski weekends. Austria has 3625 railway miles (5800km) to ride. There is an additional charge for express trains, and if you wish to reserve a seat it costs A.sch.30. Trains are clean and uncrowded, except at peak holiday periods and festivals such as Christmas and Easter, with plenty of space and hooks to hang your coat. Travelling Austrians could not be more helpful. They are pleased to talk to strangers and usually engage you in amiable conversation. Timetables indicating the arrival time and the number of kilometres between stops are distributed in main line stations and on board express trains. When it is foggy in Vienna, as it often is in winter, it is easier to take the train to Salzburg, which has a good serviceable airport with direct flights to and from London, as does Innsbruck. Skiers leaving the city centres also prefer to travel by train or bus as Austrian transportation always makes allowances for skis and ski poles. In the Alps it is commonplace to see buses with a bundle of skis up front, and cars with them on overhead racks, as well as hosts of skiers clanking down the streets with skis hoisted over their shoulders.

Austrian Airlines connect major cities; international air route green 1 goes

1 Venice-Simplon Orient Express

from east to west; amber routes 12 and 13 go from north to south, while blue routes fly to Italy and south-east Europe. Austria has six commercial airports with regular flights by 31 national airlines and 70 charter companies.

Car hire firms make it easy for the independent traveller. You can collect hire cars at airports and gateway points such as Bregenz, Graz, Innsbruck, Klagenfurt, Linz, Salzburg and Vienna. Costs are more expensive in Austria, however, than in Germany due to 30 per cent VAT, so many people hire cars in Switzerland or Germany. VAT is also added to drinks in Austria – something to watch out for in bars and restaurants.

There are currently 600 miles (956km) of motorways and over 20,000 miles (32,000km) of roads. Austria's transit network reaches into remote Alpine valleys and even glaciers. The Venice–Simplon–Orient Express operates a route from Victoria Station through Austria, which passes through the Arlberg tunnel to St Anton, Innsbruck and the Brenner Pass on its way to Venice. The one-way fare per person is £435 inclusive of meals. Passengers can break their journey at Innsbruck, if they wish. Orient Express offices can be found in most major cities of Europe and in New York. You can reach Vienna by train from a variety of European destinations: from Frankfurt – a journey of around seven-and-a-half hours – from Rome and Scandinavia. The Arlberg Express leaves from Paris, via Switzerland, to Innsbruck.

In cities like Vienna you can buy special tickets for travelling around in the city by metro. You simply punch the card in the machines before boarding the train. On all my journeys by subway I was never once asked for my ticket, so the Viennese clearly trust each other. As the trains are comparatively new, and because the Viennese are respecters of property, the coaches, to date, bear not a trace of graffiti.

Bus tours are a good way of seeing the country if you do not want to hire a self-drive car. They give you a sufficiently comprehensive view of the regions so that next time you can visit a particular region with time to spare. Bus and coach services are run by the Federal Authorities, with motor coach excursions organised by local bus companies to well-known tourist spots. Tour operators will be glad to organise individual or group tours within the country to enable you to see something beyond the major cities. Steamer services operate on the Danube and the major Austrian lakes from May to September. The main Austrian toll roads are the Grossglockner High Alpine highway, the Felbertauern highway, Gleinalmtunnel, the Brenner and Tauern motorways and the Arlberg tunnel.

Some bus trips, especially those in the Alps, take you through some staggeringly beautiful scenery. The speed limit on all autobahns is 80mph (130km); on trunk roads 63mph (100km) and in built-up areas 35mph (50km). The wearing of seat belts is obligatory. Austria has several toll roads, most of them in the mountains, and you pay to use the Arlberg tunnel. Austrians drive on the right and measure their distances in kilometres. Some Alpine passes are nerve-racking but offer spectacular views, so although the scenery may be breathtaking, it's best not to take your eyes off the road. It is also safer not to drink and drive. The legal permissible alcohol limit is 0.8 per cent. The minimum fine if you are caught breaking the law is steep, and the confiscation of your driving licence is a foregone conclusion.

If you suffer from vertigo the cable cars rushing up the mountainside may put you in mind of James Bond movies. For those who have mastered their fear of heights, rushing up and down rock faces are the least of their worries. There are close on 4000 cable cars in operation.

Limited parking zones known as Blue Zones with a maximum parking time of 1½ hours are clearly marked. You can obtain parking clocks from tobacconists. The clocks must be displayed on your windscreen. In some cities, such as Vienna and Salzburg, you will have to pay for the parking vouchers. All traffic accidents must be reported to the police. If you should break down on motorways, call the emergency breakdown service operated by the Austrian Automobile Clubs. The service can be used by anyone, not only by nationals.

Accommodation

Hotel accommodation comes in various categories from de luxe to clean, inexpensive pensions. Gasthöfe are good places to stay, many of them having fine reputations and a long history of service. For traditionalists the ambience is truly Austrian. In the Alps the friendly Gasthaus is much favoured by ski groups who can relax in a warm, cosy atmosphere after a day on the pistes.

Hotel accommodation is so comprehensive that it suits all pockets. Hotels are classified according to government standards by five to one star ratings. They range from luxury hotels, such as the Sacher in Vienna, to simple, traditional hotels, often with an excellent restaurant. Some hotels are open seasonally, such as those in winter sports areas. In peak season expect to pay more than at other times, especially in top ski hotels.

Few hotels in Austria carry the de luxe tag except in Salzburg and Vienna, which can rely upon massive influxes of tourists to fill them. First class hotels are usually centrally situated, spotlessly clean and tidy and, although your room may not be ornately decorated, the service will be faultless. Many people favour the more traditional Gasthof which is a good class, comfortable hotel with a more homely atmosphere than an impersonal, de luxe hotel. You will find Gasthöfe in rural areas too. Their atmosphere is friendly and you will probably feel at home right away. The Gasthof is not to be confused with a Gasthaus, which is a country inn, chiefly noted for its restaurant, but which also has a few beds. Smaller than the Gasthof, the Gasthaus can also be a good place to stay *en route* if you are travelling. Chalets and pensions proliferate throughout Austria and in some of the resort towns you will observe the sign *'Zimmer Frei'* (rooms to let). Apartments can also be rented. Some companies specialise in chalets in Alpine areas such as Interhome, Griesgasse 2, Salzburg 5020. If you arrive late in a town without a place to stay the local Tourist Office lists hotels and various accommodations. A Kurhaus is the name of a spa establishment which often offers accommodation and a restaurant, while a Kurhotel offers hotel rooms and cure amenities to its guests.

If you would like to stay somewhere different, and as Austria is the land of castles and ruined fortresses, castle-hotels are the answer. Many castles, some with long and fascinating histories, have been converted into hotels. Tourist Offices can help with these, but some well known ones are the Palais Schwarzenberg in Vienna, Schloss Fuschl on the Fuschlsee, and Schlosshotel Igls near Innsbruck. Austria also has inns of historic interest which you may care to stop at on your journey.

Farmhouse holidays appeal to families. More than 4000 farms all over Austria are ready to take in guests, and you should contact the Tourist Office for a brochure. There are also camping sites, Youth Hostels, and mountain huts in many areas, and should you be interested in taking a cure, spas are the ideal location. Many visitors like to combine treatment with a relaxing, restful holiday and you can do no better than to try one of the 30 Kurhaus resorts. All cures are under medical supervision.

Hotel receptionists all seem to speak English so you get little chance to practise your German unless you insist. On mountain hikes and in more remote areas, especially if you are travelling alone, German can be useful, but wherever you are in Austria, from the Vorarlberg to Vienna, Austrians are only too ready to discuss music, politics or the economy with anyone who cares to do battle with them. They consider their past, from Charlemagne to Empress Maria Theresa, has been a mere rehearsal for the future. They are tired of hearing about their glorious history, and since they hold the opinion that the new Federation of 1918 was constituted by the forces of destiny, they can hardly be to blame that things have turned out the way they have. However, visitors can be forgiven for revelling in Austria's glories and, indeed, can hardly fail to do so. As most of them arrive by air in Vienna or Salzburg they are instantly surrounded by an *embarras de richesses* in architecture, music and the arts.

While Austria relies heavily on its winter sports to bring in the tourists, other lesser known parts of the country are gradually opening up. Instead of coming just for the winter sports and *après ski* of chic centres like Kitzbühel and St Anton, tourists are arriving in summer to walk the Alpine meadowlands, to study the flora and to climb mountains and fish in clear mountain streams. Hobby holidays are on the increase too. If you are inclined you can attend wine seminars, go on archaeological digs, study sacred music (Linz and Salzburg are renowned centres for this), take art courses and study German. Some companies specialise in art treasure tours which are guided tours with an expert guide to Salzburg, Vienna and other cultural centres. Instead of staying by the Carinthian lakes or in the Salzkammergut region, visitors are looking at less lauded parts of Austria such as the Vorarlberg and Burgenland which still maintain their ancient folkloric festivals. Austria has a wealth of history at its doorstep from the magnificent treasures of Vienna and the music festivals of Salzburg to the castle-fortresses and abbeys throughout the nine federal provinces. Today some fortresses still stand; others are in ruins, but names such as Schwarzenberg, Montfort and Werdenberg fill history books.

The Austrian National Tourist Office at 30 St George's Street, London W1R 0AL can supply the latest information on visiting Austria. Once you are in the country local tourist offices – Verkehrsvereine – in cities and resorts (see page 55) can inform you about hotel accommodation, places of interest, transport and hunting and fishing licences. Spa administrations are listed under Kurkommissionen.

Travel agents specialising in Austria are:

General

   Thomson Holidays, Greater London House, Hampstead Road, London NW1 7SD

   Blue Sky Holidays, Blue Sky House, London Road, East Grinstead, West Sussex RH19 1HU.

   Cosmos Ltd, Cosmos House, 1 Bromley Common, Bromley, Kent BR2 9LX

   All branches of Thomas Cook Ltd

Winter sports

   Inghams, 329 Putney Bridge Road, London SW15

   Neilsons Holidays, International House, Granby Street, Leicester LE1 6FD

   Intasun, Intasun House, Cromwell Avenue, Bromley, Kent BR2 9AQ

Special interest holidays

   Cox and Kings, 46 Marshall Street, London W1

   Venice–Simplon–Orient Express: Sea Containers House, 20 Upper Ground, London SE1

   Dr W Lueftner Reisebuero, Sterzingerstrasse 8, Innsbruck 6020

2

FROM EMPIRE
TO
REPUBLIC

During the Bronze Age (dating from 2000 to 1000 BC) Central Europe began to see glass and pottery being produced, ornaments of gold, bronze and amber, weapons, swords and breastplates, and in the Alps copper mining. In the Iron Age (1000 to 400) the Illyrians arrived in Austria and these were the country's first settlers. They quickly established themselves as traders, and, being shrewd, saw the potential of salt deposits around Hallstatt in Upper Austria. The year 800 established the Hallstatt culture, known as Austria's cradle of civilisation, when the salt trade boomed, ironworking increased and fortified strongholds were erected.

In the Bronze Age the dead had been cremated, their ashes placed in urns; during the Hallstatt period they were buried in shallow graves.

Celts followed the Illyrians and later came the Romans in 14 BC, who incorporated the country south of the Danube in the Roman Empire. The Vienna basin was of particular importance to them and, during their period of occupation, they established roads and planted vineyards. Roman camps and forts were set up all over Austria: Carnuntum (Petronell), Aguntum (Lienz), Vindobona (Vienna), Juvavum (Salzburg) and Lentia (Linz).

Around AD 400 Germanic tribes occupied the territory in great numbers, some coming from Scandinavia, while another faction arrived from Spain. It seems these various peoples settled down together and soon developed a high degree of civilisation.

The next century saw the arrival of the Bavarians and Slavs, and by the eighth century Charlemagne had set up a border province to defend his empire in the east. At this time Austria was divided into two divisions, the Germanic sector in the Alps, and a mix of Slavs, Celts and Germans in the eastern parts. After the Battle of Lechfeld in AD 955, the Bavarians began recolonising while the Franks, who had been brought in by the margrave Burchard, began establishing territories in what today is Lower Austria. They later populated Burgenland, extending their settlements into Hungary. Today the names of Austrians follow a simple pattern; most are German – while Bavarians and Franks spoke German they had different dialects and customs – followed by Czech and Hungarian, the rest being Polish or Croatian.

During the centuries of expansion which followed, two dynasties were to dominate Austria. The first was the Babenbergs, originating in Franconia, who controlled the country for 270 years until 1246; the second, the Habsburgs, ruled for 640 years. The first Babenberg to rule was Leopold, who in 976 became the margrave of Austria. Twenty years later, early documents mentioned Ostarrichi, which in time became Oesterreich (Austria). By the twelfth century Heinrich II (Jasomirgott) – he had earned his nickname because he was so fond of proclaiming 'Ja, so mir Gott helfe' (with God's help) – was in command, and Austria was elevated to the status of Duchy. Under the Babenbergs Austria underwent great development. Gold, silver and salt mining filled the state coffers. Monasteries and churches were built and religious learning spread. Noblemen installed themselves in castles.

On the death of the last Babenberg, Friedrich the Quarrelsome, in 1246, Austria was divided between two kings; Ottokar II of Bohemia at first took only part of it (King Bela of Hungary claimed Styria) but eventually Ottokar claimed Styria and Carinthia too. By that time Vienna had become the most important German-speaking town after Cologne.

If the Babenbergs had been powerful leaders, the Habsburgs, whose name originated from Habichtsburg (Hawk's Castle), their estate in Aargau in Switzerland, were to be more so. From the beginning the Habsburgs were greedy landowners. They were also foreigners. When Count Rudolf von Habsburg, a Swiss who had been crowned in Aachen, was instated as Emperor and came to Vienna, he could claim family possessions in Aargau, Breisgau, and Alsace as well as Styria and Carinthia. However, when King Ottokar was killed in the battle of Marchfeld in 1278, Rudolf claimed the estates of his arch enemy and the House of Habsburg began its prolonged rule of Austria.

During the fourteenth century the Habsburgs extended their territory as far as Trieste, and from 1452, when Friedrich III was crowned Emperor in Rome, the Habsburgs ruled over the Holy Roman Empire until its abolition in 1806.

Whereas in the Middle Ages the Habsburgs had entered into battle to win possessions they now took to extending their already considerable holdings by a series of cleverly orchestrated marriages. When Maximilian I, Emperor of the Holy Roman Empire, contracted marriage with Mary of Burgundy, he acquired both a wife and most of the Burgundian estates in the Low Countries. His eldest son, Philip the Fair, was married to Juana, the Infanta of Spain, thus ensuring that Flanders went to Austria. Their son, Charles V, subsequently inherited all their possessions. The Habsburgs were acquiring territory in all directions. When in 1516 Maxmilian's grandson, Karl, came to power in Spain another branch of the Habsburg line was firmly established.

The Habsburgs also acquired territory by treaties. In 1526 the union of Bohemia with Hungary had been established. By that time two Habsburg lines were flourishing, one in Austria – Ferdinand I had become head of the Austrian branch on the abdication of his brother Charles V – and the other in Spain for Charles V's son, Philip, had been given Spain and Portugal in addition to the Low Countries, Burgundy, Sicily and Naples. Half a century later, in 1618, the Thirty Years' War broke out, sparked off by the antagonism between Protestants and Catholics.

In 1529 Vienna had to defend itself against Turkish attack, and hardly had Leopold I ascended the throne than the Turkish siege of 1683 began. There were further complications over Austria's political ambitions, which had been temporarily quelled by the Turkish invasion, but which, nevertheless, were causing concern in Europe. Austria had overcome the plague, which had made its appearance just as the country was celebrating a new heir to the throne, and had gained Hungary, which had fallen to the Habsburgs in 1687. The Turks had been pushed back, but during the eighteenth century a whole host of new and alarming problems arose. Chief of these was the War of the Spanish Succession which began in 1701. Three years later Vienna was saved from the French at the battle of Blenheim (1704) by the English army commanded by the Duke of Marlborough. Austria secured the Spanish Netherlands and Milan in 1713.

Another pressing problem was the Turkish threat to Austrian territory. Charles VI was obliged to waïve his right to European territories so that his daughter, Maria Theresa, could succeed as Archduchess of Austria and Queen of Hungary, and to that end he proclaimed the Pragmatic Sanction under whose terms Maria Theresa claimed the Imperial Crown of Austria and ruled for the next 40 years. Her reign was a constant battle to keep Austria's territories. In 1736 she married Francois of Lorraine, and in 1740 ascended the throne. Scarcely had she attained power than the War of the Austrian Succession began after Frederick II of Prussia seized Silesia. The war was to last eight years, with England and the Netherlands supporting Austria against Prussia, France and Spain. At the battle of Dettingen, England and Austria scored a victory over the French. It was the last time an English monarch (George II) fought personally on the battlefield. But success was reversed at the battle of Fontenoy, in 1745, when the English and Austrians were themselves defeated. The war was finally ended in 1748 by the Treaty of Aix-la-Chapelle.

Empress Maria Theresa, meanwhile, was obliged to cope with innumerable domestic problems. She bore 16 children, one of whom was Marie Antoinette, and astutely arranged dynastic marriages for them: Marie Antoinette became Queen of France and Maria Caroline, Queen of Naples; two other daughters became duchesses. She took it upon herself to sweep aside outmoded institutions and her drastic reforms were to change the face of Austria. She updated the financial system, encouraged industrial development and abolished the barbarous practice of torture. She transferred the various states into one single unit which could be efficiently administered, and established a separate legal system (previously it had been tied to the administration). But above all, her educational reforms were triumphs of her day and established her as a far-seeing and much loved Austrian monarch. She revolutionised old practices and cast aside outdated methods. Universities were wrenched from ecclesiastical grips and made into state institutions. An elementary school system was introduced.

She was sufficiently shrewd not to rush matters. Although her reforms were radical she took care not to implement them too drastically, and for this reason they endured. However, she did ban Freemasonry in 1764. During the nineteenth century Freemasonry in Roman Catholic countries was forbidden yet many leading lights, especially in Vienna, were Freemasons. Despite the ban she was a much admired monarch, judging from the number of statues erected to her memory. As for the Freemasons (whose song, *Brüder reicht die hand zum bunde* was composed by Wolfgang Amadeus Mozart) after the Empress's death in 1780 her heir and co-regent Josef II, reinstated them. Thus the rebirth of Freemasons in Austria was effected.

When Josef II ascended the throne, the examples exercised by the Empress were to some extent adhered to by her son, but while his mother had carefully calculated her influence on her people, Josef was more overbearing in his approach. He was something of an *enfant terrible*, and his word was law. But all was not lost, for it was during this period of enlightenment that the great age of Austrian classical music came into being.

Franz II acceded to the throne in 1792 and, in recompense for the territories lost under the Treaty of Pressburg, Austria was accorded the estates of the Archbishopric of Salzburg. In 1804 Franz II renounced his title of Head of the Holy Roman Empire and became known as Emperor Franz I. It was during Franz I's reign that Prince Metternich was put in charge of Austrian policy in the year 1809, the year in which the Tirolean leader Andreas Hofer led the rebellion against the French–Bavarian alliance.

During the eighteenth and nineteenth centuries Napoleon's ambitions caused ripples in Austria. In 1809 Archduke Karl succeeded in checking Napoleon at the battle of Aspern, but his victory was reversed at Wagram. However, in 1813 the allied armies, led by Prince Karl Schwarzenberg, defeated him in the battle of Leipzig and Napoleon was finally overthrown in 1814.

In the following year Prince Metternich, the Austrian State Chancellor, presided over the Congress of Vienna in which the Duke of Wellington participated. Under their terms Austria gained Lombardy and Venetia but failed to recover the Austrian Netherlands. It was to be the beginning of a new order in Europe establishing a period of peace during which Austria made immense headway on the industrial front. It was a time of great economic development. The year 1837 saw the opening of the country's first railway, and less than two decades later the world's first mountain railway, south-west of Vienna over the Semmering Pass.

With the end of the Napoleonic Wars and the establishment of the Congress of Vienna, Austria enjoyed a few golden years when the arts flourished and the Viennese, in particular, set out to enjoy themselves on a grand scale. Coffee houses were filled, and Schubert's Lieder were heard everywhere, but the relatively long period of peace was soon disrupted by revolutions within Austria itself, due to the multi-national structure on which the Empire had been founded. In 1848 there was a revolution in Vienna. Metternich fled to London and the Emperor Ferdinand abdicated in favour of his nephew, Franz Josef, who died in 1916 aged 68.

As a result of the Seven Weeks' War of 1866 with Prussia, Austria lost Venetia to Italy. In 1867 the dual Austro–Hungarian monarchy was formed. A series of governments came and went, unable to control or solve the tensions aggravated by the working classes, who were pressing their demands for better working conditions and higher wages. The disparate nations living together under the Austrian flag were growing restless and dissatisfied. When Archduke Franz Ferdinand, heir to the Austrian throne, was assassinated in 1914 it was as if everyone had been waiting for the axe to fall. With the start of the First World War the Austro–Hungarian monarchy was effectively at an end. The Emperor's successor, Karl, issued a statement in the autumn of 1918 renouncing all state duties.

Austria was now divided, with Yugoslavia gaining Serbia, parts of Romania and Poland (which had formed part of the Austro–Hungarian monarchy) being granted areas of land, and Austria, Hungary and Czechoslovakia becoming separate states. Austria, now reduced to Vienna and its immediately surrounding provinces, was declared a republic. The new boundaries with Yugoslavia, Czechoslovakia and Hungary were closed. In March 1933 the Nationalrat (Lower House of Parliament) abdicated its responsibilities and Chancellor Engelbert Dollfuss took the helm. To all intents and purposes democracy had ceased, and in February 1934 there was civil war. Meanwhile the National Socialists, allying themselves with Adolf Hitler's regime in Germany, carried out a *coup d'état* in which Dollfuss was murdered. His successor, Kurt Schuschnigg, met Adolf Hitler at his residence on the Ober Salzberg in Bavaria in 1938, but no acceptable solution was reached.

Schuschnigg was under severe pressure from Hitler who, in 1934, had made his intentions clear to incorporate Austria into Nazi Germany. Hitler subsequently told Schuschnigg that he must include a Nazi in his Cabinet, and after some deliberation Austria was reluctantly obliged to do so. Schuschnigg had no choice but to announce a referendum for 13 March 1938, in which the people themselves would vote for an independent Austria, but on 11 March, two days before the plebiscite could take place, Hitler and his Nazi troops marched into Vienna. The Anschluss was effected and Austria was incorporated into the German Third Reich.

Eighteen months later the Second World War began and the Austrians found themselves under German occupation. Eventually, towards the end of the war, resistance groups became active and the liberation of Austria began in March 1945 with the Allied forces approaching from the west and the Russians from the east. Some of Vienna's finest buildings, including St Stephen's cathedral, were badly bombed. Others, like the Opera House, were burned down. Karl Renner formed a provisional government and a few months later a second republic was instituted.

A new sense of independence was at last beginning to emerge. The termination of the Anschluss convinced even the most sceptical Austrians that a burden had been lifted and that at last they could get on with repairing the physical and psychological damage. For the first time since 1918 there was a unique sense of identity and purpose. During the dark days of the Second World War, Austria had been governed from Berlin. Now the union with Germany was over. There was hope.

There was also a new economic stability in the second republic which had been patently lacking in the first. In eastern Austria oil had been discovered, which gave the new republic a boost of confidence. Added to that was the wave of tourism on which Austrians could begin to build an economic future. In 1946 special postage stamps were issued to celebrate Austria's first anniversary and everyone rushed out to post offices to buy them. A new sense of patriotism filled the country. The war was finished and Austrians were ready for the next move.

It was the start of a strongly felt nationalism. At last Austrians had a common destiny and they dedicated themselves to building up their new republic and embracing a new ideology. With the Anschluss behind them they were determined upon unity and a lasting independence. Thus the provisional government headed by Karl Renner (who had led the Austrian peace negotiations during the First World War) was recognised by Britain, France, the Soviet Union and the USA – the four occupying powers. The National Assembly held the first election, in which the Christian Democrats took 85 of the 165 seats. Both Houses of Parliament – the Nationalrat and the Bundesrat – elected Karl Renner as President. A coalition government was formed to represent the country, which was divided into four occupied zones, with Vienna split into four sectors. A European Recovery programme was set up which gave Austria's economy a chance of revitalisation.

At the Moscow Conference in 1943 the Allies had undertaken to give back to Austria, on the cessation of hostilities, its independence and its frontiers, but it took 12 years to materialise because the Soviet Union refused to move its troops until a German peace treaty was signed. No such treaty was ever signed and Austrian Chancellor Julius Raab was called to Moscow, where he was informed that the Soviet Union would withdraw its troops providing Austria maintained neutrality between the Eastern and Western blocs. Austria pledged to do so, thus declaring itself a permanently neutral state. Finally, on 13 May 1955 at Vienna's Belvedere Palace, the former home of Prince Eugene of Savoy, the USA's John Foster Dulles, Britain's Harold MacMillan, France's Antoine Pinay, and the Soviet Union's Vyacheslav Molotov put their names to the Austrian State Treaty, known in Austria as the Belvedere Treaty, which became effective on 27 July of that year, thus giving the Austrian nation its post-war independence. Austria's Foreign Minister, Leopold Figl, appeared on the balcony of the Belvedere Palace, held up the newly signed document, and announced '*Oesterreich ist frei*' (Austria is free).

A federal constitutional law on the neutrality of Austria came into force on 26 October 1955, which since then has been recognised as Austria's National Day. Austria had suffered 17 years of occupation, from 1938–1945 under Hitler's Anschluss and from 1945–1955 by Allied forces of Britain, the USA, USSR and France.

The State Treaty of Vienna lays down that Nazi Germany annexed Austria by force. It further guarantees human rights and the rights of Croat and Slovene minorities. Above all it outlaws all fascist organisations. In accordance with the Potsdam Agreement, Austria retrieved property seized as German assets which included oil fields and industrial plants. Article 1 of the constitutional law on Austrian neutrality states:

> For the purpose of permanent maintenance of her external
> independence and for the purpose of the inviolability of her territory,
> Austria of her own free will declares herewith her permanent neutrality
> which she is resolved to maintain and defend with all the means at her
> disposal.

The signing of the Treaty of Vienna had been one of the great moments of the second republic. After the treaty the last foreign soldier left Austrian territory.

Furthermore the constitutional law on Austrian neutrality declared that never again would Austria accede to any military alliances nor permit the establishment of military bases by foreign states on her territory.

Austrians today are committed to the policy of *détente*. They uphold that constitutional law which declares the establishing and maintaining of good relations with other states, on pursuing policies designed to maintain peace, and on participating in any humanitarian action, particularly within the framework of the United Nations.

3
MUSIC
AND THE
ARTS

Music

In the Middle Ages the Minnegesang (folk songs), sung by minstrels and later the Meistersinger, was fostered by the Church and the Court. Folk ballads had a wide following, and by the fifteenth century Emperor Maximilian had established a Court orchestra. Folk music continued to flourish alongside classical compositions, merging with French and Italian influences, resulting in the Singspiel which roughly conformed to the operas we know today.

During the seventeenth century the baroque era was at its height, with architecture and the arts – particularly music – prospering in Vienna. The Imperial Court of Vienna actively encouraged all manner of musical compositions and no less than four emperors manifested a keen musical knowledge. While Emperor Josef II, when asked to comment on Mozart's symphonies, may have been a trifle non-plussed, he had little alternative but to set his seal of approval upon the high standard of music he heard, for Austria was about to embark upon a golden age of music and art.

Opera, whose natural home was Italy and Germany, was beginning to gain ground in other parts of Europe and quickly reached Vienna. The German composer Christoph Willibald Gluck recognised both music and dramatic art in opera. In 1754 he was Kapellmeister of Opera at the Imperial Court. With the encouragement and patronage of the Habsburgs, themselves proficient performers, his opera *Orfeo ed Euridice* was performed in 1762, and *Alceste* in Vienna in 1767. By now opera had gained in popularity and court musicians vied with each other trying to topple Italian compositions by introducing German ones.

During that period of intense competition, Wolfgang Amadeus Mozart was born in Salzburg in 1756. By the time he was five years old he could play both piano and violin by ear without having been taught a note, and his father, recognising his son's precocious gifts, gave Wolfgang music lessons over a period of five years and then arranged a tour of Europe which took in Vienna, Frankfurt, Munich, Paris and London. The boy genius became ill and on his return to Salzburg remained there for the next three years. Meanwhile, Josef Haydn, born in 1732, was composer and conductor in the service of Prince Esterhazy in Eisenstadt, where he remained for 30 years.

Emperor Franz Josef II had conceived the notion of departing from Italian opera and introducing German opera to Austria. Wolfgang Amadeus Mozart was summoned to the Court and enjoyed a brief spell of adulation before returning to Salzburg. By 1782 he was back with some of the music which he had composed in Salzburg. In that year his *Il Seraglio* had its first performance in Vienna. Four years later his *Le Nozze di Figaro*, initially unpopular, was performed at the old Burg theatre, then on Michaelplatz. *Cosi Fan Tutte* followed in 1790 (but the first performance of *Don Giovanni* was in Prague at the Tyl Theatre). When Mozart died on 5 December 1791 he was Kapellmeister of St Stephen's cathedral and lived close by on Schulerstrasse, where he composed *Le Nozze di Figaro*; sadly, he died in poverty, and is buried in a pauper's grave in St Mark's cemetery.

By the end of the eighteenth century the Romantic Movement was underway and Vienna was the music capital of Europe. Foreign musicians, mainly from Germany, began making their way to the city, including Ludwig von Beethoven, born in Bonn in 1770. He arrived in Vienna in 1792, aged 22, and in 1801 composed the *Moonlight Sonata* for his lover Giulietta Guicciardi. Seven years later he composed his Fifth and Sixth Symphonies, and in 1824 the Ninth Symphony. He died in the city in March 1827, and is buried in the corner of the city cemetery known as 'musicians square'.

It was left to Franz Schubert, born in Vienna in 1797, to rediscover the lieder (songs) which had been so popular during the Middle Ages. Schubert died at the early age of 31 and his *Unfinished Symphony* was discovered four years after his death, in 1832. It was Franz Schubert who drank to 'the one who will follow *him*', at Beethoven's funeral, speculating on whoever had genius enough to follow in the great composer's footsteps.

By 1820 there was a new mood in Vienna. Suddenly folk music was fashionable again, the minuet and the Styrian polka setting the pace. Soon the Viennese waltz, introduced by Johann Strauss the Elder, and Josef Lanner, followed. In 1867 Johann Strauss the Younger composed the *Blue Danube* for a Carnival Ball – the melody that would forever be associated with Vienna. His *Emperor Waltz* and *Tales from the Vienna Woods* firmly established him as the 'waltz king' surpassing his father. His operetta *Die Fledermaus* would enchant audiences for generations to come, while Franz Lehar's *Merry Widow* and Ralph Benatsky's *White Horse Inn* would further endorse Vienna as the musical capital of the world.

The city's musical progress had been advanced in its initial stages by royal patronage. From then on it was the genius of composers like Gustav Mahler, Franz Liszt, Anton Bruckner and Richard Strauss who ensured that Vienna remained the most popular venue of the music scene. In the past, Austria's music had seemed inextricably bound-up with opera. In the nineteenth century Richard Wagner exclaimed: 'The opera in Vienna is divine, the orchestra splendid'. His *Ring* cycle, based on the ancient Nibelung saga, was performed in Vienna in 1879, but *Tristan und Isolde* did not make its debut in Vienna until four years later.

Opera was also closely connected with the orchestra, which had many distinguished conductors, amongst them Giuseppe Verdi who had been known personally to conduct his opera *Aïda*. Gustav Mahler, when appointed as director of the Viennese Opera, was remembered by Franz Schmidt, a cellist and composer, as 'a great musical force', but others considered him a dictator:

'Mahler seemed to dominate the whole musical life of Vienna' Schmidt observed. In 1919 Richard Strauss became the orchestra's director, remaining until 1924. His *Der Rosenkavalier* continued to be one of Austria's most famous operas and is today performed in all the world's opera houses.

However, orchestra music was to continue to play a large part in Austria's musical development. In the era when the waltz was at its most popular, Anton Bruckner was born in 1824 in Ansfelden, a village near St Florian in Upper Austria, and in 1856 became organist at Linz cathedral. As well as church music he composed nine symphonies and eventually became Professor of Music at the Vienna Conservatory. During Bruckner's time, Johannes Brahms settled in Vienna, composing many of his works there. In 1842 the Vienna Philharmonic Orchestra was founded and was conducted by many illustrious composers, such as Richard Strauss and Wilhelm Furtwaengler.

It was while Gustav Mahler was director of the Opera that Arnold Schönberg discovered the twelve tone technique which revolutionised twentieth-century music. Schönberg was a Viennese who emigrated to America in 1933 and died 18 years later in Los Angeles. Following Schönberg's lead, Alban Berg, the traditionalist of modern music, adapted his twelve tone technique, though his most famous work, his opera *Wozzeck*, used atonal expression. His contemporary, Anton von Webern, developed still further atonal and polytonal music.

A succession of innovative musicians followed, including Karl Heinz Fussl and Erich Urbanner. Born at the turn of the century, Gottfried von Einem is perhaps the best known of these. *The Trial*, based on Franz Kafka's novel, and *Danton's Death*, based on one of Büchner's dramas, are two of his best-recognised works. It is difficult to follow in the footsteps of Wolfgang Amadeus Mozart but, even so, there is no shortage of contemporary Austrian composers. Fridolin Dallinger makes use of the twelve tone technique while Friedrich Cerha concentrates on complex tonal structures.

The walz established Vienna as a music centre but, as well as orchestral music, Austria also takes delight in· spontaneous music like the songs of the Heuriger and the simple folk melodies heard throughout the nine federal provinces. In the Tirol, especially, folk music has a long tradition, and nowhere more so than in the Zillertal. While there may not be so much thigh slapping as in Bavaria, folk songs and dances are as popular as ever. One of the Zillertal's songs, 'Auf der Alm, da gibst koa Sünd' (on the Alpine pastures sin is non-existent), is purported to have greatly moved Napoleon when he heard it. Queen Victoria was also said to have been impressed by a group of Zillertal musicians who visited London.

At the grand Fasching Balls of Vienna, waltzes are played just as they were during the Austro–Hungarian monarchy. Even the Lippizaner stallions of the Spanish Riding School are familiar with them, for traditionalism is the underpinning of Austrian society.

The Vienna Boys Choir has been in existence for close on 500 years and can number Franz Schubert and Josef Haydn amongst its famous 'old boys'. It was first formed because Emperor Maximilian I wanted a group of choristers to sing at his table and to sing daily mass as well. Originally it was maintained by the

Court but when the monarchy came to an end the choir became an independent association. Today the Vienna Boys Choir travels the world performing to vast audiences.

Silent Night, one of the best known of all carols, was first sung in 1818 at Oberndorf near Salzburg at the Christmas Midnight Mass and these days it is the highlight of the Christmas masses, not only in Salzburg, where it is especially poignant, but elsewhere in Austria too.

The Viennese Philharmonic (whose musicians also comprise the State Opera Orchestra) is just one of the many orchestras playing not only classical works but modern symphonies too. The Musikverein in Vienna is the scene of Sunday mid-morning concerts which attract large audiences. In Bruckner's day the Philharmonic was the only fully fledged orchestra in Austria. These days Austria can muster at least eight orchestras, including the Vienna Philharmonic, the Vienna Symphony, the Salzburg Mozarteum Orchestra, and the Graz Philharmonic. There are also numerous chamber ensembles which play at music festivals. Operettas still have a part in Austria's musical traditions, from Franz Lehar who incorporated Bohemian, Hungarian and Slovak strains into his works, to Robert Stolz, the last of the great operetta composers.

All kinds of festivals proliferate in Austria so that if you miss one musical event in one city you can catch up with it in another. The Vienna Symphony Orchestra can be heard at the Bregenz Festival as well as in Salzburg and Vienna. The establishment of the Salzburg Easter and Whitsun festivals has placed the Austrian musical tradition firmly in the vanguard.

After the Second World War the Opera moved from its temporary headquarters, the Theater an der Wien, where Franz Salmhofer had been the director. The restoration of the Opera House on the Ringstrasse had cost 265 million Austrian schillings and was re-opened in November 1955 with Beethoven's *Fidelio*, an opera which had had its premiere in 1805 at the Theater an der Wien, where it had met with little success. So closely connected with the Opera was the Viennese Philharmonic Orchestra that the appointment of the conductor became central to the Opera House itself.

A series of conductors followed Richard Strauss (who left in 1924) and, given the Viennese's reputation and inclination for disagreeing with everyone about everything, each encountered a different reaction. The Opera House was starting to attract international artistes which meant the selection of the right conductor was of paramount importance.

In 1954 Karl Böhm was appointed director, and was followed by Herbert von Karajan who freed the Opera from its narrow traditionalism and began engaging singers with international reputations. Leonard Bernstein often visited as a guest conductor, and the pattern continued under Egon Hilbert. Heinrich Reif-Gintl was appointed director upon Hilbert's death, and from 1972 Rudolf Gamsjager took over and remained for four years, handing over the baton to Egon Seefehlner, who was director until 1982. In the 1980s the familiar disputes began all over again and the American-born Lorin Maazel, who had been appointed director immediately after Seefehlner, resigned. The reaction in Austria was that it took a Viennese, or at the very least, an Austrian, to control the Opera which had earned itself quite a reputation, thanks to tenacious press coverage. Yet despite the disputes the Opera remained as popular as ever.

Architecture and interior design

As in the case of music, architecture in Austria underwent a series of progressions from Romanesque, to Gothic, then Renaissance, to baroque. The Romanesque period saw its flowering in such churches as St Stephen's – the main entrance is a good example – and Cistercian, Benedictine and Augustinian monasteries such as Melk, Klosterneuburg, Zwettl, Gurk cathedral in Carinthia, with its fine frescoes dating from the mid-thirteenth century, and Seckau Abbey in Styria. In addition to architecture the Romanesque period was characterised by sculpture, altars and religious reliquaries, though none as fine as the Tassilo chalice, the work of medieval goldsmiths. It was also a period of illuminated manuscripts which included the Admont bible.

Between the thirteenth and fifteenth centuries Gothic architecture took over and led the way to new styles in both art and architecture. Early examples of Italian Gothic can be seen at Krems and Friesach. The Cistercians favoured French Gothic, examples of which can be seen at Zwettl and Lilienfeld. St Stephen's, a cathedral incorporating many styles, perfectly illustrates Austria's Gothic Age, and the Goldenes Dachl at Innsbruck, with its roof of gilded wooden tiles, is another good example.

Architects of the time who worked on St Stephen's included Anton Pilgram and Ullrich Helbling, while artist Michael Pacher worked on altarpieces such as that at St Wolfgang. The late Gothic in Austria was the antithesis of that seen in France. Austria's Gothic style was represented by paired naves, which can be seen to advantage in the church at Feldkirch in the Vorarlberg, and the overall style was one of clear-cut austerity.

Once Gothic architecture lost favour, the Renaissance quickly replaced it, due largely to the patronage of Maximilian von Habsburg who became Emperor in 1493. The aristocracy began to build castles in Renaissance style, but whereas Italian Renaissance inspired some architects to build Italianate palazzi (such as Schloss Porcia in the town of Spittal an der Drau in Carinthia, the Landhaus in Graz, Rosenburg castle in Lower Austria, and in Salzburg where the Prince-Archbishops conceived the grand notion of making their city into another Rome), the Italian style did not predominate, and the German Renaissance style prevailed.

The Renaissance, however, was not confined to palaces. It revealed its splendours in the tomb of Emperor Maximilian I at the Hofkirche at Innsbruck, the Residenz and the cathedral in Salzburg. A Renaissance school of painters was also prevalent, pioneered by artists and sculptors like Lukas Cranach and Albrecht Altdorfer. The Danube School was represented by Max Reichlich and Wolf Huber, who painted the St Florian altar. Italianate art mingled with Austrian traditions. There was a distinct feeling of optimism and growing confidence, and never more so than during the baroque period that was to follow.

The Thirty Years' War had taken its toll on Austrian resources, but by the end of the seventeenth century, Austria was beginning to build again. While palaces were paid for by the nobility, urban buildings relied on the Crown, the State, or aristocratic families to pay. Funds for such monasteries as Gurk were often donated by the people or by benefactors like Countess Emma of Friesach-Zeltschach, later to become St Emma, who founded the first monastery at Gurk.

While baroque architecture went ahead in leaps and bounds in Italy and France, high baroque in Austria was late in coming. There is hardly a baroque building to be found in Austria before 1680. France and Italy, meanwhile, were developing sophisticated styles, and although Austria, too, began to produce architecture in the manner of the French and Italian baroque, it advanced with caution. Thus today you can see buildings of great aesthetic beauty, and others which manifest all the shortcomings of baroque art.

Baroque originated in Italy and was introduced into the Habsburg Empire, which spanned Central Europe, by Charles V. The majority of Austrians were Roman Catholics, as they are today, and baroque art served a religious purpose, coming as a welcome change after the austerity of Lutheran buildings. The extravagances of the baroque age were to continue under Charles V's successors, but Austrian baroque would never be as ornate as that of Italy, as Austrian architects exercised characteristic restraint.

Three such architects dominated Austria's baroque era. They were Johann Bernhard Fischer von Erlach, Johann Lukas von Hildebrandt and Jakob Prandtauer, and yet their designs were considered so Italian in style and extravagant that they came to be talked of as sculptors and decorators rather than architects.

In the vanguard of the new movement was Fischer von Erlach, born on 3 March 1656 at Graz, Styria. He had left Austria at the age of 24 to study in Italy and had returned five years later to a steady stream of commissions. While Fischer von Erlach was influenced by Italian and French design, he nonetheless was ready to experiment, and his architectural innovations became the model for Central European architects. Some accused him of lacking true artistic imagination and of exerting too intellectual a discipline, but his architecture was to withstand the test of time. The ornate plague column in the Graben in Vienna was the first of a series of monuments designed by Fischer von Erlach, and little by little he transformed Vienna.

His most remarkable example of church architecture is the Karlskirche, built between 1715 and 1733 in thanksgiving after the plague of 1713 which had swept through Austria. In Fischer von Erlach, Austrians realised they had found an architect who would reflect their ideas and ambitions better than imported foreign architects with great reputations. Fischer von Erlach was familiar with architecture in France, Italy and Central Europe and he set about constructing the Austrian National Library (Oesterreichische Nationalbibliothek) on Josefplatz (whose cupola is one of Vienna's instantly recognisable landmarks) and the Collegiate Church in Salzburg. He was also responsible for part of the Hofburg – the Imperial Palace. In 1705 he was made architect of the Imperial Court, a title he held until his death in 1723.

Lukas von Hildebrandt, 12 years younger than Fischer von Erlach, was an

Italian by birth. Born in Genoa in 1668 he studied under the architect Carlo Fontana in Rome. He was made engineer to the Imperial Court and was subsequently knighted by the Emperor. Lukas von Hildebrandt favoured the Italian style. The Belvedere, the summer residence of Prince Eugene of Savoy, was constructed by Hildebrandt, and is considered by some to be the loveliest palace in Vienna. Lukas von Hildebrandt also designed the Kinsky palace, the Peterskirche and the Schloss Mirabell in Salzburg.

Emperor Leopold I had wanted Johann Fischer von Erlach to design Schönbrunn Palace, believing that in his skilled hands the palace would become one of the finest residences in Europe, surpassing even that of Versailles; but it was not to be, and a less grandiose building was constructed from 1695 to 1700 by another architect.

Between two such architects as the intellectual Fischer von Erlach, and the younger, dynamic Lukas von Hildebrandt there was bound to be rivalry and a fierce sense of competition, but each went on to design some of Austria's most prestigious buildings. Fischer von Erlach designed the Schwarzenberg Palace which was completed after his death by his son Joseph Emmanuel.

Completing the trio was Jakob Prandtauer who had initially been trained as a craftsman-sculptor. Unlike Fischer von Erlach and Lukas von Hildebrandt, Prandtauer did not become an architect until he was in his forties, but he went on to design some of Austria's greatest baroque buildings. His masterpiece was Melk Abbey, begun in 1702, and thought to be the finest baroque church north of the Alps. With flair and imagination Prandtauer made the best possible use of the site. The Abbey sits resplendent above the Danube, a monument to all that was best in Prandtauer's architectural concepts.

While the above three architects were building abbeys, palaces and churches, sculptors and interior designers were working alongside. Frescoes proliferated in the interiors of palaces, castles and monasteries. Plague columns (Pestäule) began to enhance towns and cities. Each main square of any city of importance had its fountain and its Pestäule, in celebration of the end of the plague. Painters like Johann Michael Rottmayr, who was highly valued by Fischer von Erlach, and Franz Anton Maulbertsch, one of the finest painters of the baroque period, and others, added to collections of baroque art, paintings, frescoes and altar pieces. During the late baroque period artists like Kremser Schmidt and Paul Troger dominated. Such artists as Balthasar Permoser, whose work decorates the Museum of Baroque Art in Vienna, collaborated with architects like Fischer von Erlach; Georg Raphael Donner designed fountains like the Neue Markt in Vienna, while Daniel Gran painted the frescoes of the dome of Fischer von Erlach's National Library in Vienna.

Empress Maria Theresa's reign saw the development of rococo, a style inspired by the French *rocaille*. Medallions, stylised garlands and baldachins, adopted by the stuccoists, overloaded interiors. Every niche, every spare space was covered by what was considered at the time to be decorative refinements, but which in a later period were to be dismissed as vulgar indulgences.

It was not, therefore, surprising to find the period of neo-classicism that followed, and which took as its influence the examples of Greece and Rome, resorting to functional simplicity both in architecture and the arts. Buildings like the Mint and Vienna's Technical University are typical of the trend towards modernism, after the excesses of the baroque age. The nineteenth century introduced the most fundamental change of all with the building of the Ringstrasse in Vienna. The old city walls were pulled down and suddenly Austria emerged from the chrysallis of the Austro–Hungarian monarchy into a modern state, with some of the more impressive architecture of the time – such as the Votive Church, the Parliament building, the Burg theatre and the Opera House – appearing during the latter half of the century when Franz Josef was Emperor.

Between the Congress of Vienna in 1814 and the 1848 revolution, the Biedermeier style flourished. In complete contrast to the ornate architecture of the baroque era, Biedermeier was essentially bourgeois, embracing homely comforts and bric-a-brac. Rudolf von Alt's watercolour paintings are representative of Biedermeier art, as are the paintings of Friedrich Gauermann and Ferdinand Georg Waldmüller. Bent wood furniture with its curved design bore the indelible stamp of the period. The firm of Thonet has been producing it since 1830.

Just as the Biedermeier period, epitomised by its simple, homespun designs, was a revolt from the extravagances of baroque, so twentieth-century architects and designers saw the need for new expression. Thus the Viennese Secession Movement was formed and under one of its most famous founders, Gustav Klimt, was born Jugendstil (art nouveau). The Secession was a group of architects and artists who had broken with tradition in 1897 and had opened up the field for a new school of architectural visions and forms. One of the group, Joseph Olbrich, designed the Secession building in Vienna, and soon architects like Otto Wagner and artists like Klimt developed international reputations. Functionalism and restraint were the Secessionists guidelines. Clemens Holzmeister, who was to follow Otto Wagner, designed the new Festival Hall in Salzburg and also accepted many commissions abroad, in addition to working on church designs. Roland Rainer designed the Stadthalle in Vienna and Karl Schwanner the Museum of the Twentieth Century.

Otto Wagner's Post Office Savings Building on Georg Coch Platz, his metropolitan railway stations and Adolf Loos's Steiner building led the way to the modernistic architecture which appeared after the First World War. Housing schemes, such as the Karl Marx Hof in Vienna, which extends nearly 1 mile (over 1 km) and earned itself the derisory tag of a horizontal Manhattan skyscraper, and Johann Staber's Vienna International Centre at Donaupark, are typical of the futuristic architecture seen in Austria today, although not to everyone's taste.

Art and sculpture

During the Renaissance, the Danube School of Painting, with its representatives of Max Reichlich and Wolf Huber, had enjoyed limited success, but began to flourish under the Regensburg artists Albrech and Erhart Altdorfer whose altarpieces, such as the one at St Florian's Abbey, became well known.

With the founding of the Secession Group, painting in Austria began to develop new trends, led by such exponents as Gustav Klimt, who became one of Austria's leading expressionists though he was essentially a mural painter. Hans Makart, born in 1840, whose *Entry of Charles V into Antwerp* hangs in the Belvedere Palace, had a considerable influence on Klimt's work. Gustav Klimt's *Kiss, Judith* and *Death and Life* paved the way for the surrealist movement. Today Klimt's work reaches a wide audience (largely due to the poster reproductions of his original paintings) while surrealist artists like Oskar Kokoschka (born in Pöchlarn, Lower Austria in 1886, and died in 1980) and Alfred Kubin (born in 1877, and died in 1959) are internationally admired.

Before the First World War, Austria held a strong position in the art world, but the post-war years brought a series of changes, not just in art. Architecture had made brave advances, with such designs as Josef Hoffmann's Purkersdorf sanatorium and Joseph Olbrich's Secession building, and somehow expressionism managed to remain. While the older generation of painters had, in the main, shunned French and Italian influences, the succeeding generation adopted a more cosmopolitan stance, giving exhibitions in Europe and the USA. Abstract art, art nouveau and graphic art became the vogue.

Abstract painters like Gustav Beck and Johann Fruhmann introduced a new sense of energy, while graphic artists produced several original and highly individualistic artists like Kurt Moldovan. The Vienna School of Phantastic Realism, founded by Albert Paris Gutersloh, further advanced the switch to modernism by its close relationship to surrealism. In Austria today a multiplicity of styles can be seen in city art galleries and art museums from foremost impressionists like Egon Schiele (who was a pupil of Gustav Klimt) to abstract artists like Josef Mikl and Herbert Boeckl, one of the country's best-known modern artists.

New trends also surfaced in the field of sculpture. Today Austrian sculptors are eschewing traditionalism in favour of a modernistic or avant garde approach. Foremost of those who made an earlier breakthrough was Fritz Wotruba, who had spent the war years in Switzerland. When he returned to Vienna it was largely due to his influence that Vienna developed into a sculptural centre. Karl Prantl was another such innovator. When he began his sculpture symposium in the sandstone quarry of St Margarethen, Burgenland, in 1959 it began attracting artists from all over the world, and spawned similar symposiums in Mauthausen in Upper Austria, and others in Lower Austria and Carinthia.

Wotruba was best known for his figures and in that area has been compared to Britain's Henry Moore. His pupil, Joannis Avramidis, sculpted the bronze *Polis* which stands in the Vienna International Centre plaza. Alfred Hrdlicka, Otto Eder and Bruno Gironcoli are just some of the outstanding sculptors found in Austria today alongside painters of the School of Phantastic Realism such as Ernst Fuchs and Rudolf Hausner.

Distinctive church sculpture had been prevalent in Austria throughout the Renaissance. Though Michael Pacher, one of the best known of Austria's Gothic painters, also carved in wood, seventeenth-century sculptors like Georg Raphael Donner and Balthasar Permoser made their names by specialising in fountains and statues. Austria's museums (like the Baroque Art Museum, and the Museum of Modern Art in Vienna) are representative of past and present trends, while the Museum of Applied Art, the oldest museum of applied art in Central Europe, has a special exhibition of art nouveau representing architects like Otto Wagner and the Secessionist school of thought.

Literature

Just as the *Minnegesang* had introduced musical ballads to audiences in the Middle Ages, so story-telling progressed to its present, sophisticated form. The earliest example of Austrian poetry dates from the twelfth century. During the sixteenth century, Emperor Maximilian I, himself an accomplished poet, lent his support to the literary arts.

With the collapse of the Austro–Hungarian monarchy new literary forms took hold. Writers such as Franz Kafka and the psychoanalyst Sigmund Freud exerted considerable influence on Austrian writers. The end of the monarchy and the First World War were still popular themes; Stefan Zweig and Robert Musil both wrote about the breakdown of the Empire. Some went on to experiment with new trends, but the Salzburg-born poet Georg Trakl grew depressed by the coming of the First World War and committed suicide in 1914; his literary reputation was established during his lifetime, but his lyric poetry was most appreciated posthumously.

By the end of the Second World War writers were beginning to look beyond Austria for inspiration. Elias Canetti, born in 1905, who had achieved international success with novels like *Die Blendung* (published in 1936) which had been translated into several languages, won the Nobel Prize for Literature in 1981. Strange as it may seem in a society rooted in tradition, Odon von Horvath in his plays spoke out against contemporary society. Anti-theatre began to catch on. Peter Handke's *Insulting the Audience*, which enjoyed a certain success in Europe, triggered lively debates on modern theatre and would never have been staged before the 60s revolution in the theatre.

The religious dramas of the Middle Ages had spawned works such as *Jederman* (*Everyman*) still performed each year in Salzburg. The seventeenth and eighteenth centuries introduced the popular comedy to wider audiences. A century later came the dramatists Ferdinand Raimund and Johann Nestroy, known as the Viennese Aristophanes, both of whom are still amongst the most popular dramatists in the German-speaking theatre.

When, in 1776, during the reign of Emperor Josef II, the Burg Theatre became the National Theatre, farces, comedies and dramas were performed. During the baroque era, Austria had become one of Europe's chief artistic centres where theatre, opera and ballet could be enjoyed regularly. Today the Burg Theatre in Vienna is considered one of the best in the German-speaking world, while provincial theatres run by provincial and local authorities, like the Vereinigte Bühnen at Graz, the Landestheater at Linz and the Tiroler Landestheater at Innsbruck, put on a range of operas and dramas.

Austrians have always preferred popular comedy to high drama so visitors are often surprised to find that while opera and light dramas are well-subscribed, there are no Austrian musicals. In general, Austrians are sceptical about anything new, which probably accounts for the fact that there are few new dramas. Private theatres, many of them showing *avant garde* works, are, however, making a comeback, which is good news for anyone looking for a successor to Johann Nestroy.

The same is true of the Austrian cinema, which is of poor quality compared to Italy or France. Any rising star of the theatre was shrewd enough to go to Hollywood; two who did were Romy Schneider and Oskar Werner. In 1981 the Austro–Hungarian production *Mephisto* won an award for the best foreign film of the year. While queues of eager cinema-goers waited around the block in New York to see the film the critics had praised, the Austrians went back to their opera and forgot about it.

The establishment of Salzburg's Easter and Whitsun Festivals has been instrumental in bringing music lovers to Austria from all over the world, not only to listen to Wolfgang Amadeus Mozart, but, as much as anything, to see world-class conductors, like Leonard Bernstein and Herbert von Karajan, perform. As the Austrians cheerfully admit, they don't go to the theatre for the drama but to see the artists; and the big names draw the biggest crowds.

4
PRACTICAL NOTES

Food and restaurants

Magyars, Slovenes, Franks, Bavarians and Turks all left their imprints on Austria, so it is not surprising that Austrian cuisine should be a *mélange* of many countries. Hungarians introduced their Gulasch, the Czechs Bohemian pastries, the Germans Sauerkraut and sausages. Later arrivals were the Italian pizza and the American hamburger. All over Austria today you will find pizzerias alongside hamburger restaurants, but none more common than the MacDonald chain. There is even an upmarket pizzeria right opposite Peterskirche, just off the Graben in Vienna, the grey marbled portico of which was fittingly designed by an Italian. But you will also see Hungarian, Nordic, French, German, Chinese and Russian restaurants. Almost every national cuisine is represented somewhere in Austria, but it is refreshing to note that the majority of Austrians still prefer their own wholesome cuisine, served in generous proportions, and often incorporating, or refining, another country's traditional cooking.

Without exception Austrian food throughout the nine federal provinces attains a high standard, and with so many dishes to choose from, selection can be bewildering. In the Alps, food tends to be heartier still, with plenty of Knödel (dumplings). Austrian Knödel are the best in the world, but that does not stop Austrians from eating potatoes as well. Austrian housewives pride themselves on cooking delicious meals and feather-light pastries, so don't pass up the chance of eating as a guest at home. The meal will be superb, the recipe probably originating from the lady's grandmother.

Some restaurants, particularly in the Salzkammergut region, will even cook the fish you catch for dinner, or the wild mushrooms you gather – there are infinite recipes for wild mushrooms in Austria – and will be only too delighted to arrange special dishes. You may find your platter brought to the table by a waitress wearing national dress, or, if you are dining at a wine tavern, by a young man in knee breeches and leather waistcoat. You may decide to opt for a banquet fit for an emperor at one of the many castle hotels scattered around the countryside, or in an atmospheric Heuriger in one of the wine growing areas. Whatever you settle for, you will be presented with a veritable feast, for above all, Austrians eat well and frequently.

Austrians believe in starting the day with a hearty breakfast. Breakfasts often amaze guests because of the staggering choice placed before them. In addition to all kinds of bread, from Schwarzbrot (black rye) to brioches, croissants and Austrian pastries, there will be baskets of fruit, mountain cheeses, hams, salamis and, in the Alps, bowls of freshly-picked mountain berries.

At 11 a.m. it is time for a hot snack known as Gabelfrühstück, which can take the form of an omelette, spicy sausage, or even soup. In the mountains after a hike you will see Austrians settling down unashamedly to this hot knife-and-fork meal. Don't mistake it, as I frequently do, for an early lunch, for that starts around 12.30 p.m. In restaurants on the ski slopes the food, although simple, is delicious, with superb crusty rolls, homemade soups and local specialities, with good local wines and Schnaps to help it along. Afterwards there will be pastries and coffee both topped with generous portions of whipped cream. After a morning's skiing this is the kind of food to enjoy as you bask in the warm Alpine sunshine. Food in Austria is more expensive on the whole than in Britain, but the servings are generous and most dishes well worth the price.

All kinds of restaurants from Gasthöfe, wine taverns, five star gastronomic temples, inns and restaurant chains like Wienerwald offer a variety of local dishes as well as the usual fare. Of course you can eat international cuisine, but when you see the range of Austrian dishes you will probably change your mind.

Soups are eaten a great deal in winter, and range from the highly seasoned Hungarian style Gulaschsuppe, Schwammerlsuppe made from wild mushrooms and Kartoffelsuppe (potato soup), to farmhouse soups and the popular Leberknödelsuppe (a meat broth with liver dumplings). Sometimes Frittate (pancake strips) are put into soups; on other occasions soups are accompanied by Gebäck (rolls).

In Vienna the Wienerschnitzel (veal in breadcrumbs) reigns supreme and is present on every restaurant menu, but alongside it you will find Holsteiner Schnitzel, Pariser Schnitzel, Schnitzel Cordon Bleu, Schnitzel Natur (fried without breadcrumbs) and a variety of other Schnitzels including the spicy Paprikaschnitzel. Knuckle of veal is also a popular dish.

Austrians are not particularly partial to lamb, with the exception of Steirisches Schöpsernes – the mutton ragout found in Styria. They prefer pork, which, like veal, is regularly consumed. You can choose from a selection of smoked pork, roast pork, grilled pork, pork with prunes, pork with dumplings, and in Vienna, Wiener Krenfleisch (stewed pork served with horseradish). For a rustic banquet try Bauernschmaus which is roast pork and ham served with Sauerkraut.

Every Austrian will have his favourite restaurant in which to introduce you to a welter of local specialities; but no matter where you dine, chicken is sure to appear. In Styria the favourite speciality is Backhendl (fried chicken in breadcrumbs). Elsewhere, Brathuhn (roast chicken) often cooked on a spit is greatly enjoyed. You will also find a variety of game, especially in Styria and Alpine areas. Wild boar, venison, pheasant, hare and quail are frequently encountered in the hunting season. Two typical Austrian game dishes are Rehfilet (fillet of venison with cranberries) and Wildschweinbraten (roast wildboar with dumplings).

Gulasch, originating in Hungary, is often highly-peppered and garnished with onions and tomatoes. As the Austrians have discovered, Gulasch is ideal for cold winter days. Another great Austrian dish is Tafelspitz (boiled beef) served with sauté potatoes and a variety of sauces from horseradish to apple. Faschiertes (meatballs) are delicious. Just remember that any bread you eat in restaurants is not included in the price of the meal. Dinners tend to be lighter than lunches, when cold meats and sausages are favoured. With no seacoast, Austria relies on its lakes for carp and trout, while Krebs (crawfish) and pickerel are popular delicacies. Knödel are found all over Austria, but if you are watching your waistline – beware. Knödel come in a variety of styles from unsweetened (when they accompany meat or soup), savoury or sweetened (when they are eaten as a dessert).

Balkan-style cooking lends itself to the way in which vegetables are prepared and you will find plenty of stuffed, spicy peppers, puréed spinach, to which, in true Austrian style, a dollop of cream has been added, stuffed cabbage and mushrooms. Gebackene Champignons (button mushrooms) fried in bread-crumbs and served with tartare sauce are a delicacy. Salads or crudités accompany some dishes, and it is customary to add a little sugar to salad dressing in Austria. Potatoes are sautéd, roasted, or grated and mixed with flour, then made into dumplings and noodles. As for sausages there is a wide selection from Frankfurters (known as Wieners) to spicy Salamis, Burenwurst, Krakauer, Polnische, liver and blood sausages. Cheeses vary from mountain cheeses – you can sample these at their best in some of the Alpine villages – to gruyères and a multitude of German style Käse (cheeses).

Cakes and coffee houses

Austrian bread is arguably the best in the world. You buy it in a Bäckerei (bakery) and wherever you find it, on the main street of a large town or in the back street of a small village, the choice is staggering. In Salzburg the ancient monastery of St Peter's still bakes bread on the premises for the monks, and any bread left over can be bought by the public. The loaves are large, the bread deliciously spicy and many local inhabitants make a special effort to buy it at the monastery rather than from a regular bakery.

To stand outside the window of an Austrian bakery gazing at the innumerable kinds of bread therein is an experience. There in front of you are plaited loaves of all shapes and sizes, bread twisted into the most intricate shapes, flat loaves, round loaves, oblong loaves, square loaves, some decorated with poppy seeds, others with salt crystals and rolls so exquisitely crusty you can hardly wait to bite into them. There are Buchteln (buns), Golatschen (plaited pastry), Striezeln (crispy rolls), Krapfen (doughnuts) and Mohnboutiz-zen (poppy seed cakes).

For cakes and gateaux you will need to find one of the many excellent pastry shops or Konditoreien, where you can also have coffee as you eat your warm Apfelstrudel. In patisserie shops you can buy Torten, layer cakes (like the cream filled Doboschtorte), nut-filled pastries, Pischingertorte with roasted almonds, marzipan, cream filled dates, and a superb selection of mouth-watering sweets. If you are in a restaurant you might order a Strudel filled with white cheese, cherries, apple or apricot; Pfannkuchen (pancakes filled with anything from cream to raisins), Salzburger Nockerl (a soufflé flavoured with lemon), Semmelschmarren (bread pudding), crêpes known as Palatschinken,

Kaiserschmarrn (a sweet omelette filled with raisins) or Marillenknödel (sweet dumplings with breadcrumbs outside and whole apricots within). Strudel comes in many varieties such as Millirahmstrudel (made from sour cream) to Griesstrudel (made with semolina). From soufflés to Torten, Austrian desserts are world famous, and with justification. Often coffee houses will place neat little blackboards outside their premises announcing 'warm Apfelstrudel' and that alone always causes a rush, for who can resist hot Austrian apple Strudel?

Torten take their names from their places of origin such as Linz (Linzer Torte), Ischler Torte, which is almond cake with apricot jam and so on. Some are named after great families like the Esterhazys. There are Indianers (pastries covered in dark chocolate), light airy crescents scattered with flaked almonds and others filled with walnuts and marzipan.

The coffee house is the ideal place to sample Austrian patisserie, and is a remnant from the time of the Turkish presence in Austria. After the Turkish sieges, when the last Turk had left Austria, some coffee beans were discovered. An Austrian from the Turkish camp had learned what to do with them and thus was born the coffee house in Austria which, in 1983, celebrated its three hundredth anniversary. Coffee houses, ranging from splendid emporiums with umblemished reputations like Demel, Heiner, and Sacher in Vienna to Tomaselli in Salzburg and Zauner's in Bad Ischl, are institutions. No matter what time of day you drop by such venerable establishments you will find them full. There is always something to pass the time, from gossip to the days' newsprint. Most regulars, however, are too busy eating their Sachertorte to notice what is going on at the adjacent tables.

In all coffee houses, from chains like the Aida Konditorei to Demel's the coffee is excellent, and there are innumerable varieties listed on the menu. These range from a simple Espresso to Mokka, Turkischer (Turkish coffee), a Melange (half coffee, half milk) to a Kapuziner and the famous Viennese coffee with its mountain of whipped cream called Kaffee mit Schlag. Schlag is a byword in Austria and most Austrians order a sickly pastry (also 'mit Schlag') with their coffee or hot chocolate. If you like cream, order a 'Doppelte Portion Schlag'. If you prefer black coffee in a glass with a single blob of whipped cream, ask for an Einspänner. In winter hot grogs are also served, so you can safely order a Mazagran (black coffee with rum) and in summer, Eiskaffee (iced coffee).

For anyone with a sweet tooth it must be purgatory to dismiss the confections winking at you from beautifully arranged shop windows. The displays in patisserie shops are more awesome than the Bäckerei in their variety. The dainty confections are brought to you on a silver tray with a small glass of water accompanying your coffee. Having ordered, the place is yours. You can help yourself to any of the newspapers suspended from their wicker racks and even start a political debate with your neighbour. Across the street more confectioners offering even more piles of delicacies from dates to Nusstorte are guaranteed to distract you.

It is amazing to me how such institutions have strenuously resisted change and are still enjoying as much of a vogue as they did in their heyday; yet it would be a strange visitor indeed who did not sample the wicked delights of Demel's, or take home a box of pastries from their infinitesimal selection.

Beverages

Weinstuben (wine bars) – known in Vienna as Beisels – often have quite a history. Home cooking is usually served, together with the local wines. Such places are packed by six p.m., but the atmosphere is hale and hearty. If you prefer beer there are plenty of inns, taverns and Keller all with a pleasant, lively atmosphere. Food is good and simple, and sometimes there is music too. The Viennese in particular become attached to certain hostelries, just as Franz Schubert did.

Austrian beer is excellent and is drunk in quantities at fêtes and festivals. The province of Styria alone produces three kinds of beer – Reininghaus and Puntigam are made in Graz, and Gosser beer in the industrial town of Loeben. If you are looking for soft drinks you can find those in many self-service chains, like Nordsee, where you can buy snacks and salads. Most countries have adopted Coca Cola almost as a national beverage, but not Austria. The Austrians' national drinks remain wine, beer, apple-juice and coffee.

Austria can trace its vineyards back to Roman times. Today wine growing areas in Lower Austria, the Weinviertel of Vienna, Styria and Burgenland cover 90,000 acres (46,000 ha). Eighty-five per cent of the wine produced is white, and although Austrian wines are made for easy drinking there are some excellent ones amongst them, including Gumpoldskirchen and Grüner Veltliner. Whites to look out for are Rheinriesling, one of the best dry wines, and Gewürztraminer. The red wines tend towards softness. Neither reds nor whites would be so presumptuous as to compete with the world's finest wines. Austrian table wines were not created to rival a Chateau Latour or a Mouton Rothschild. However, if your taste is for dry wines, you will find Austrian wines much drier than their German counterparts.

The Wachau region of the Danube valley is noted for its wines, such as Krems and Langenlois, both of which have a delicate bouquet. Grinzing, the wine village in the Vienna Woods, makes a sparkling wine. In Burgenland the wines from Rust are noted and the white Styrian wines from Leibnitz can be recommended.

Some of Austria's best white wines are produced at Mailberg on the Czechoslovakian border where the climate and the quality of the soil combine to make this area one of the best for white wine production. Some red wines, like the Blauer Burgunder from the pinot noir grape, are produced, but are less popular with Austrians and foreign visitors. The Blaufränkischer and Blauer Portugieser are high quality red wines, the latter being an old Austrian grape which produces a robust wine. The red wines of Bad Vöslau, south of Vienna, and Retz in the Weinviertel are also popular. Very few Spätlese and Auslese wines are produced.

Austria's largest wine producer, Lenz Moser, exports to Britain, West Germany, the USA and Canada. The Lenz Moser vineyards at Mailberg were once owned by the Knights of Malta. The Gruener Veltliner is produced there. Not far away at Lake Neusiedl, close to the Hungarian border, another well-known wine, the Gewürztraminer, is produced, popular with both Austrians and foreign visitors. As well as white and red wines, Austria makes Sekt, a version of champagne. The dry Henkell Schlumberger is especially good.

Austrians are not great wine exporters; should they become so, their white wines in particular might compete with the Germans. Wine making is a risky business, dependent upon many factors, not least the weather. Harsh winters can wreak havoc in the vineyards. In 1984 Austria produced 250 million litres, while the previous year's total had been almost double that, causing a surplus of stocks. At present it does not look as if Austria will add to the EEC's wine lake, but wherever you travel in Austria you can be assured of finding good local wines. The 1986 anti-freeze scandal will doubtless affect sales and production for a long time to come.

Distilled liquors, like Kirschwasser made from cherries, Obstbranntwein made from pears and apples, Wacholder from juniper berries and Himbeergeist from raspberries, are very much liked and bought by tourists to take home. Slivovitz (plum brandy), which is found throughout Yugoslavia and parts of Eastern Europe, is also frequently drunk in Austria. There is also an apricot brandy known as Hungarian Barack. Apfelsaft (apple juice) is drunk widely, often with soda added, when it is called Gespritzter (as is any wine mixed with soda water). Mineral water is easily obtainable in restaurants and supermarkets. A popular brand is Römer Quelle.

Austrian beers are good and inexpensive. Stiegelbräu and Augustiner Bräu, produced in Salzburg, are two of the best. Styria produces three beers, Innsbruck brews Adambräu and Vienna, Ottakringer. German beers are also popular.

Naturally enough the best places to sample wine are the wine taverns, or Heurigen. These venerable places are as much part of the Austrian way of life as the coffee house. Heurige can mean both wine tavern and last year's wine pressing, but usually you drink the year's wine, the Heuriger, in the Heurigen. The suburbs of Vienna are strewn with Heurigen which are indicated by a strip of pine or wine shingle. Grinzing, Sievering and Heiligenstadt are favourite areas. You can catch a number 38 streetcar from the centre of Vienna to Grinzing and spend the day wandering from tavern to tavern sampling the wine. You may drink inside or out, and in summer the outside benches are full of merry drinkers, who often improvise their own Heuriger songs.

The Heuriger is served either by the quarter litre, known as *ein Viertel*, or by the glass. Although the wine may seem light and fairly innocuous you will soon realise that it is, in fact, quite potent, which is why many regular Heuriger drinkers dilute their drinks with soda. The old Heurigen are for the most part rustic inns with wooden tables and old beams – rather like a rural English pub. Saturday and Sunday afternoons are the most popular times to visit the Heurige, for at weekends there is often Schrammel music and the crowd is free and easy and ready for amusement. The Heurige is a friendly informal place, and at night, when the gardens are illuminated by lanterns, the drinkers sitting at the rustic benches put you in mind of a Brueghel painting.

Winter sports

Austrians welcome the opportunity to be out of doors, and the Heurige provides the perfect excuse for getting out of town. Hospitality is second nature to

Austrians, and visitors will be invited along not just to the Heurige but to sporting events too. To the uninitiated it seems as if every Austrian was born on skis, had climbed mountains since infancy, and taken to curling as a babe in arms. It is certainly true that it is a rare Austrian who does not take part in one sport or another, often three or more, and at a serious level.

As two-thirds of the country is mountainous, winter sports are popular and important. Austrian ski pioneer Hannes Schneider gave his first ski lesson in the Arlberg in 1907 and ever since then St Anton has been well known. Skiing in Austria is by no means just for experts and stars of international downhill races – though during those events every Austrian who cannot be spectating on the ski slopes is glued to either his TV set or car radio – but is for everybody, whether a beginner, an intermediate or a professional skier. Most Austrian ski resorts have their own ski schools, the larger fashionable resorts often having six or more, where you can test your abilities under the expert eye of qualified instructors. In 1945 Austria had 12 cable cars, 6 ski lifts, and 8 mountain railways. Today it has 314 cable railways and some 3500 chair lifts and T-bars. Yet, despite new cable installations, there are still queues for the cable cars, thus underscoring the huge popularity of skiing in Austria.

The ski season runs from December to April, the most popular periods being Christmas and the New Year (when an even livelier atmosphere than normal prevails), February, March, and the first week in April. Some prefer the off-peak season when the crowds are fewer and it is easier to reach the pistes without long lines forming; but if you are going for ambience and some great *après ski*, then go during the peak periods even if it does cost more. Nothing quite equals chic resorts like Kitzbühel when they are in full swing!

Several companies operating in Britain organise ski packages to Austria, including Inghams, who have been sending tourists to Austria for 50 years. Ski package holidays include flights from Britain, transfers to the ski areas and accommodation in good class hotels. The advantage of ski packages is that you will be with a group of people of varying ski standards with whom you can swop tall stories at the end of the day as well as on the pistes. Bar crowds excel at

2 Skiing at Kitzbühel

talking over their thrills and spills and a mixed group of varied abilities can often be more fun than a holiday alone. Skiing is fun and is a sport in which everyone mixes in, no matter what his nationality or ability. Of course you can travel to the resorts as an individual, picking your hotel and flight and one of a number of first class ski resorts. Package tour brochures clearly state what the resort offers and the type of skiers it is best suited to, the class of hotel, amenities and so on. If you want *après ski*, clearly Kitzbühel, St Anton and Zürs would head the list, while quieter spots – like Gaschurn and Alpbach – are ideal for those seeking a less hectic atmosphere. If you choose a reliable tour operator you will have no worries. Please note that the longest ski slope descent in Austria is a staggering 8000ft (2440m) and is definitely not for beginners!

If you are a good skier you may, for added excitement, decide to learn to ski jump, and you can do this in the Montafon valley of the Vorarlberg, Mitterndorf in Styria and Villach in Carinthia. Austrian ski instructors undergo rigorous training, so once you are in their hands you can trust them. For all-round events and amenities, Kitzbühel is one of the very best. Its ski school, with its Red Devil team of ski instructors, offers special racing courses, and for expert skiers the Ski Circus – a series of marked trails which are floodlit by night – will take you through the Alps.

The Arlberg school still adopts the methods of Hannes Schneider teaching the Kurzschwingen-style (short and fast swinging), and those taught this way will countenance no other. Ski instruction costs vary, but if you want to learn it is wiser to start off the right way, despite the cost. Skiing is an expensive sport and you must be prepared for that before you go. In addition to the initial package you will be paying for ski passes, chairlifts, and the hire of ski equipment. Skis of various lengths can be hired. They come in a variety of materials from wood to plastic and fibreglass. Beginners usually start off with shorter skis and graduate to longer ones.

Austrian National Tourist Offices have a variety of brochures on winter sports which will assist you in making your final choice. Each province has its choice of ski resorts and the Tirol is often a favourite with visitors. It has Kitzbühel, St Anton and Mayrhofen as the major attractions. Well-known ski resorts in the Vorarlberg are Zürs, Lech and Tschagguns (which has two ski jumps used regularly in international competitions). In Styria, Tauplitz and Bad Mitterndorf are the best known; in Salzburg, Saalfelden; in Carinthia, Heiligenblut and Mallnitz; in Upper Austria, the Dachstein plateau, and in Lower Austria, Semmering.

The nursery slopes are the Austrians' kindergarten. Every weekend finds them racing down mountainsides. They drive out from the cities, with their skis jutting from the roofracks of their cars. They take their vacations on the ski slopes. It is therefore not surprising that ever since competitions were first introduced, from downhill racing to slaloms and ski jumping, Austrians have been very successful in the Winter Olympics.

You can even ski on Vienna's doorstep. Semmering, west of the city, is a popular weekend spot. Mariazell in Styria is another favourite, and for good skiers there is the Schneeberg. Winter finds Vienna isolated at weekends, except for the tourists, as Austrians have gone to the ski slopes. And who could blame them? With such a wealth of ski areas at their disposal it would be mad to stay in cities when they can get a winter sun tan and breathe fresh Alpine air.

Cross-country skiing is becoming increasingly popular although ski experts prefer to stick to downhill racing. However, cross-country skiing is quite a good way to become familiar with basic ski techniques, and it provides good exercise. You can practise cross-country skiing in Carinthia, Styria, Salzburg, Lower and Upper Austria and the Vorarlberg, trekking over 400 tracks.

Skibob and tobogganing can be fun, too, and are popular in most ski resorts, while curling and ice hockey definitely have their supporters. Curling is a sport that appeals to all age groups, but more particularly the middle age bracket who, in Austria at least, seem to thrive on it. It's a sport the Austrians do well at – both at amateur and professional levels – and it's a good spectator sport too. These days it is a rare ski resort that has no posters of forthcoming curling events. Austria has a staggering 250 ice skating rinks and, if you want to have a go at something different, try ice sailing on the frozen lakes.

Other sports and outdoor pursuits

Mountaineering and camping

Austria is also a major centre for mountaineering. There are several sporting organisations that climbers and hikers can join. The largest is the Öester-reichischer Alpenverein, the Austrian Alpine Association, which has 210,000 members. These various associations are responsible for the hundreds of Alpine huts scattered across the Alps. While the best of Austria's climbers take themselves off to far flung corners of the earth to scale the highest and most difficult mountains, others with more modest ambitions are content to walk the foothills of Vienna to the Swiss border; others to amble through flower-strewn meadows with the soaring Alps as a backdrop. Tiroleans are natural hikers and seem to have an advantage over the rest of us. In 1978 Reinhold Messner from the South Tirol climbed Everest without the benefit of oxygen.

Alpine peaks and glaciers are a great incentive for visiting climbers. If you don't want to climb all day, mountain railways and cable cars will take you part of the way and you can stop off at refuges, hotels and restaurants to catch your breath and admire the view. Austrian mountain guides are superb and the Austrian Mountain Refuge service ensures that climbing in the Austrian Alps is as safe as it could possibly be. Cinematic visions of the heroine falling over a cliff can be dispelled from your mind! It goes without saying that you have to be fit and active to scale mountains, but it would be foolhardy to set off without a guide. They are the experts who know the terrain; and it is the best possible experience, not to say pleasure, to climb with someone who really knows what he is doing.

There are more than 40 mountain climbing schools in Austria. Two excellent schools exist at Innsbruck in the Tirol, another in Land Salzburg. The Bergsteigerschule Heiligenblut in Carinthia is at the foot of the Grossglockner, Austria's highest mountain, and the Bergsteigerschule Dachstein is at the foot of the Dachstein mountain in Ramsau. The Austrian Alpine Club has branch organisations abroad, and if you wish to climb in Austria it is wise to contact the Club in advance, as such clubs own mountain huts right across the Alps which are vital for emergencies, and which can be used at the climbers' convenience. Mountain schools organise special climbs from June to October. Some provide climbing equipment, others do not. The climbs are for both beginners and regular climbers and are usually arranged a month in advance.

Fitness and leisure have become commonplace in any country these days, with many people turning into fanatics – visiting gymnasiums, forcing themselves to play squash and tennis and jog each day. The Austrians have a natural aptitude for this healthy living, and the necessary facilities abound. Today tennis is a feature of most cities and holiday resorts, while golf is available in Vienna, Salzburg, the Tirol and the other federal provinces.

Austrians are also keen athletes and riders. Even in the Alps you will find plenty of stables where you can hire horses to ride. In fact many equestrians like the frozen wastes of such resorts as Kitzbühel. Swimmers enjoy the heated indoor pools as alternatives to the pistes. Money allocated to sports promotion – some 80 million Austrian Schillings each year – goes towards the cost of facilities and sports centres. As well as the major sports are roller skating, bowling, power boat racing on the lakes, waterskiing, shooting, badminton and many others.

The great outdoors has always appealed, and camping is a good way of relaxing, as well as of being thrifty. Austria has many camping grounds, all with running water and the usual amenities set in woodlands, beside rivers and lakes. If you camp by a mountain stream, fishing is a sport you can do almost from your tent, providing you remember to get a licence first. The same applies to hunting. It is illegal to do either without permission. Trout is plentiful in mountain streams, rivers and the Salzkammergut lakes. Lakes like the Traunsee, Attersee and Mondsee also provide perch, carp and other varieties of fish, while Styria – particularly the Salzkammergut region – has some of the best fishing in Austria, and you can prove it by dining out on locally-caught fish in Styria's restaurants. Huchen, a salmon found in some of Austria's rivers, does not need to reach the sea to spawn, but breeds well in the tributaries of the Danube.

Water sports

Rivers provide the ideal locale for canoeists too. The Danube is a great starting point; or you can try lakes, mountains, streams and valleys. Experts go for the Enns river where the world kayak races are held each year. In contrast the Inn river is safe for beginners, and most of it is navigable. Its tributary, the Ziller, is one of the most scenic regions and if you are a leisurely canoeist this is an ideal area, while mountain streams are exhilarating partly on account of the stunning Alpine scenery. It is logical to choose rivers which have good clear stretches and the minimum number of locks, otherwise you will spend half the time stationary.

Austrian watersport enthusiasts compensate for their lack of coastline by using their lakes and rivers to the full. In summer the Carinthian, Styrian and Land Salzburg lakes are filled with waterskiers, sailboats and windsurfers all anxious to make room for their own preference. If you are a fledgling sailor it's advisable to take a sailing course; finding yourself in the wake of the experts is a daunting experience. Lake Constance and Lake Neusiedl provide excellent sailing possibilities and you can hire boats at a reasonable cost. If you have friends who are members of one of Austria's 40 yacht clubs, then you will do better still. In any event, lakes like the Mondsee in the Salzkammergut offer plenty of scope for sailors of all standards.

Windsurfing is popular in the warmer lakes, such as those in Carinthia. As beginners are likely to spend more time in the water than on a sailboard it is useful to know that the lakes reach temperatures of 26 °C (79°F) in mid-summer. Although depending on the individual, experts calculate that it takes between seven to ten hours to learn the basics of windsurfing. The art, of course, is to stay upright, but this is much easier said than done. From the shore you may think it is all a matter of balance, but wind direction is important too. Windsurfing is frustrating, but can also be exhilarating.

Gliding

Of all the outdoor sports to gain popularity in Austria, gliding has been the most surprising. A few years ago no one would have given it a chance, but today in Austria, gliding is ferociously pursued to such a degree that several holiday resorts actually have glider landing stages. Graz airport is quite accustomed to getting gliders airborne, which could not please the enthusiasts more. Föhn gliding is a speciality in Austria, the dry southern wind keeping the glider aloft and at the same time giving the pilot fabulous views over the Alps. There are a handful of gliding schools in Austria, varying from the Wien-Donauwiese on the outskirts of Vienna to the Zell-am-Zee gliding school in Land Salzburg. If you have never tried gliding before you will find it fascinating! Gliding is not as soundless as you might expect, as the wind makes unexpected noises. There seems to be a great deal of steering to be done, at least initially. Gliding is an acquired taste, quite different from piloting a small aircraft, but quite addictive, judging by the number of enthusiastic glider pilots all over Austria.

Hunting

Hunting has always been popular in the mountains, with a range of game from roe deer to chamois, and these days archery is high on the list of popular sports. The Öesterreichischer Bogenschützenverband (The Austrian Archery Association) has its headquarters in Bad Goisern in Upper Austria, but its ten archery clubs are dotted all over the country, from Vienna to Styria where the European Archery Championships are held. Visitors are welcome at the clubs. If you would like to become an archer in your spare time, courses are held three times a year.

Golf

Austria has 17 golf clubs, all of them private, but visitors are welcome on a green fee basis. Of the 17 courses, seven have 18 holes. The Vienna Golf Club in the Prater is one of these, so that visitors to the city can play their golf close at hand. The course at Seefeld in the Tirol has stunning scenery and, according to golfers, is one of Austria's hardest courses. Some travel operators arrange special sporting holidays with courses in sailing, fishing, mountaineering, skiing and tennis. The Austrian National Tourist Office is the place to find out full details about sports vacations.

Football

Football stadiums are found in all provincial capitals and towns for, like the rest of Europe, football attracts the crowds. Vienna's stadium in the Prater is the biggest, with a capacity of 72,000. The Prater has been developed as a sporting complex. There is an indoor stadium, a cycling track, an indoor athletics track and facilities for tennis and volleyball. The Austrian Football Association comprises 2000 clubs. Since Austria took part in the playoff rounds of the World Cup in Argentina in 1978 there has been a marked increase of interest in the sport. In 1982 Austia qualified for the World Cup in Spain and since then everyone who could get into a pair of football boots did so. Winter sports, however, still remain firm favourites.

Cycling

Two sports Austrians excel at are judo and cycling. In judo Austria is unsurpassed, while cycling could not be more pleasurable anywhere. The stunning scenery provides a spectacular backdrop – at least for spectators. The Tour of Austria punishes competitors for almost 935 miles (1500km), over such passes as the Grossglockner, the highest stage of the run.

Motor racing

Austria has produced many sporting heroes, but none more popular than Nicki Lauder, the world motor racing champion. Motor sport is now very popular, with two racetracks – Oesterreichring in Styria, and Salzburgring in Land Salzburg – often making the headlines. Another well-known Austrian driver, Jochen Rindt, was killed in 1970.

Casinos

While Austrians are not particularly noted for gambling, there are ten casinos, all run under government licence and most of them open from 4 p.m. daily, where you can play roulette, blackjack, and baccarat. You can find casinos in smart resorts like Baden, and Bad Gastein, in hotels like the Hotel Winkler in Salzburg, in Linz, Kitzbühel, Bregenz, Seefeld in the Tirol, and Velden on

Carinthia's Wörthersee. The entrance fee is about £2.50 in most casinos, but in Vienna's Cercle it is twice the price.

Shopping

Shopping is a favourite pastime for many visitors to Austria. There is a wide range of merchandise from inexpensive souvenirs to classic Loden coats. Austria's textile industry is concentrated on three principal centres: the Vorarlberg where cotton, woven goods and the famous Vorarlberg lace are produced; the Inn valley of the Tirol where Loden cloth is manufactured, and Vienna, home of Austria's fashion industry. Austrian fashion designers have, in the main, concentrated on sports and leisure wear, leaving the more avant-garde styles to the Italians and French, yet Austria's Women's Fashion Weeks held each year in Vienna attract buyers from many parts of the world, including the USA and Japan. Truly innovative fashion is rarely produced, Austrian designers preferring to concentrate on traditional designs and good quality products. Their fur industry, on the other hand, turns out some superbly original designs. You will also find distinctive and unusual jewellery, especially in the smart jewellers of Vienna and Salzburg which can rely upon a discerning, international clientele.

Top ski resorts exhibit some of the best ski wear to be found in Europe. As most Austrians spend time on the ski slopes at some time in their lives, the ski designers must be inventive to keep up with their European competitors. As for ski equipment, skis, poles and all other equipment are superbly made in Austria. You can buy all makes of skis from the Austrian company Heads, to Rossignol and Atomic.

Austrian chocolates are amongst the best in the world; Austrian patisserie a foregone conclusion. Nowhere else will you sample delicacies equal to those bought at Demels, Heiners or Zauner's. Sachertorte, mailed all over the world in its sophisticated, chocolate-coloured boxes, is internationally acclaimed, thanks to Prince Metternich's chef who devised the confection. Cowbells, wooden carvings and porcelain are still bought by the dozen by foreign visitors. As for Tirolean hats, if there was ever a national symbol, it is surely the Alpine hat with its chamois brush. You have only to look around you in a crowded street to know you are in Austria by the headgear sported by old and young alike.

Your duty free allowance is that of the EEC countries. You will find duty free shops more expensive in Austria than England. Vienna airport has a wide range of boutiques from Cartier to a comprehensive international bookshop, and a delicatessen where you can buy Mozart sweets, Austrian chocolate, wines and a variety of edible exotica from smoked hams to patisserie.

Shops open from 8a.m. until 6p.m. Most operate until noon on Saturdays, when those Austrians who can, take off for the mountains. No one wants to be seen in Vienna when there are pistes waiting to be tackled. Post offices open from Monday to Friday from 8 a.m. to noon and from 2 p.m. to 6 p.m., banks from 8 a.m. to 3 p.m. Between 7 a.m. and 8 p.m. there are seven radio broadcasting hours in English and French starting with *Good Morning Vienna*.

The Blue Danube Magazine contains news reports and reviews, and goes on the air between noon and 2 p.m., terminating with the *Evening Round-up* from 6 p.m. until 7.30 p.m., a programme consisting of news bulletins, sports round-ups and interviews.

The clothes you pack for a visit naturally depend upon the areas in which you plan to stay. Austria enjoys a moderate Central European climate. If you aim to climb in high altitudes, protective clothing such as raingear is necessary, along with emergency provisions. It is also essential to check weather reports frequently. In most ski resorts, even the most fashionable ones, you will not need to dress in the evenings, casual wear being appropriate for most *après ski* events.

By contrast, should you be invited to the Viennese Opera you should sport your glitziest wear, for the Viennese treat their opera with respect and dress accordingly. Black tie for men and long evening dresses for ladies are no longer obligatory, but the occasion is definitely dressy and jeans would be frowned upon. This too applies to any grand occasion such as a ball or gala evening, when best clothes are worn. For sporting occasions and general day wear, casual clothes, shorts and sneakers and T shirts are usual. Most people bring their own ski wear, but if you want to wait until your arrival on the slopes you will find Austria's boutiques among the best in Europe. You can hire ski boots, poles, etc. at reasonable prices which obviates the necessity to transport them by air.

Tipping

Tipping can be a sore point in some foreign countries, but in Austria everything is made simpler by hotels and restaurants including service charges in their rates, with few exceptions. However, despite that, it is usual to leave a small tip in restaurants. You should tip porters, taxi drivers and cloakroom attendants.

Health and insurance

Although it is wise to take out holiday insurance, you need have no qualms about falling ill. Austria has plenty of English-speaking doctors and a list can be obtained from the IAMAT (International Association of Medical Assistance for Travellers). You can safely drink the water, and it's not likely you will suffer from sunburn, although you can get scorched beside the lakes and in the mountains. Pharmacies (Apotheken) abound, operating on a rota system for night and Sunday duty. Emergency medical services (Ärztedienst) can be obtained from the telephone directory or local police station. All mountain resorts operate a mountain rescue service (Bergrettungsdienst).

If you plan to ski you should take out an insurance policy which covers you for all eventualities both on and off the ski slopes, for while Austrian doctors can patch you up so that you are back on the pistes in three days, after care costs money.

Austria has a number of health resorts and spas which provide treatment for all complaints, such as rheumatism and asthma, which respond to climatic therapy. You don't have to go to spas for cures only. Many go purely for rest and relaxation in attractive, peaceful surroundings.

Entertainment

Austrian National Tourist Offices in the main cities publish pamphlets on music festivals, dramas and entertainments. In Vienna, *Rendezvous Wien* tells you all you want to know about forthcoming events from new art collections to exhibitions and charity concerts. Artists as diverse as Eugene Ionesco, Edward Albee, Julio Iglesias and Frank Sinatra are just some of the illustrious names to be seen on theatre bills. The *Veranstaltungsvorschau Wien* also lists forthcoming attractions from balls to trade fairs and sporting events.

During the Vienna Festival there are operas, concerts, and theatre productions all listed in the Vienna Festival Preview. *Wien Programm*, a pamphlet enumerating each month's cultural events, can be obtained at Information Offices or theatre ticket booking agencies. Another useful leaflet is the *Wiener Musik-Sommer*, which lists summer concerts from Kirchenkonzerte (church music) to Schrammelabende (Viennese Schrammel music played by a group including at least one violinist and one accordionist), symphony concerts, palace concerts and operettas, as well as special events which include anything from military music to the European Youth Orchestra. Renowned conductors such as Claudio Abbado, Leonard Bernstein and Herbert von Karajan are regularly seen conducting orchestras at music festivals throughout Austria.

Similarly in Salzburg all cultural information can be obtained from the local Tourist Information Office. Pamphlets on hotels, Salzburg Panorama Tours listing the tours of the region including the popular 'Sound of Music tour', museums, winter and summer events and city maps can also be obtained there. The booklet *Salzburg Events* is useful to have around as it lists each year's main attractions from palace concerts to Festival Hall productions, concerts in churches and in the Mirabell palace, theatres, carnivals and Mozart week productions. During the Salzburg Easter and Whitsun festivals, as well as musical concerts there are operas and ballets and you can hear some of the world's finest orchestras directed by international conductors.

Festivals

The Salzburg Summer Festival takes place from the last week in July to 1 September. During the opening, festivities in the streets and squares celebrate the event, rendering it a colourful and joyous occasion with all nationalities taking part. There are more than 140 festival performances from operas like Verdi's *Macbeth* to sacred dramas, Lieder recitals, chamber and choral concerts. If you should miss the Summer Festival, Salzburg holds a Cultural Week from mid-October to mid-November, where you can see Salzburg folkloric events combining poetry, song and dance, operas, plays and concerts. Salzburg holds summer courses from June to August in fine arts (painting, architecture, sculpture and design), drama and language courses.

Festivals in the various provinces are listed overleaf.

Vienna
Festival of Vienna
Viennale (Film Festival)
Ballet Festival
Music Summer Viennale

Salzburg
Mozart Week
Hellbrunn Festival
Easter & Whitsun Music Festivals
Summer Music Festival

Vorarlberg
Bregenz Festival

Carinthia
| Ossiach | Carinthia Music Festival |
| Millstatt | International Music Weeks |

Burgenland
Eisenstadt	Haydn concerts (Esterhazy Palace)
Morbisch	Lake Festival
Wiesen	International Jazz Festival

Upper Austria
| Linz | Bruckner Festival |
| Bad Ischl | Operetta Festival |

Lower Austria
| Baden | Summer operetta |
| Langenlois | Brass Bands Festival |

Styria
| Graz | Styrian Festival |

Tirol
| Ambras | Palace concerts |

Tourist information offices

Vienna (Wien)
Fremdenverkehrsstelle der Stadt Wien (Vienna City Tourist Information)
Opernpassage. (open daily from 9a.m.–7p.m.)
Österreichische Fremdenverkehrswerbung (Austrian National Tourist Office)
Margaretenstrasse 1. 1040 Wien

Salzburg (City)
7 Auerspergstrasse

Land Salzburg (province)
Landesverkehrsamt in Salzburg. Mozartplatz, 5010 Salzburg

Upper Austria
Schillerstrasse 50. 4020 Linz

Lower Austria
Paulanergasse 11. 1040 Wien

Carinthia
Kaufmanngasse 13. 9010 Klagenfurt

Styria
Herrengasse 16, Landhaus. 8010 Graz

Burgenland
Landhaus 7000. Eisenstadt

Tirol
Boznerplatz 6. 6010 Innsbruck
Kitzbühel
6370 Kitzbühel. Tirol.

Vorarlberg
Römerstrasse 7. 6901 Bregenz

Further information about Austria can be obtained from the Austrian National Tourist Offices in Europe and the USA (New York and Los Angeles).

5
UPPER AUSTRIA

The province of Upper Austria (known in Austria as Oberöesterreich) covers 4625 square miles (11,980sq. km) and can be split into three very different kinds of landscape. The Danube Valley divides Upper Austria into areas of limestone Alps, granite hills in the north, and the Salzkammergut, the southern lakeside region which possesses some of the most dazzling scenery of the province. With a population of over a million, Upper Austria relies on tourism and agriculture. Most tourists head for the Salzkammergut, which also spreads itself over the two neighbouring provinces of Land Salzburg and Styria. Land Salzburg can claim the delightful Fuschlsee, the largest proportion of the Wolfgangsee; Styria has the Aussee and the Grundl and Toplitz lakes, while Upper Austria possesses the two largest lakes, the Attersee and Traunsee, as well as the Mondsee.

The Salzkammergut

These days the Salzkammergut is well equipped to deal with tourists and although you will find a few castle-hotels, the emphasis is placed on Gasthöfe and moderate to inexpensively priced accommodation. Furthermore, the weather is generally warm during the peak season of the summer months of July and August, and the Salzkammergut offers plenty of opportunities for sports and relaxation. The season for most lakeside hotels is from May to September and if you plan to spend more than a month in the region, many hotels offer reduced rates. The ski season is at its best from December to April, but in the Dachstein region the season can last until the end of May.

At Obertraun you can ski the Dachstein plateau at heights ranging from 5000 to 9000ft (1525–2750m) in splendid glacial scenery. The Dachstein ice caves are enjoyable to visit, and the hotels in the area are excellent, serving good, wholesome mountain meals. Even in Linz, the capital of the province, the visitor will find hotel accommodation prices well down by comparison with those in Vienna and Salzburg, and as there is a lot to explore in Upper Austria, travellers consider their money well spent. Restaurants and Gasthöfe offer local specialities and, in lakeside locations, freshly caught fish and good homecooking.

Reaching Upper Austria presents no problems by road or rail. The public transport system is good, with three main railway lines criss-crossing the province. Local bus services usually run on time, and Information Offices are only too happy to recommend the best and fastest routes. In the Salzkammergut, steamer services operate from May to October. Additionally there are many side trips the visitor can enjoy all within easy reach, including the city of Salzburg. Upper Austria offers a wealth of possibilities from the salt mines of Hallstatt, which played a prominent part in Austria's economy, to spas like Bad Ischl, which once attracted emperors and prelates and which now caters for the more discerning tourists.

Lake Mondsee and the town of Mondsee

It comes as no surprise to discover that the Salzkammergut is the province's chief tourist area. Its largely unspoiled landscapes of lakes, wooded slopes and meadows provides the perfect spot for relaxation. Each visitor will have his favourite lake, either for vistas, hotel accommodation, sports or atmosphere and many prefer Lake Mondsee, 5 miles (8km) long and shaped like a crescent, which the Romans called Moonlake, simply because, despite its chilly sounding title, it has the warmest water of any of the three lakes in Upper Austria's Salzkammergut. However, it has changed considerably since the eighteenth century when Mondsee had close ties with the Benedictine Abbey.

The town of Mondsee is approached through an avenue of lime trees, and sooner or later visitors usually arrive at the lakeside where they can dawdle the hours away beneath the trees. Lakes such as the Mondsee offer a truly relaxing ambience, and mercifully there is no pressure on the tourist to go all out to enjoy himself.

For those who are decidedly energetic and who like to wander around towns, their efforts will be rewarded by Mondsee's parish church, once a former abbey church dating from the fifteenth century. Although the façade has been reworked, the interior has preserved its original Gothic vaulting. In the local museum you can learn all about the history of the church and glimpse an interesting exhibit, a boat cut from a single tree (Einbaum). Such boats can occasionally be seen today.

Lake Attersee

Attersee, twice the size of the Mondsee, is much beloved by fishermen due to its lake trout which like the cold, clear waters. Lake Attersee, sometimes called the Kammersee, has, on its west bank, an area of sunny orchards, while the lake itself is crowded in summer with vacationers who come to stroll along its banks, or to enjoy the watersports. Some lakeside accommodations have garden terraces and restaurants which, as well as locally-caught fish like trout and pickerel, often serve game.

Lake Traunsee and the town of Gmunden

Like Attersee, the Traunsee, the second largest lake, measuring 7 miles (11km), has its steamer traffic during the summer months. There is nothing like sailing the lakes of the Salzkammergut with their sun dappled shores and clear, still waters. Being marooned on a steamer in the lake affords splendid views of the surrounding areas. One of the most idyllic is Traunkirchen, situated on the peninsula which stretches into the lake. The Corpus Christi processions which take place from late May to early June are a big feature of this charming village, attracting scores of visitors. A climb above the town gives you an overall view. One of the most notable spots is the Kalvarienberg which is particularly favoured in good weather when sunsets flare over the Traunsee.

The lakes have their associations with musicians, some of whom, like Brahms, lived for a time on the Traunsee; Richard Wagner composed *Tristan und Isolde* there. Beyond Traunkirchen lies Gmunden, a resort of the Salzkammergut, with wonderful views of the Traunsee. The town is noted for its pottery. It has a delightful esplanade along the shores shaded by chestnut trees. As it is the chief resort of the Traunsee, Gmunden has several hotels and Gasthöfe as well as restaurants, some of which serve locally caught fish. It also has some of the best equipped lake beaches and an unusual costume parade in April, known as the *Liebstattsonntag*, when girls in national dress hand out gingerbread hearts with messages inscribed in pink icing sugar. In high season Gmunden celebrates with brass bands and fireworks.

The two castles of the area the Seeschloss and Landschloss (or Ort Chateau) are joined by a 400ft (122m) wooden bridge and are much photographed by tourists to the area. A nephew of Franz Josef bought the estate in the late nineteenth century and lived there under the name of Johann Ort. Like the beautiful Elizabeth of Bavaria, he met an untimely end. He vanished on a cruise in South America and was never heard of again.

Salt

The Salzkammergut made its reputation on its salt. The Kammergut was crown land and its revenue boosted the exchequer or Kammer. Salt was so precious a commodity that Emperor Maximilian decided to put the salt industry into State hands. The Habsburgs had been quick to recognise the value of salt and they were so worried that the salt might be illegally spirited away from the Salzkammergut without *their* taxes being imposed upon it that the region was banned to visitors, while the local people were obliged to remain within that limited area and were even restricted from marrying outside it. Clearly some of them managed to avoid this restriction, but the ban was not relaxed until the nineteenth century. By then Emperor Franz Josef had discovered that salt also had curative properties and thus Bad Ischl became famous.

Bad Ischl

The Emperor established his summer court at Bad Ischl. He had met his wife, Princess Elizabeth of Bavaria (the doomed 'Sissi'), at Bad Ischl and romance blossomed. Once the Imperial villa was built in 1853 – it was a wedding gift to the Emperor from the Archduchess Sophia, who was also a fervent believer in the saline cures – Bad Ischl suddenly acquired a fashionable image which sent everyone from artists to musicians, and royal hangers-on scurrying to the spa. Nineteenth-century artists like Rudolf von Alt and Ferdinand Waldmüller were soon setting up their easels. Franz Lehar had a villa in Bad Ischl, which has been turned into a museum, where he composed the *Merry Widow*. He died at Bad Ischl in 1948. Anton Bruckner, in whose music you can visualise the hills and lakes of Upper Austria, played the organ in the local church.

The landscape is as delightful today as it was then; from the park of the Imperial villa you can glimpse the Dachstein mountains. Johann Strauss the Younger soon arrived there, while the nineteenth-century Viennese playwright, Johann Nestroy, was also attracted by the spa town. King Edward VII visited Bad Ischl in 1905, 1907 and 1908, on one occasion sharing a car with Emperor Franz Josef. Unwittingly the Emperor had established Bad Ischl as one of the most chic spas in Austria and it was not long before its saline baths and, in particular, the treatment of Dr Wirer from Vienna, who was a keen believer in the salt cures, were all the rage.

The brine baths date from 1840 when the Biedermeier style was at its height. These days the spa has built a reputation for the treatment of diseases of the respiratory system and certain vascular conditions. It is situated in parkland surrounded by wooded mountain slopes. Like the brine baths, the pump room and the theatre are in the Biedermeier style.

Away from the spa, the town of Bad Ischl is worth browsing in. The Esplanade, a boulevard beside the Traun, was once the area favoured by the salt refiners of Bad Ischl, and one of these houses, easily identified by its rococo façade, remains. On the main shopping street, the Pfarrgasse, you will find the Zauner cafe and patisserie dating from the nineteenth century. It served the Imperial Court when it was in residence in summer. Bad Ischl's summer season is a good time to be in town. From June to September there are concert performances and regular productions at the Lehar Theatre, once the old Imperial Court Theatre.

The Kaiserville (Imperial villa) standing on the left bank of the Ischl can be visited from May to October. Despite its colonnaded exterior and some fine interior decorations, the Kaiserville emphasises Franz Josef's love of hunting and his own modest taste in standards of comforts. The reception rooms contain his hunting exhibits, paintings and personal memorabilia. The villa evokes memories of the doomed House of Austria, for though the Imperial villa is today in the possession of Franz Josef's great-grandson, Markus von Habsburg, the Grey Salon used by Empress Elizabeth remains exactly as she left it on 16 July 1898. She never returned, for the beautiful Sissi, who was noted for her quick changing moods, was assassinated in Geneva that same year.

Leaving behind the sad memories of Empress Elizabeth's early death we enter the world of operetta at St Wolfgang. If you enjoy romance you may stay at the updated Weisses Rössl (White Horse Inn) which was the location of the operetta of that name. Before the operetta left its mark St Wolfgang was noted for what is popularly held to be one of the finest Gothic carvings in the world, that of its winged altarpiece sculpted by Michael Pacher. Born around 1435, the artist was commissioned to make the now famous carving and he completed the work in 1481. You can see Pacher's masterpiece on request only, except on popular festivals, for it is closely guarded by its custodians and with good reason, for although St Wolfgang parish church has two other altars, the Pacher carving, representing the coronation of the Virgin, easily surpasses them.

3 Hallstatt

The Dachstein range

Like the Salzkammergut, the Dachstein massif – vast limestone cliffs which form the eastern Alps – extends over Land Salzburg and Styria as well as Upper Austria.

Hallstatt

The town of Hallstatt, which is recognised as dating from Austria's earliest period of civilisation and thus the oldest community in Austria, is situated in a foothill of the Dachstein range, and acquired its name from the Halstättersee. Salt mines had been Halstatt's wealth since neolithic times and today they are still being worked. The museum contains relics of the Halstatt period at its height between the years 1000–500 BC and reveals that in prehistoric times piles were driven into the lake for support. Even today the town, in the shadow of the mountain, is built up on terraces. If you wish, you can take guided tours of the salt mine from May to October. Another worthwhile trip is to the ice caves of the Dachstein glacier. You will find Gasthöfe and pensions in Halstatt, should you wish to extend your stay. Halstatt once needed every inch of space for the living and thus did not have a graveyard. The remains of the dead were preserved in the charnel house.

Spital-am-Pyhrn

Spital-am-Pyhrn, where the Steyr and Enns valleys meet, would probably be bypassed were it not for the Stiftskirche built in baroque style with its altarpiece paintings by Master Schmidt of Krems. It gained a reputation as a resting place due to its monastery, founded in the twelfth century by Otto von Bamberg for the purpose of providing a refuge for travellers using the Pyhrn Pass. So perhaps would Pfarrkirchen, the parish church of Bad Hall 1 mile (1.6km) distant from the spa, if it were not for the spa itself. However, Spital is on the main Linz-Graz railway line and has several Gasthöfe where you can stay. It is also a good spot for ski beginners. It has mountain lodges, a ski jump and toboggan run.

Bad Hall

Bad Hall, on the other hand, is noted for its iodised springs used to treat circulation, metabolic and glandular disorders. They are thought by many to be the strongest in Europe and as a result many go there seeking a cure not only for the aforementioned ailments, but also for heart and eye diseases. The wooded surroundings of Bad Hall make the spa especially attractive. A good place to stay is the castle pension of Schloss Feyregg with its period-style furnishings. There are government-owned hotels in and near the spa park. Bad Hall also has good sporting facilities, including tennis, riding and shooting.

Kremsmünster

Five miles (8km) west of Bad Hall stands one of the most famous abbeys of Austria – Kremsmünster, overlooking the Krems valley. It contains the Tassilo chalice, the oldest example of goldsmiths' art in Austria, ascribed to the year AD 769 and named after the founder of the abbey, Tassilo II of Bavaria. His son, Gunther, was fatally wounded in a hunting accident and his father had the abbey built in the eighth century to his memory. In the eighteenth century the architects Antonio Carlone and Jakob Prandtauer worked on the abbey's restoration. As well as the Tassilo chalice the monastery contains a vast art collection, including a twelfth-century reliquary and an illuminated Bible dating from the eighth century, among the 100,000 volumes in the library.

Steyr

Nearby is the town of Steyr and the village of Christkindl, which takes its name from the Infant Christ. At Christmas every year the children of Christkindl send their messages to the Weihnachtsmann (Father Christmas). Whether or not they are granted their requests is another matter, but nevertheless millions of letters each year are forwarded by the good auspices of the Austrian Post Office.

4 *Pilgrimage church at Christkindl, Steyr*

Pilgrims still visit the baroque church built by architects Jakob Prandtauer and
Antonio Carlone which is dedicated to the Christ child.

Steyr is considered by many to be the finest preserved of any German-
speaking town, with an impressive assortment of old buildings. Moreover it
still continues to work iron, a tradition which has persisted for 800 years. Today
Steyr had added vehicle factories. Since 1945 the Steyr-Daimler Puch plant has
been producing engines, tractors and trucks. Once the town's iron was used for
making arms which went to Venice and Constantinople, and Steyr considered
itself a worthy rival to Vienna. These days it is the industrial centre, and the
second largest town of Upper Austria, which has resulted in industrial suburbs
spreading out around the city; but the old city has remained more or less intact.
Steyr can claim to have given its name to the province of Styria – Steirermark.

The Stadtplatz, with its great display of late Gothic and Renaissance houses,
is the focal point of the town. In the centre of the street-cum-square you will
find the seventeenth-century Leopold fountain. Two main buildings in the

Stadtplatz immediately catch your attention. They are the late Gothic-styled Bummerlhaus mansion, considered to be the finest Gothic house in the city, and the rococo Rathaus (town hall). The courtyard of many of the houses are of special interest. They have wrought iron balconies, pillars and arcades. The town's old granary is now a museum.

Anton Bruckner

Although Anton Bruckner was born in Ansfelden, a village to the west of St Florian, he composed his Sixth Symphony in Steyr. When he was 13 years old his father died and Bruckner was taken in as a chorister by the St Florian monastery school. This was perhaps his first contact with sacred music. He taught for a time near Freistadt but eventually returned to the monastery, where he first taught, before being appointed organist in 1848 when he was 24 years old. Bruckner later became organist at Linz Cathedral but in 1868, like so many musicians and composers of his day, made his way to Vienna where he took up the post of Professor at the Conservatory in 1871.

But Bruckner was an unwordly man who never reconciled himself to Vienna. By all accounts he appears to have been an isolated figure, a loner whose heart remained in St Florian, for he never forgot his association with the abbey and desired to be buried there. His years in Vienna were the scene of triumphs and disappointments and by the time he died on 1 October 1896 he had composed nine symphonies as well as numerous choral works. Today he is recognised as the greatest exponent of nineteenth-century church music in Austria. His memorial slab lies in the crypt of St Florian's, beneath the organ loft with its 7000 pipes and 103 registers. In summer there is a daily organ recital which no doubt the serious and totally dedicated composer would appreciate.

St Florian's monastery

St Florian, Upper Austria's patron saint, who gave his name to the largest abbey in the province, was converted to Christianity. He was martyred in 304 under Diocletian, and his body cast into the river Enns. The legend says that his body was buried at the spot on which the present abbey stands which is about 10 miles (16km) from Steyr. The architect Carlo Antonio Carlone began the building of the modern day abbey, one of Austria's greatest baroque edifices, in 1686, though an abbey had stood on the spot since the year 880. However, before Carlone could finish the work, he died and Jakob Prandtauer was brought in to supervise the completion of the building.

St Florian's monastery includes a Marmorsaal (marble hall) and library attached to the inner courtyard at the edge of which stands the Eagle's fountain. The library is noted for its early manuscripts while the marble hall was dedicated to Prince Eugene of Savoy to commemorate his role in defending the Austrian Empire against Turkish attack. Today, like the Marmorsaal of the Mirabell Palace in Salzburg, it is used for concert performances.

Albrecht Altdorfer, a painter of the sixteenth-century Danube School, who painted the 14 pictures of the St Sebastian altar in St Florian's abbey, is commemorated in the Altdorfer Gallery. Born in Regensberg in 1480 Altdorfer

5 Monastery of St Florian

6 *View of Enns and St Michael's church*

is noted for his landscape paintings and, as well as being an artist, Altdorfer was an architect and wood engraver.

On the same side of the inner courtyard as the Altdorfer gallery lie the imperial apartments and church. You reach the sumptuous apartments by a grand staircase and as you make your way through the halls and state rooms you are reminded of the fact that visits from royalty were not uncommon. Until the end of the eighteenth century a succession of emperors and princes had occasion to visit St Florian's.

Enns

East of St Florian lies Enns, which was granted a charter in 1212, thus making it the oldest town in Upper Austria. It developed from the old Roman camp of Lauriacum and eventually emerged as the capital of the Roman province of Noricum. In the municipal museum there are discoveries of the old town of Lauriacum.

The early Gothic Parish church at Enns was originally Franciscan and is noted for its double nave. Like Steyr, Enns has several well-preserved baroque houses, some with oriel windows, but the focal point of the city is the Stadtturm, the 200ft (61m) high tower in the main square, erected at the command of Emperor Maximilian II in the sixteenth century.

Linz

Twelve miles (19km) west of Enns lies Linz, the fast expanding industrial town, Austria's third largest city and capital of Upper Austria, with a population of around 212,000. The city was built on both sides of the Danube. In the Middle Ages Linz was an important crossroads, but long before the thirteenth century the Romans noted that not only did Linz command the Danube valley, but it was also the route by which that precious commodity, salt, travelled from Halstatt on its way to Bohemia. Shipping became important during the Middle Ages and through the centuries shipping on the Danube increased so that today the port of Linz is by far the most significant of the middle Danube. Moreover Linz is a major centre for iron, steel and chemicals. The Austrian United Steelworks and Chemie Linz AG possess the most modern factory equipment in Austria.

Industry's growth has swallowed up the southern suburbs, but miraculously the centre of the old town has survived the onslaughts of industrialisation. Linz takes its name from the Roman encampment of Lentia, which dates from the fifth century. A slave trading centre is known to have existed there, and during the sixth century Bavarians settled in the region. Three centuries later Linz had transformed itself into a market town and had begun to expand. It was Emperor Friedrich III who put his seal of approval on the city by residing in the castle there for a period of four years during the late fifteenth century. Today his castle is given over to the State Museum (Oberösterreichisches Landesmuseum). The coming of the railways – the first train in Austria ran from Linz to Budweis, now Ceske Budejovice, in Czeckoslovakia, in 1832 – assisted industry. Soon textile industries were underway in the city and with the end of the Second World War, Linz was concentrating on steel and chemical output.

From the 1762ft (537m) high Postlingberg Hill overlooking the Danube valley you can see Linz, spreading like an octopus below, incorporating the industrial suburbs. Those who consider industrial towns an anathema will take the quickest route out of Linz. From the railway it looks drab and unattractive with its MacDonald hamburger advertisements; but it would be a pity to let first impressions cloud your judgement for the medieval town, which clusters around the fifteenth-century Schloss, burned down in 1800 and not rebuilt until 1904, is quite different.

The Hauptplatz possesses some remarkable Gothic and Renaissance houses. Central to the square is the Trinity column by Beducci and Stumpfegger, which, just as in many other Austrian cities, represents deliverance from the plague. The Renaissance Landhaus, which dates from the sixteenth century, might be overlooked if it were not for the fact that the mathematician and astronomer, Kepler, was a teacher at Linz college between 1612 and 1626 which, at that time, was part of the Landhaus. However, next door the Minoritenkirche, founded in the thirteenth century by the Franciscans or Minorites, should not be bypassed as, apart from being a rococo building, it possesses paintings by two acclaimed masters, Kremser Schmidt and Bartolomeo Altomonte whose altarpiece represents the annunication.

Nor were the Jesuits to be outdone. The former cathedral, Alter Dom, or

Jesuit Church, dedicated to St Ignatius, although four centuries older, can lay claim to being the largest baroque church in Linz and to having had Anton Bruckner as its organist; while the little church of St Martin, perched above the Schloss and built by Charlemagne in the eighth century on Roman foundations, is one of Austria's oldest churches.

The Neue Dom (New Cathedral), beside the Bishop's palace, whose architect was Jakob Prandtauer, dates from 1832 and was designed by the German architect Vinzenz Staz. The tower of the New Cathedral is a symbol of Linz and was the forerunner of many of the new buildings such as the Central Station (1946) and the Post Office (1951).

The New Gallery at Urfahr on the left bank is an interesting stop as it specialises in Austrian painters such as Kokoschka, Klimt and Schiele, most of the works comprising nineteenth- and twentieth-century artists.

Linz has limited hotel space, but its restaurants, cafés and wine taverns are plentiful. The Kremsmünsterer Weinstube, at Altstadt 10, is an old wine restaurant where you can be sure of good food and wine, while the Klosterhof on the Landstrasse, if you are looking for a place with historic associations, was once the library of Kremsmünster Abbey. Its hunting decor would appeal to the Habsburgs as well as modern-day travellers. The Cafe Konditorei Tautermann has won many awards for its patisserie and should you want to try the local speciality Linzertorte, you will find it both at the Tautermann cafe and the Konditorei Wagner. In the Weinstuben you can be sure of good, wholesome Austrian wines made for easy drinking rather than intoxication. If you have shopping in mind, the Landstrasse running from the Taubenmarkt to the station is Linz's main shopping street, with several side streets offering a range of goods from dirndls to ceramics, glass and handicrafts. Linz also has a flea market held every Saturday from March to November.

Linz offers a selection of entertainments from plays and opera at the Landestheater to musical concerts. The concert season runs from autumn to spring with concerts in the Bruckner Haus. The Linzer Bruckner Festival is held in September. The festival spills out to St Florian's Abbey, 8 miles (13km) away; and it is not just Bruckner's music you will hear, but a wide range of musical performances, including jazz. The whole city is swept up in the festival, with radio and television stations bringing you the latest updates. Summer concerts are also held in the Landhaus. The Linz City Information Office can give you the latest information on sightseeing tours, car hire, special events and any other details you may need.

Wilhering

Higher up the Danube valley from Linz lies the twelfth-century Cistercian monastery of Wilhering, situated in a remote valley and named after its founder Cholo von Wilhering. The founding of the monastery brought a sudden interest in monastic building, and a rash of religious houses soon appeared elsewhere. In the early eighteenth century the monastery was destroyed by fire and the church was rebuilt in rococo style, by Linz architect Johann Hasliger, and is today considered one of the finest rococo churches in all Austria. Of the original building only the cloisters and the Romanesque door remain. The Counts of Schaunberg are remembered by their fourteenth century-tombstones. Schaunberg castle is associated with King Wenceslas IV of Bohemia who, after being deposed in Prague, was sent to Vienna. He made his escape across the Danube and is thought to have hidden in the castle before he was captured.

Mauthausen

East of Linz lies Mauthausen, noted for its granite quarries – indeed much of its stone was used to pave the sidewalks of Vienna – but after the Anschluss of 1938, one of the Mauthausen quarries was used as a Nazi concentration camp. Today there is a more optimistic note in the town with the growth of a sculptor's symposium, but in 1949 the Austrian government decided to preserve the camp as a grim testimonial to the annexation of Austria to Nazi Germany. It is a pity that such a pretty village as Mauthausen should be associated with such a sad past. Braunau-am-Inn, in the Innviertel region, which did not become part of Austria until 1779, also has a Nazi connection; for this town, which still preserves its medieval character, is Adolf Hitler's birthplace.

The Mühlviertal region

The Mühlviertel region, which lies above Linz, north of the Danube, takes its name from the river Mühl, and borders Czechoslovakia. The farmhouses of the Danube plain are quadrangular buildings and are frequently seen in the hill areas around Linz; in the Mühlviertel, two-storey houses are more regular. The Mühlviertel is a windswept area of granite hills and forested valleys and if you drive in the Mühlviertel you will notice the distance between towns is greater than in the Danube valley.

Freistadt

The town of Freistadt in the Mühlviertel, sitting on its granite plateau on the old salt route to Bohemia, emphasizes the essential bleakness of the region. Anton Bruckner arrived at Windhaag near Freistadt at the age of 24, but little is recorded of what he found to do there. The main square of Freistadt has a Rathaus, a new castle (the Neue Burg), some houses with oriel windows and the expected parish church. Apart from that there is nothing to linger for and most visitors press on through the Danube Valley which reaches into Lower Austria.

The Innviertel region

Wels

The northern part of the Danube plain, known as the Innviertel, is farming country lying between the Inn and the Danube, so it is not surprising to find

Wels, the third largest town in Upper Austria and chief town of the Innviertel region, holding an agricultural fair. Wels is also noted for its Welser Volksfest, a popular folk festival held every other year in autumn. Apart from that, Wels has a medieval castle, now a museum, in which Emperor Maximilian I died in 1519. This Maximilian of Habsburg, dubbed 'the last knight', wanted to be buried in the Hofkirche at Innsbruck, but when the town gates of Innsbruck were closed against him, Maximilian left the city, made Wels his capital, and was eventually buried at Wiener Neustadt in Lower Austria. Wels can claim yet another castle, the Renaissance-styled Schloss Polheim at the corner of Polheimstrasse and Ringstrasse, only a stone's throw from the Kaiserliche Burg where Maximilian died.

Hans Sachs, the shoemaker who lived in Wels and was believed to be the origin of the character in Richard Wagner's *Die Meistersinger von Nurnberg*, was clearly a character in his own right, for a memorial tablet in the town commemorates him. The old part of Wels is the most interesting with its arches and arcades, while the main square or Stadtplatz, as is usual in many Austrian towns, has its fountain.

Wels's largest hotel is the Greif, and the town has several restaurants where you can try Austrian specialities served with dumplings. Just outside the town a well-known spot for game is the Wirt am Berg which has been a Gasthaus since the seventeenth century. Emperor Maximilian I, like most Habsburgs, enjoyed hunting, and the hunting tradition in Austria has ensured that on the menu of at least one restaurant in most towns, there will be one game dish, be it saddle of hare, quail or venison.

Lambach

South-west of Wels lies Lambach, and few visitors would think of leaving Wels without stopping there, for its Benedictine abbey is on most people's itineraries. First a monastery founded in the eleventh century by the Frankish Counts of Wels and Lambach, it was later granted to the monks of Münster-Schwarzach. Few traces remain of the original Romanesque monastery, but the frescoes depicting the infant Christ, the Virgin, and the three kings are amongst the best preserved of the medieval period and thought to be the oldest in Austria. They had remained hidden, but were rediscovered and restored in 1968. The architect Fischer von Erlach designed the high altar. Lambach Abbey was the mother house of the magnificent baroque abbey of Melk in Lower Austria, and as such received its fair share of attention.

Stadl Paura

On the other side of the river Traun, a short distance from Lambach Abbey, lies the Trinity church of Stadl Paura. As its name suggests, everything in the church is symbolised by the number three: the church has three doors, three fonts, three altars dedicated to the Father, Son and Holy Ghost, and even three organ lofts. Trinity church was built in the early eighteenth century by the Linz architect Johann Michael Prunner for Lambach Abbey to commemorate the end of the plague. It displays fine altar paintings, by the architect Carlo Antonio Carlone, and the painter Martino Altomonte.

Upper Austria may have the largest aluminium plant in the country at Ranshofen, and the region between the Salzkammergut and Bohemia is highly developed both industrially and agriculturally, but the province is balanced by spas, mountains and lakes where visitors can forget all about chemicals, cellulose factories and cars. Festivals such as the amusing Holznechtnockenessen (dumpling festival) at Bad Goisern in June, July and August, and the joyous Corpus Christi processions remind you that Upper Austria is also a province where tradition and jollification exist side by side with industrial progress.

Upper Austria can claim some magnificent abbeys, churches, and monasteries from St Florian's to Lambach, but it is an abbey in Lower Austria that takes precedence over all the rest. That is the fine baroque Abbey of Melk, considered the greatest abbey – at least by the Austrians – north of the Alps. To catch one's first glimpse of Melk one must follow the Danube as it flows eastwards.

6

LOWER AUSTRIA
AND
BURGENLAND

Lower Austria

Over 500 castles and fortresses in various states of repair pepper the landscape of Lower Austria, Austria's largest province, and known by its German name of Niederöesterreich. Austria's capital, Vienna, lies in Lower Austria, although many of those who comprise the province's population of a million and a half would like to see Krems as their chief city, since they believe that Krems is now more representative than Vienna, which, after all, is international.

The name Lower Austria originated as a result of most of the province being below the Danube's course at the time when Austria was an archduchy, but today its 7402 square miles (19,160sq. km) are almost equally situated above and below the Danube. Lower Austria is divided into administrative areas known as Viertels, which explains regional appendages like Weinviertel, the wine growing area, and Waldviertel, the wooded area. Vineyards like those of Wachau and Gumpoldskirchen, one of Austria's best wine-producing villages, lie in this province, whose landscape ranges from agricultural pastureland to wooded slopes in the Waldviertel, and rising Alpine foothills.

You will notice that the farmhouses in Lower Austria are usually lower than the chalets found in the Tirol and the Vorarlberg. In the wine-growing areas the villages have their Heurigen – where you can sample the year's new wine –

7 Wine harvest

which are often simple, whitewashed buildings strung around an open space or courtyard, and you will spot them all the way to Vienna. Spas are also a feature of Lower Austria attracting many foreign visitors. The thermal spa of Baden, for example, is not only well known in Austria, but one of the most renowned in Europe.

Reliable and fast train services make access simple. Once you are in Lower Austria, trains from Vienna connect you with St Pölten, Wiener Neustadt and Semmering. By car you can reach Melk, Baden and any other town or village that appeals. Many Viennese spend weekends in their province without bothering to go farther afield, as Lower Austria offers plenty of sporting facilities from skiing to mountain climbing. Outside Vienna hotel rates are lower and the pace slower. As in the rest of Austria, hotel rooms, even the cheapest, are wonderfully clean. Roadside Gasthäuser serve good, simple lunches if you are *en route*, and restaurants in many of Lower Austria's towns serve local specialities. Even abbeys sometimes have their wine cellars where you can sample monastic wine! Lower Austria is the land of the Nibelung, so for those interested in myth and magic you could do no better than visit this province, where you often get the feeling that the race of dwarfs is watching strangers.

Castles and abbeys

Whether you choose to enter Lower Austria from neighbouring Burgenland, Upper Austria or Styria, by which the province of Lower Austria is bordered, castles and abbeys will astonish you. In the north-eastern part of the province which borders Czechoslovakia you will find Schrems castle where Mozart spent a night on his way to the première of *Don Giovanni* at Prague's Tyl theatre. Also near the Czech border is Falkenstein castle, built in the eleventh century and today largely in ruins, while almost within Czechoslovakia lies twelfth-century Hardegg on the Thaya river. Like many of Lower Austria's ancient castles, Hardegg was rebuilt during the last century. In the parish church at Hardegg you can find a wooden cross which was carved from the ship *Novara* on which the brother of Franz Josef, Emperor Maximilian, sailed to Mexico where he met his death. Also on the Bohemian frontier stands Heidenreichstein, one of the finest moated castles in Austria, complete with drawbridge and massive walls measuring 15ft (4.5m) wide and 125ft (38m) high; it could almost be a fairy tale castle.

If you ever doubted that Lower Austria was the land of castles and romance, driving through the province will dispel all such suspicions. In fact it seems, on occasion, as if history looms up at every corner. At Breiteneich near Horn in the far north, lies the oldest Renaissance castle in the province, and 8 miles (13km) from the Benedictine abbey at Altenburg, in the region known as the Waldviertel, is Greifenstein castle with its medieval judgement chamber. West of Altenburg, Zwettl can boast a Cistercian abbey about 1 mile (1.6km) outside the town. The church dates from the Middle Ages, and has some interesting Gothic window glass paintings. It also has baroque additions dating from the eighteenth century. The abbey's chapter house is one of the oldest in existence

8 *Hardegg castle*

with late Romanesque cloisters and a fine library possessing over 3000 volumes, of which more than 400 are old manuscripts.

South-west of Zwettl lies Rappottenstein castle, erected in the twelfth century and possessing Austria's best-preserved torture chamber. Additions were made in the sixteenth century, but Rappottenstein still maintains its medieval aura. Another castle of interest in the area is the Rosenburg which also dates from the twelfth century. In 1620 300 people were murdered there. Rosenburg at that time was the chief centre of Lutheranism in the north of Austria. In 1809 much of the castle was destroyed by fire. Today the restored castle is one of the most splendid in the Kamp valley with a collection of weapons dating from the sixteenth century.

All 500 castles and abbeys are far too numerous to mention, but some like Rohrau, south of the old Roman town of Carnuntum, are especially worthy of note. Rohrau was the town in which Josef Haydn was born and its castle is today Austria's only private art museum. Castles, castles, and more castles, whether ruined or restored, are inescapable; but then it is impossible to avoid history, especially in Austria, and the castles are an intrinsic part of the Austrian heritage.

9 *Maria Taferl, Marbach an der Donau*

Pöchlarn

From the Strudengau in the Waldviertel, the Danube passes through Persenbeug. Schloss Persenbeug, built in the tenth century and rebuilt seven centuries later, overlooks the river and is chiefly remembered because Emperor Karl I, the last Austrian emperor, was born there in 1887. It also heralds the end of the Nibelungau, the valley between Persenbeug and Melk, and home of the Nibelung. According to legend the Nibelung haunted the valley in their search for knights to bring to Attila's court in the west of Hungary. Theirs were stories of conflicts and revenge and some of the knights of the legend were said to have stayed in Pöchlarn, then known as Bechelaren. Apart from the Nibelung, Pöchlarn was the seat of the Babenbergs who settled there in the tenth century and founded Melk Abbey. But it is the Nibelung who are remembered even to this day when each June a pageant celebrating their arrival by ship is a big event, when the banks of the Danube are set aflame with bonfires and fireworks.

A little inland, on top of a hill, stands the church of Maria Taferl which is still used by pilgrims. Maria Taferl is a summer resort village, and if you are still in the mood for castles, 5 miles (8km) north-east of the town lies Artstetten in which Franz Ferdinand, who was assassinated in Sarajevo, is buried.

From Pöchlarn the Erlauf valley can easily be explored. It is full of old towns and churches. In the Ybbs or Ebbs valley lies Waidhofen on the Thaya river, with its sixteenth-century gabled houses. To the north sits Seitenstetten, a Benedictine abbey founded in 1112 with frescoes by Master Schmidt of Krems. The library contains over 70,000 volumes including 300 ancient manuscripts. The present monastery dates from the eighteenth century.

Nearby the town of Neuhofen claims that Austria (then known as Östarrichi from which came the present day Öesterreich) was first mentioned in a document dated 1 November AD 996 in reference to a property at Neuhofen.

10 *View of Waidhofen an der Thaya*

Melk

The next place of interest is Melk, the gateway to the Wachau, which the Nibelung knew as Medelike. The Babenbergs who had come from Bavaria established their court at Tulln before moving to Vienna. Leopold III of Babenberg handed over the Babenberg castle at Melk and its extensive lands in the early twelfth century to the Benedictine monks, who by the fourteenth century had so extended it that it had been transformed into a monastery. It was largely due to the Benedictines that the fame of Melk spread throughout Lower Austria.

However, for a time the Reformation hindered the further development not only of Melk Abbey, but of many monasteries throughout Austria. In the early eighteenth century Melk was ravaged by fire, and the baroque building seen today was designed by Jakob Prandtauer after the fire; the foundation stone of the new monastery was laid in 1702 by Abbot Dietmayr. The abbey, built originally on the site of a Roman stronghold, is in a commanding position high above the Danube, its buildings spanning 400 years. Above the terrace lies the church, with its twin towers and octagonal dome. St Peter and St Paul, to whom the church is dedicated, appear above the high altar in the midst of a group of statues as they go to face their martyrdom.

From the terrace built on a jutting rock you will have an excellent view of the muddy brown Danube and the wooded countryside before you turn back to the library and marble hall. The library is one of the most acclaimed in Austria containing 2000 manuscripts and 80,000 books, some of which date from the ninth century. It is noted, too, for its ceiling by the artist Paul Troger.

In the marble hall you will find paintings both of the abbey's Babenberg

11 Melk Abbey

founder, Leopold III, and its architect Jakob Prandtauer. Guests of the abbey pass through the Emperor's Gallery (Kaisergang), which is hung with paintings of the rulers of Austria, on the way to their chambers. The abbey has received many notable guests in its time, some more welcome than others, including Napoleon I, who established his headquarters there during his campaigns against Austria in 1805 and 1809.

Melk Abbey has managed to retain some of its artistic treasures, but decay is already beginning to eat away at some of the buildings. However, the abbey has a wine tavern which serves the abbey's wines and provides a pleasant break from sightseeing. The monastery and church can be visited between 11 a.m. and 2 p.m. for most of the year when there are guided tours given in various languages. In town you will find several small hotels and inns and a couple of very good restaurants. There is also a camping site on the Danube.

Wachau region

South of the Danube lies Schloss Schallaburg, thought to be one of the finer Renaissance castles in Lower Austria, with its central courtyard and 48 colonnades. Downstream from Melk Abbey on the opposite shore is Schloss Schönbühel, perched high on a rocky bank. Schloss Schönbühel originates from the twelfth century and was rebuilt in 1820 in neo-Classical style. Its domed belfry and distinctive five-storey towers make it easily identifiable.

You are now in the Wachau region – the stretch of river between Melk and Krems — which is one of the chief wine-growing areas of Lower Austria. Following the course of the Danube, on its right bank you can make out the ruined castle of Aggstein, built in the twelfth century and rebuilt in the early seventeenth century. Now you will see what is meant by castles! From Aggstein there is one of the finest views of the whole picturesque Wachau region with its

12 Schönbühel castle, Aggsbach

13 Grape pickers at Wachauertracht

terraced vineyards, orchards and fields of maize and tobacco. This is the Austria of fairy tales with its enchanting villages and ruined castles atop rocky hillsides.

On the opposite bank of the river at Willendorf, a limestone figure dating back some 25,000 years and known as the Venus of Willendorf was found at the turn of the nineteenth century and now reposes in Vienna's Natural History Museum. Upstream lies Spitz, a small town, fringed by orchards of just over 2000 inhabitants. Spitz is typical of many of the Wachau villages, with its ruined castle of Hinterhaus, braced against the wooded hillside, overlooking terraced vineyards. Master Schmidt of Krems (Kremser Schmidt) was also once in Spitz for in 1799 he designed the altarpiece in the Gothic parish church.

Passing the fortified church of St Michael you reach Weissenkirchen, a charming town of old houses and steep, climbing vineyards. Weissenkirchen also has a church built in the fifteenth century, fortified so as to ward off Turkish invasions. The interesting aspect of many of these churches, and in particular the pilgrimage churches in Austria, is that often they are reached by ancient staircases, sometimes indoor, sometimes outdoor. The church at Weissenkirchen has a sixteenth-century covered stairway, and when you have looked inside the church, you can make your exit by an open-air staircase back to the charming streets of the town. Right in the heart of the Wachau, it seems as if Weissenkirchen is thoroughly fortified, for even its museum is housed in a sixteenth-century fortressed farmhouse.

Dürnstein

Leaving Weissenkirchen the Danube makes a loop before reaching Dürnstein. The fortified town is well known to historians, and is also a renowned wine-producing area of the Wachau, making white wines which are noted for their delicate bouquet. Terraces pile up around the town, dominated by the ruined castle overlooking the Danube which claims to have held Richard Cœur de Lion a prisoner.

During the King of England's crusade at the Seige of Acre in Palestine, he offended Leopold V of Babenberg, Duke of Austria, by tearing down the Duke's colours from the tower. By ill chance Richard was shipwrecked in the Adriatic and was forced to make his way back to England through Austria. In the disguise of a peasant he reached an inn at Erdberg, near Vienna, where he was recognised, delivered to Leopold V and brought to Dürnstein on 22 December 1192. The King's whereabouts were discovered in the spring of 1193 by the minstrel, Blondel, who played his mandolin and sang a tune familiar to the King beneath the castle walls, and thus alerted Richard. But fate took a hand, for the King was moved to Trifels castle in the Rhineland where he remained in captivity for another 12 months. The English were obliged to pay a vast ransom to secure his release and the money financed much of the town of Wiener Neustadt, assisted with the cost of building the walls around Enns, and even paid for the construction of a moat around Vienna. There are other towns which also claim to have received part of the ransom, but such stories have yet to be substantiated.

The town of Dürnstein extends along the main road, the Hauptstrasse, which has at its east end a fortified gate. Quaint old houses, many of them dating from the sixteenth century, overhang the streets of the town, giving Dürnstein a romantic appeal which inspired many artists, among them Rudolf von Alt. With their oriel windows and flower-strewn balconies they make a delightful setting. As in most wine villages the shingles of the wine inns, where you taste the Heurige, are proudly displayed. Those wishing to rekindle the legends of Richard the Lionheart can climb up to the castle ruins by taking the path which starts in the town. There is even a Richard the Lionheart hotel in town, the Richard Löwenherz, which was formerly a convent.

Dürnstein's parish church was originally a monastery founded in the fifteenth century and revamped in baroque style during the eighteenth. Both from the church and the castle ruins there are splendid views over the Danube valley. The Richard Löwenherz Hotel has a garden terrace overlooking the river and a restaurant which serves local wines, game, and fish from the Danube. If you like castle hotels, Schloss Dürnstein, also overlooking the Danube, will interest you.

Krems and Stein

At the easterly end of the Danube lies Krems and Stein, once separate towns now combined to form the main wine town of Lower Austria. Its vineyard-covered hills produce some of the best-known Austrian wines, which you can sample in the inns and taverns of the city. The Wachau Keller not only serves good honest Wachau wine but is noted for its game, and fish from the Danube.

14 Oriel window, Krems an der Donau

Danube fish is a speciality of the region and you should not leave Lower Austria without trying it.

The Benedictine Abbey of Göttweig across the Danube from Krems originated in the eleventh century and its baroque buildings were constructed to plans made by Lukas von Hildebrandt. The abbey also possesses a wine tavern which serves its own wines.

Krems dates from the tenth century and has managed to preserve part of its walls. Master Schmidt of Krems, whose baroque paintings appear throughout Lower Austria, has a place in Krems Historical Museum, formerly an austere Dominican monastery, in whose gallery his paintings are well represented. His name was plain, Martin Johann Schmidt, but for the purposes of religious art he became known as Kremser Schmidt. Some of his frescoes can be seen in the Paris church and his ceiling painting in the church of St Veit. The museum is open from spring to autumn. For wine enthusiasts it is essential to visit the Weinbaumuseum housed in the cloisters of the museum, as it not only displays everything connected with viticulture, but also illustrates the extent of the Danube valley's vineyards.

Täglicher Markt is Krems' oldest market square noted for its Gogelhaus which possesses frescoes dating from the fifteenth century. In the Hoher Markt in summer open-air plays are staged at the Renaissance Gozzo Palace. From Krems you can take steamer trips through the Wachau. August and September are good months to visit for then the Krems County Fair, which incorporates a wine fair, takes place. Although not as riotous as Rhineland fairs it is well patronised. Krems holds an annual wine fair in May.

From the Kremser Tower in the east to the western Bruckentor, the Landstrasse runs through Stein. Situated on this street is one of Stein's most remarkable buildings, the imperial tollhouse with its Renaissance façade, oriel windows and turrets. In the narrow streets, interested visitors will find other examples of Renaissance architecture as well as baroque and rococo.

Krems Valley

Above the Danube at Krems and Stein lies the Krems Valley with its vineyards and orchards of plums, peaches and apricots growing on terraces in the loamy hills. As you climb the valley you can see the ruined castle of Rehberg and, after Imbach, Senftenberg's ruined fortress on an escarpment above the charming village. The valley, although rocky and inhospitable beyond Senftenberg, is a landscape of startling beauty, combining orchards, bluffs, and rocky outcrops with fabulous monasteries, abbeys and ruined fortresses. Small wonder the Nibelung legend persisted! One glance at the Danube at Wachau stirs reminiscences.

The legend says that Siegfried, possessor of the Nibelung treasure, marries Kriemhild, sister of Gunther of Worms, wins Brunhild as a bride for the latter, and is murdered by Hagen, Gunther's vassal. Kriemhild obtains vengeance for Siegfried's death by marrying Etzel (Attila) of the Huns, at whose court Hagen and Gunther are slain. It was on the Danube that Kriemhild sailed to meet Attila.

From Krems the Danube flows to Tulln where the Babenbergs established their court, but it is worth making a detour up the Traisen valley to the Augustinian Abbey at Herzogenburg on the right bank of the Danube. The monastery was founded by Bishop Ullrich of Passau at the beginning of the twelfth century. Today its baroque architecture by Fischer von Erlach and Jakob Prandtauer, together with its frescoes and paintings by Altomonte, are its star attractions, not forgetting its magnificent library which contains over 400 old manuscripts and 80,000 books, while the monastic buildings house a sixteenth-century collection of paintings on wood belonging to the Danube School.

Tulln

Tulln, noted today for flower cultivation was, according to the Nibelung saga, where Kriemhild met King Attila. Tulln originated on the Roman site of Comagena and is known best for its twelfth-century Romanesque church of St Stephens, which was rebuilt in Gothic style and renovated in baroque during the eighteenth century. Over the Romanesque portal sits the double headed eagle which represented the Holy Roman Empire.

The Weinviertel region

From Tulln the Danube sweeps majestically on to Vienna, but before setting out for the Wienerwald, the Weinviertel or wine district north of Vienna is of interest. It is an area of small market towns like Korneuburg, and grand castles, many of them in ruins. The castle of Kreuzenstein was built in the twelfth century, destroyed during the Thirty Years' War by Swedish invaders, and restored in the nineteenth century. One of the most interesting towns of the Weinviertel is Eggenburg, once a fortified town, which has preserved most of its fifteenth-century walls, marked out by towers. Eggenburg is unusual in that it has preserved its sixteenth-century pillory. It also has the customary Trinity column and some good examples of baroque and Renaissance houses.

North of Eggenburg lies the Pulkau valley, where some of the best wine of the Weinviertel is made. Pulkau is a wine town with a population of 1500 and its Rathaus is the chief focal point – apart from its wine cellars. The nearby wine town of Retz can boast medieval town walls and two gate towers as well as a Town Hall which was formerly a Gothic church. Its tower is said to be the best of its kind in Austria.

Marchfeld

Marchfeld, the wide plain to the east of Vienna and south-east of the Weinviertel, is hunting country, as well as producing most of Austria's grain. It is an area of hunting lodges, one of which, Schloss Marchegg on the Czech border, has been turned into a hunting museum. Castles such as Eckartsau, given by Archduke Franz Ferdinand to his nephew Emperor Karl, a noted eighteenth-century hunting castle, and Schlosshof on the Slovak frontier, once owned by Empress Maria Theresa but now neglected, testify to the amount of

15 Orth castle

hunting done in the region. The Habsburgs adored the hunt, while Archduke Johann was said to enjoy it so much he loaded his own rifle. Empress Maria Theresa and Josef II were both keen falconers who spent much time in the Marchfeld.

The oldest castle in the region, first mentioned in 1021, is Schloss Sachsengang. Closer to Vienna lie twelfth-century Orth castle, and, at Dürnkrut an der March, the thirteenth-century Renaissance Schloss Dürnkrut. At the battle of Dürnkrut in 1278 Rudolf von Habsburg killed his opponent, King Ottokar of Bohemia II, which assured Rudolf's supremacy. It also proved a turning point for Austria for it meant that Austria need no longer be linked to Bohemia. Thus began a 640 year rule by the House of Habsburg.

Carnuntum

The Roman town of Carnuntum lies across the Danube from Marchfeld, and dates from the first century AD. Carnuntum has been the scene of a number of excavations which have revealed remains of Roman houses, and various objects of the period which can be viewed in the Museum Carnuntium at nearby Bad Deutsch-Altenburg, known in Roman times as a thermal spa which produced sulphur springs. These days the spa is noted for its treatment of rheumatism and disorders of the circulation. Carnuntum's amphitheatre stages dramas during July and August and attracts a good many visitors interested in seeing Roman plays.

Hainburg and the Vienna Woods

In earlier days Hainburg, east of Vienna, attracted visitors for its medieval walls, its castle fortress and the ruined Rothenstein castle perched on a hilltop outside the town. Nowadays it is better known for being the proposed site of the hydroelectric power plant which brought such a stream of protests that the scheme was temporarily abandoned. Vociferous protestors are determined to preserve Hainburg from the inexorable march of progress. Most Viennese want to protect, at all costs, their beloved Vienna Woods, or Wienerwald, the name by which the rolling wooded area around Vienna is known. The idea of Vienna without its woods is unthinkable, but they were threatened long before the Hainburg issue, for in 1870 it was announced that the Crown Estates of the Wienerwald, all 80,000 acres (32,000ha), were to be sold. Such a prospect aroused the ire of the staid Viennese who usually prefer anything rather than bold confrontation. They petitioned against the sale and won. The woods were saved.

Nowadays the Wienerwald, for so long part of the city's heritage, are composed of beech, elm, oak, maple, poplar, aspen and birch. In the Middle Ages the forests were predominantly oak and in the twelfth century a primeval forest. During the two World Wars there was extensive felling, but the trees which were axed have now been replaced. Having preserved the Wienerwald in the nineteenth century it is not hard to understand why the Viennese are ready to fight over the Hainburg proposal.

The Vienna Woods are dotted with inns, monasteries, picturesque villages and market towns spread out around Vienna. The southern wine villages of Grinzing, Sievering, and Nussdorf, as well as Klosterneuberg, situated in the east, are all easily reached from the city, and the Viennese and visitors alike take their ease in the Wienerwald, especially at weekends. It is a great place for relaxing from city tensions.

The annual grape harvest in Vienna yields 660,000 gallons (30,000 hectolitres) of wine. Some 700 wine-growing families in Vienna alone grow vines over an acreage of 1800 (730ha). Most of the vineyards are planted on the slopes of Kahlenberg and Nussberg. The Heurige or current year's wines are usually a blend of several different wine varieties and you can get carried away trying them out in one tavern after another. The wine bought at a Heurige is usually served in a Viertel, a quarter litre measure. Wine taverns are easily identified by a sprig of pine hung above the door, illustrating that the tavern owner serves local wine on the premises. At Grinzing you will find taverns dating back to the twelfth century and these have spawned many a Heurige song, for drinkers are usually merry souls. Grinzing can claim more than 20 wine taverns. Most display plaques stating *Eigenbau* indicating that the wine grower serves his own wine. If you want to let your hair down the Heurigen are the places to do it!

Klosterneuberg

Klosterneuberg is also an important wine centre with a variety of Heurige, but is best known to visitors for its Augustinian Abbey (converted to baroque style) which, incidentally, is the biggest wine producer. In the abbey's restaurant, the Stiftskeller, you can sample the abbey's wines. Klosterneuberg is noted for its fine collection of ancient manuscripts – 230 in all, 140,000 volumes, – and in particular for its altarpiece by Nicolas of Verdun, a wonderful example of the skilled craftsmanship of twelfth-century goldsmiths. The town holds a picturesque fete on 15 November each year to celebrate St Leopold, Lower Austria's patron saint, which incorporates a strange practice dating from 1702, known as barrel sliding, in which participants climb up one side of a barrel measuring 14¾ by 11½ft (4.5 by 3.5m), and slide down the other. The ritual is said to be connected with ancient pagan fertility rites.

From Klosterneuberg a string of villages are notable for their fine views over Vienna. In the eastern sector lies Leopoldsberg with its vista over the plain of Wagram. From Kahlenberg you can pick out the spires of St Stephen's cathedral. South of Vienna lies Perchtoldsdorf, another well-known wine village much frequented by the Viennese, who refer to it as Petersdorf. Many visitors, especially music lovers, make the detour to the little seventeenth-century house at Heiligenstadt where Beethoven lived in 1817. (Today the house is a Heurige, which gives them an even greater excuse to celebrate!)

Another interesting spot is Heiligenkreuz, whose Cistercian Abbey of the Holy Cross was founded in the twelfth century. The abbey is of historic interest as it was ransacked during the Turkish siege, but managed to preserve its Romanesque nave. Its altar paintings are by Altomonte and Rottmayr.

Mödling

Mödling is yet another wine-growing village. Founded in the tenth century, Mödling merits attention on account of its Gothic parish church and for the two castles, Liechtenstein and Schloss Laxenburg, both within easy reach of the town. The former was constructed in Romanesque style in the twelfth century and was besieged by Turks during the invasion of Lower Austria. However, it was rebuilt in its original style. East of Mödling lies Laxenburg castle, comprising a small fourteenth-century castle, a considerably larger new castle in baroque style and a neo-Gothic castle. Some of the Habsburgs stayed in the Neues Schloss, and today the large park surrounding it is well stocked with game.

Mayerling

As hunting was a sport much beloved by the Habsburg monarchs it was perhaps fitting that the ill-fated Archduke Rudolf, the only son of Emperor Franz Josef and Empress Elizabeth, should choose to take his life at his shooting box at Mayerling. The heir-apparent to the Austro–Hungarian throne was already married when he fell in love with the 17 year old Maria Vetsera, and was found dead beside her body on 30 January 1889 at Mayerling. A Carmelite convent marks the spot where the hunting box stood, constructed on the orders of Emperor Franz Josef as a memorial to his son's tragic death.

The story of Crown Prince Rudolf still puzzles and fascinates people, with all manner of wild theories being advanced. The romantic image of dying at dawn, and for love, appeals to all ages, and as a result Mayerling remains on the tourists' itineraries.

The road from Mayerling runs to the spa of Baden and on to the village of

16 Mödling

17 Gumpoldskirchen

Gumpoldskirchen, whose vineyards produce one of Austria's most drinkable wines, the white, aromatic Gumpoldskirchner.

South of Baden lies another vineyard, that of Vöslau which can claim to produce some of Austria's best red wines. The Weinstrasse runs directly to Gumpoldskirchen where you can sample the good white wine, which can range from dry to slightly sweet, before you continue on to Baden.

Baden

Baden was known in Roman times for its hot sulphur springs, which reach a temperature of 36°C (97°F). Today the 15 springs pour out close on 1,500,000 gallons (6,800,000 litres) of thermal water. The Roman spring is thought to have been used for 2000 years, thus proving Baden's antiquity. Cures are taken in the form of the waters, or by mud applications in the treatment of rheumatism. The beautiful, restful surroundings of the spa make it one of the most frequented in Europe. Baden not only attracted those searching for a cure, but became so well known and fashionable that aristocrats and café society of the day flocked to it.

During the tenth century the Babenbergs had favoured Baden, but the seal of approval was placed on the spa when Peter the Great of Russia visited Baden in the seventeenth century. It was not long before Baden became the summer residence of the Imperial Court. Emperor Franz Josef II spent several years at Baden before his death in 1835, and just as Bad Ischl in Upper Austria had become fashionable, so Baden began to be patronised by the rich and famous of the day. Ludwig von Beethoven spent his summers at Baden where he composed parts of his Ninth Symphony. Wolfgang Amadeus Mozart was another of Baden's notable guests, as were the masters of the waltz, Josef Lanner and Johann Strauss, who both composed some of their waltzes there.

In summer, visitors to the Kurpark can listen to concerts in the most idyllic surroundings, and in winter can watch drama and operettas at the Stadtheater. In January and February during the Fasching (Lent season) Baden holds many glittering balls and concerts, and when the main season starts in May another round of balls and concerts gets underway.

18 Kurpark, Baden

19 Church at Semmering

For sporting fans, Baden provides plenty of distractions. There is an open-air swimming pool, and a riding ring at Reitstall Baden. There is also a casino open from 4 p.m. daily. The town and outskirts have a variety of restaurants and Gasthöfe where you can sample good Austrian cuisine, including the Sauerhof zu Rauhenstein, a charming Biedermeier palace furnished in period style.

South-west of Vienna lie the highest mountains of Lower Austria, the Schneeberg, Wechsel, Semmering and Rax, their highest ridges snowcapped in winter. This is the winter sports region of the province, easily reached from Vienna and Baden. Semmering enjoys plenty of sunshine, its hotels and chalets hugging the slopes of the Semmering Pass. With the beginning of the New Year torchlight ski races liven up the resort, making the first two months of the year a good time to be in Semmering.

Between the two massifs of Schneeberg and Raxalpe lies the Hollental or Hell's valley. The limestone massif of Raxalpe is a favourite with climbers, who can reach it quickly from Vienna. The views from the mountains are stunning, and visitors can stay in some of the mountain refuges if they wish. Tourist Information Offices will advise you on their locations and accommodation facilities.

Wiener Neustadt

Lying east of the Schneeberg range is Wiener Neustadt. Emperor Maximilian I, who failed to end his days in his waiting mausoleum at Innsbruck, has his resting place beneath the high altar at Wiener Neustadt in the Gothic Georgskapelle. Wiener Neustadt was founded in the twelfth century by Leopold, Duke of Burgundy, and became the imperial residence during Friedrich III's reign in the fifteenth century. His son, Emperor Maximilian I, was born there in 1459. The Georgskapelle, or Church of St George, built during Friedrich III's reign, was damaged and restored during the Second World War. The presence of the Habsburgs is ubiquitous; their coats of arms decorate both the central window and the base of Friedrich's statue. The tombstone of Friedrich's wife, Empress Eleanor of Portugal, can be seen in the Neuklosterkirche, the New Abbey church.

Wiener Neustadt suffered much damage during the air raids of the Second World War, necessitating considerable rebuilding of the city. As a result it is a changed city, but has managed to maintain some of its churches, such as the thirteenth-century Church of Assumption. Parts of the original city walls remain including the twelfth-century Reckturm, a tower which stood at a corner of the ancient fortifications. It is thought that part of the ransom the English paid to Leopold of Babenberg for the release of Richard the Lionheart was used in building the Reckturm, and Empress Maria Theresa established the Austrian Military Academy at Wiener Neustadt, in the thirteenth-century Burg, which had to be enlarged for the purpose.

St Pölten

We have bypassed St Pölten, on the main railway line between Vienna and Linz, a town that can trace its beginnings back to Roman times, and which deserves to be mentioned for its Romanesque cathedral and seventeenth-century Bishop's Palace. St Pölten also has a famous hotel, the Pittner, which once entertained imperial visitors, though looking at the town today one cannot imagine why. Nearby Annaberg is noted for its pilgrims church, dedicated to St Anne. It was there that pilgrims passed on their way to more famous Mariazell in Styria. Visitors to the area should try to see the moated castle of Pottenbrunn, open from March to November. The castle's parks are delightful and if you are interested in historic battles, the tin soldier museum is an essential stop. Higher up the Traisen valley is Lilienfeld with its medieval Cistercian abbey and priceless library. It is built in Romanesque style and is well worth a visit.

Burgenland

Like Lower Austria, the adjoining province of Burgenland, whose name derives from Burgen (castles), has its castles and vineyards. The province is also a noted agricultural area producing wheat, maize, vegetables and wine, and has earned itself the reputation of being one of the hardest working provinces, for although small – 1530 square miles (3960sq. km) – it is highly productive.

20 Pottenbrunn castle, St Pölten

Burgenland, Austria's most easterly province, is a long, skinny, irregularly-shaped piece of land, only 40 miles (65km) at its widest point, bordering Hungary, and touching on Czechoslovakia and Yugoslavia. It also shares common borders with Lower Austria and Styria.

As it was formed by the German-speaking border areas of what had previously been Hungary, Burgenland is Austria's newest province, having been created as late as 1921. Much of the countryside is still Hungarian in style and appearance, with the Neusiedler see in the north forming Central Europe's sole steppe lake. As well as its lake region being a sanctuary for numerous species of birds, Burgenland produces wines and vegetables, especially sweet corn, much of which finds its way to Vienna. In spring, Burgenland is a mass of almond and cherry blossom.

As Burgenland is less peopled by tourists, visitors will delight in its largely unspoiled and unsophisticated way of life. Pretty villages, their houses hung with corn cobs strung out to dry, make a welcome change from tourist traps with their gaudy souvenirs. Simple village churches are enchanting too after a plethora of baroque abbeys. Burgenland is unpretentious, and proud of it. You will find its small hotels charming and appreciably cheaper than those of other provinces.

The population of the province numbers over 270,000 and is composed principally of farmers, foresters and wine makers; 88 per cent of them are Germans, a small percentage are Croatians who settled there in the sixteenth century, and an even smaller percentage are Magyars from Hungary. Burgen-

21 Ice sailing, Neusiedler See

land has seen a host of nationalities, from the Celts in the fourth century, to Romans, Huns and Goths. Next came the Bavarians, and later the Turkish invaders. Burgenland was Hungarian territory until after the First World War when the 1919 Treaty of St Germain ceded it to Austria, and two years later it become one of the nine provinces that make up present-day Austria. Since the Second World War, Burgenland has undergone many changes, but is still regarded by many as a mysterious province, due, not least to its Neusiedler See, a shallow salt water lake in its northern territory.

The lake measures 200 miles (320km) in length, but its depth is no more than 7ft (2m) at any given point. Three-quarters of the Neusiedler See is in Austria, one quarter in Hungary. The lake is considered unpredictable as winds can whip the waters into one end, leaving the other end at half its original depth. Legends and myths sprang up around the Neusiedler See, and its melancholy appearance, especially on grey days, only served to fuel the most outlandish of them. Salt marshes line one side of the lake while tall reeds grow at its edges. Birds and wildfowl, from wild duck to teal and egrets, inhabit the region, and fishing and shooting are popular sports. As it is so close to Vienna, many visitors make their way to the Neusiedler See at weekends and holidays to bathe and fish in the warm salty waters. Flat-bottomed boats prowl the reed beds. The lake is a natural beauty spot when there is no wind. Once the wind gets up, the face of the Neudsiedler See changes rapidly and you can find yourself beginning to believe some of the myths which have sprung up about it. Around the Neusiedler See you will find vineyards, wine cellars and spicy Hungarian cuisine – a legacy left from the Magyars – while the Rosalia region is a mass of strawberry fields in June.

Rust

High above the lake lie terraced vineyards and orchards where fruit ripens fast in the sunny climate. Wine villages like Rust and Mörbisch produce excellent red and white wines on their sun dappled slopes. Rust is a true wine-growing village with the wine growers' homes guarded by tall wooden gates which lead into cool, shady courtyards. The town is noted for its storks' nests, and rumour has it that the birds return each year. It also has a sailors' church, the old thirteenth-century Schifferkirche.

Wine drinkers, anxious to try the Heuriger or last year's wine, make their way to the Rathauskeller. If you think you are dreaming as you spy storks on some of the roofs of the old building, you might be right; but then again you might not. Storks are almost as much a feature of Rust as its wine taverns. If you wish to sample Hungarian dishes, Rust has restaurants specialising in them. You may even hear gypsy music.

Mörbisch

Mörbisch, a neighbouring village, is noted for its wines and its lake festival as well as for its Hungarian cuisine. Mörbisch has a lakeside beach and a sailing school. At Mörbisch you are almost on the Hungarian frontier. The village is the last on the western side of the lake before the border, and its whitewashed houses with their outside stairways are a focal point. In Burgenland you often see bunches of maize hung up to dry outside farmsteads and the houses in Mörbisch are beautifully decorated, with drying corn cobs hanging beside the shutters. Mörbisch is noted for its operettas performed by the Neusiedler See in July and August. It is a curious sensation to realise that no more than 1 mile (1.6km) away lies the Iron Curtain.

Across the Neusiedler See, at Illmitz, is a vast, natural wildlife sanctuary whose desolate marshes are noted throughout Europe for their flora and fauna.

Forchtenstein

West of Mörbisch lies Forchtenstein castle, an old fortress set on a bluff and looking towards the Hungarian Plain. The castle is noted for its fine collection of arms and armour. Forchtenstein, built in the fourteenth century, was extended by the Hungarian Esterhazys in the early seventeenth century and was in the firing line of the Turkish sieges of the sixteenth and seventeenth centuries.

Eisenstadt

The Esterhazys were a powerful faction who claimed their descent from Attila the Hun and, while loyal to the Habsburgs, had been known to stand up for no less a personage than Napoleon I. They made their base at Eisenstadt, at the foot of the Leitha mountains, which in 1924 became Burgenland's capital. Today Eisenstadt with its Biedermeier houses is an important wine centre with a population of around 10,000. Since 1296, under the Esterhazy princes, it had been noted for its protection of Jews and even before that date there had been a synagogue in the town.

Josef Haydn, one of Burgenland's most noted citizens, was in the service of the Esterhazys, and resided partly at the Esterhazy castle, and partly in Eisenstadt. During his time there he composed music and conducted the orchestra. In 1766 at the age of 34 he became the musical director. With an orchestra to conduct, and various other business to attend to – he was also music librarian and administrator – Haydn still produced an impressive number of compositions which established his fame. He was later to be of assistance to Mozart. Since 1982 Eisenstadt has held an annual Haydn Festival. Haydn, who died in 1809, is buried in the Kalvarienbergkirche, the hilltop Calvary Church. His house at 21 Haydngasse – where the composer lived from 1766 to 1778 – contains the memorabilia of his work and lifestyle. The Haydn Room is on the first floor of Schloss Esterhazy and can be visited from June to September. During the Esterhazys' time it was a grand state hall, where Josef Haydn contributed evening concerts.

The castle itself was built during the seventeenth century by the Italian architect Carlo Antonio Carlone on the site of a medieval fortress. Early in the eighteenth century the castle's architecture was modified by the French architect Moreau, as the original building was considered a little too ornate with its great dome.

Not far from Eisenstadt, at Raiding, Franz Liszt was born in 1811. His father was employed by the Esterhazys as bailiff to the estate and with his job went the small house where his son Franz was born, and which is now a museum. (The Esterhazy chateau was at that time part of the Austro–Hungarian empire.) There you can see the organ Liszt played. If you want to transport yourself back to Liszt's time you can rent horsedrawn gypsy wagons which have accommodation for four people and from which you can view the Burgenland countryside with its simple villages, *Gasthöfe* and castles. Hotel bills are considerably

22 Esterhazy castle, Eisenstadt

cheaper than those in Vienna, and Eisenstadt has several typical wine taverns and restaurants where you can try out local wines and specialities.

North of Eisenstadt pilgrims make their way to the baroque church of Loretto. A Roman settlement is being excavated nearby where Bronze Age graves and Illyrian burial mounds were found earlier. Although by no means as well known as Baden, Burgenland's best rated spa is Bad Tatzmannsdorf. The spa has hotels, pensions and the usual spa facilities. Two castles lie close by: the thirteenth-century Burg Lockenhaus on the Hungarian border, and the fortress Burg Schlaining. Austrian and Hungarian nobility constructed their castles all over the Burgenland, and many of them, built on hilltops, were marvellous vantage points.

The province has its own small industry, a kind of yellow jade, in the village of Bernstein, which takes its name from the village. In English Bernstein means amber. This particular stone is found only in Burgenland so if you buy it as a souvenir you will be sure of something different. Bernstein is exported in the form of jewellery and ornaments. If you decide to stay in town, Burg Bernstein is a thirteenth-century castle, now transformed into a castle-hotel. It has its own hunting grounds and torture chamber, so beware!

At the end of September, Lower Austria and Burgenland celebrate the grape harvest with street processions and fireworks. In November there are Martinmass Goose Weeks (goose fairs). Martinmass is also significant at the *heuriger*, for after 11 November the wine from the last vintage becomes *alter wein* (old wine). Apfelsaft is stowed away and out come the wines of Bad Vöslau, the spezi (special) wines of Retz, Pöttelsdorf, and Rust. The town of Neckenmarkt upholds the curious ceremony of banner waving, which dates back to the Thirty Years' War when the soldiers of the town commandeered 14 enemy standards in 1620. To commemorate the event Neckenmarkt holds a procession in which banners are paraded on the eve of the first Sunday after Corpus Christi.

As nothing that happens in Burgenland is very far away from Vienna – Burgenland is a mere 15 miles (24km) distant – and since buses and trains can transport you there in no time at all, it is perhaps surprising there is so little interaction, yet Burgenland remains largely unknown to the majority of tourists who arrive in Austria each year. But those who do discover it, usually go back for a further visit.

7
VIENNA

There is a widely supported belief in Austria that the country consists of only eight provinces, excluding the ninth which is Vienna. The Viennese relish the dubious reputation of being different and disgruntled about everything, yet in their once imperial city, tradition remains almost a religion. You will see more Loden coats, more Tirolean hats, more Alpine patisserie (even discounting the Sacher hotel, where once the saying went 'The Sacher is Austria') than anywhere else in the country, as well as a mania for diplomatic solutions rather than argument.

To arrive in Vienna is to step back into the past, for Vienna's past is inseparable from its present. Under the Habsburgs, and especially during Empress Maria Theresa's reign, the city saw massive expansion, and by the time Emperor Franz Josef II took the throne, Vienna was on the verge of yet another transformation. It was during his reign that Vienna, with the creation of the Ring, became the city we know today. Buildings like the Votive church, the Town Hall, the Parliament building and the Opera House were built along the famous Ringstrasse which characterises Vienna as much as the memorials to Empress Maria Theresa and Johann Strauss.

Musicians and artists were drawn to the city. Franz Schubert was born there. Mozart came to Vienna and was buried in an obscure grave in St Mark's cemetery. Beethoven and Johannes Brahms settled in Vienna, while Anton Bruckner ended his life as professor at the Vienna Conservatory. Wherever you go in Vienna you sense the presence of such musical giants, particularly in such venues as the Figarohaus, where Mozart composed the *Marriage of Figaro* between 1784–87.

History, tradition and cliché salute you at every turn. This is the city of the waltz and of the Vienna Woods, of which more than enough has been sung and written. It is the city of Franz Josef and Empress Maria Theresa, of Sigmund Freud and of stately palaces like Schönbrunn and the Belvedere where ghosts still linger.

Palaces – some of them six storeys high – mostly date from the baroque age when Vienna earned itself the tag *Vienna Gloriosa*. Majestic palaces like the Kinsky, built by Johann Lukas von Hildebrandt, and the Starhemberg Palace, now the Ministry of Education and Arts which belonged to the Count von Starhemberg who had defended Vienna with his 24,000 strong troops during the Turkish siege of 1683, are two of the finest. The Schwarzenberg palace, designed by Fischer von Erlach, now operates as a hotel, while the Lobkowitz palace, also known as the Dietrichstein, was the venue of the first performance of Beethoven's *Eroica Symphony* in 1804.

Schönbrunn

Emperor Leopold I had envisaged an Austrian answer to the palace of Versailles when he invited Fischer von Erlach to design a summer residence for him at Schönbrunn, but it was to be Nikolas Pacassi who created the ochre-washed palace, a colour that came to be known as 'Schönbrunn yellow'. Charles VI was not enraptured by Schönbrunn, but his daughter Maria Theresa was. She spent much of her time in the palace with its 1440 rooms set in nearly 500 acres (200ha). Her daughter, Marie Antoinette, spent her childhood there. Wolfgang Amadeus Mozart gave a concert for the Empress at Schönbrunn when he was six years old, and later his *Don Giovanni* was performed there.

Schönbrunn was the birthplace of Emperor Franz Josef. He died in the palace in 1916, and it was at Schönbrunn that Karl I, the last of the Habsburgs, signed his abdication two years later. Napoleon had used the palace as his headquarters in 1805, and his son, the Duke of Reichstadt, languished there in stately exile, forbidden all contacts with France by Emperor Franz.

Of the many rooms of the palace (one wonders if the Empress Maria Theresa herself ever visited all of them) only 45 are open to the public, but these include the Empress Maria Theresa's apartments; the private apartments of Emperor Franz Josef and his Empress Elizabeth (with the two Chinese rooms, and the bed on which he died); the fabulous Million Room decorated by Persian miniatures; the Gobelin Salon with its Flemish tapestries; Napoleon's room, and the chamber in which his son, the Duke of Reichstadt, died of tuberculosis at the age of 21. Guest apartments include the luxurious Blue Room and Old Lacquer Room with its miniatures. Portraits of Empress Maria Theresa and her daughters hang in the State apartments.

Many visitors go to Schönbrunn, which is only a subway ride from Karlsplatz, just to stroll in the remarkable park designed by Ferdinand von Hohenberg. On a fine day (in winter it can be so foggy even the colonnaded Gloriette with its imperial eagle is obscured) you get a magnificent view over Vienna. The Schöner Brunnen (beautiful fountain) gave its name to the palace and was believed to have been discovered by Emperor Mathias during the seventeenth century. The beautifully landscaped gardens, with their arbours and flower beds, house one of the oldest zoos in Europe, founded in the mid-eighteenth century.

The Belvedere

It is not known exactly what kind of palace Prince Eugene of Savoy had in mind after his defeat of the Turks in 1683, but the two palaces of the Belvedere were built as his summer residence by the architect Lukas von Hildebrandt; the Lower Belvedere was begun in 1714, the Upper Belvedere in 1721. Two centuries later, in 1955, the State Treaty was signed at the Belvedere, and it is commemorated by a painting of those present at the event.

Terraced gardens link the two buildings, both of which contain splendid art collections. In 1734 the Upper Belvedere was the venue for balls and banquets given by Prince Eugene, and is still, on occasion, used for State functions. However, it is chiefly known for its nineteenth- and twentieth-century art

23 Belvedere castle

collections which include paintings of both the Biedermeier and the Ringstrassenzeit periods, of which the latter symbolised the art of Franz Josef's reign. The paintings of Hans Makart, Herbert Boeckl, Gustav Klimt, Egon Schiele and Oskar Kokoschka are well represented.

The Lower Belvedere, which originally comprised the apartments of Prince Eugene of Savoy, is now a museum of baroque art, while the Orangery contains Austrian medieval art, including the work of Michael Pacher. Artists of the stature of Franz-Anton Maulbertsch, one of the most prolific of the eighteenth-century Austrian painters, and great exponents of baroque religious art, such as Kremser Schmidt, Michael Rottmayr and Martin Altomonte, can be viewed.

Pestäule

During the seventeenth century Vienna defeated two scourges, the plague and the Turks, with the result that Pestäule (plague columns) went up throughout Austria to commemorate Austria's deliverance. The highly-decorative plague column designed by Fischer von Erlach was erected in the Graben in 1682. Charles VI pledged that a church would be built, and thus one of Vienna's greatest churches, the Karlskirche, was begun by Fischer von Erlach in 1716, and this massive church, which dominates the Karlsplatz, has become a symbol of baroque art with its 236ft (72m) high copper dome.

St Stephen's cathedral

Although Charles VI had an undoubted influence on the city it was Rudolf IV who was most ambitious for Vienna. He wanted to see the city expand on all fronts, and the magnificent St Stephen's cathedral testifies to his soaring ambitions. It began as a simple village church outside the Lichtensag at the old gate of the city, in the time when it was customary for a priest to live outside the walls of his parish. From 1263–1611 expansion began, first in late Romanesque

St Stephen's cathedral,
Vienna

Kitzbühel in spring

A Lippizaner stallion

A festival in the Wachau

and then in early Gothic style until St Stephen's rivalled in grandeur the great cathedrals of Germany. Today it ranks as one of the chief cathedrals of central Europe. Its southern steeple soars to 450ft (137m) while the northern tower, though never completed, contains what purports to be the largest bell in Europe, called the Pummerin, weighing 21 tons.

St Stephen's was damaged during the Turkish siege of 1683, and also by bombs during the Second World War. Standing right in the heart of the medieval city on the Stephansplatz, the cathedral is the focal point of Vienna. Its interior contains a sixteenth-century pulpit and the tomb of Emperor Friedrich III. The cathedral is a place for reflection, but it is also put to practical use. As well as the permanent crowds, film companies shoot there, musical programmes are broadcast, and church services go on as usual. There are guided tours of the cathedral and the catacombs, with English speaking guides. You can also ascend the tower from where you will get a magnificent view over the city.

Old Vienna

Old Vienna, the area which lies between St Stephen's and the Danube canal, is the ideal place for strolling. The narrow streets evoke the spirit of medieval Vienna, while the Stephansplatz is a pedestrian precinct abutting the busy Graben and Kärntnerstrasse, the chief shopping areas of the city. A few blocks to the east lies the great Gothic votive church on Rooseveltplatz, built at the time of the Ringstrasse in 1860, its steeples soaring 325ft (99m). The architect was von Ferstel, who built the church on the instructions of Maximilian von Habsburg, to commemorate the deliverance of his brother Emperor Franz Josef from an assassination attempt. It was the first neo-Gothic building in Vienna, and emulated the great Gothic cathedrals of France. The sixteenth-century tomb of Count Niklas Salm, defender of Vienna during the first Turkish siege, lies behind the pulpit.

Churches

Of all Vienna's baroque churches, Peterskirche, built by Lukas von Hildebrandt in the early eighteenth century, is acknowledged to be the most sumptuous. Just off the Graben, it has some of the finest frescoes in Vienna, these frescoes on the cupola being attributed to Michael Rottmayr. Rottmayr and Martin Altomonte also painted the altarpieces in the side chapels.

Two more churches deserve mention, both of them quite different from the mixed splendours of the Karlskirche and St Stephen's. They are the Ruprechtskirche, built on the site of one of the gates of the old Roman city of Vindobona during the eleventh century, and Vienna's oldest church with a Romanesque clock tower; and the unusual twelfth-century church of Maria am Gestade, alternatively called Our Lady of the Steps, or Our Lady of the River Bank, because although in the heart of the city, the church stands on a branch of the Danube. Both churches have their own special charm, and come as a pleasant surprise after the excesses of baroque art. St Rupert, after whom the Ruprechtskirche was named, was the patron saint of the Danube salt merchants. Check before you visit, as the church is often locked.

Viennese architecture

Vienna comprises 160 square miles (256sq. km), and has a population which has constantly fluctuated until it now stands at over one and a half million. It is also a federal province, a mere 40 miles (65km) from the borders of Czechoslovakia and Hungary, and surrounded by the province of Lower Austria. Vienna is a Congress Centre and is the headquarters of OPEC. It has its own United Nations Building – Vienna is the third UN capital after New York and Geneva – at the Vienna International Centre, a modernistic Y-shaped block of concrete standing at Donaupark on the Danube.

Ever since the Habsburgs became patrons of the arts, Vienna has been a cultural centre and it is not surprising that in these times the Vienna Festival and the Vienna Film Festival draw the crowds. An international Trade Fair is held biannually.

But despite its attempts to push itself into the future, Vienna remains an essentially baroque city where for all its charm such effects can seem overpowering. The Habsburgs haunt you. Their portraits eye you in palaces and museums. They lie silent in their tombs, in the ten rooms of vaults that comprise the imperial crypt (Kapuzinerkirche). In short the Habsburgs symbolise Vienna.

During the nineteenth century Vienna began expanding, developing its industries and taking in a stream of immigrants which increased its population overnight. Art nouveau buildings heralded a rise in the city's fortunes. All manner of architectural styles suddenly began changing the face of the old city, noted for its traditionalism.

Otto Wagner and the Kirche am Steinhof

Otto Wagner was in the vanguard of these original architects of art nouveau who turned traditions on their heads, but like all innovators he had his critics. Nevertheless it is impossible to ignore his influence. One look at his Stadtbahn is sufficient. While Otto Wagner experimented with art nouveau, Gunther Domenig specialised in contemporary architecture. His bank building in the Favoriten area of Vienna is reminiscent of the work of the Spanish architect Antonio Gaudi. Fritz Wotruba, better known for his sculptures, designed the Georgenberg church.

It was to the Vienna Woods that Otto Wagner went in order to establish a thoroughly modernistic piece of architecture that would get him talked about for years to come – the Kirche am Steinhof, built on a steep rise in the grounds of a psychiatric hospital. The church, constructed like a mosque, with a gilded dome, is an eye-catching construction. The interior is stark, but striking, with its modern stained glass windows depicting contemporary characters, the white marble dome fretted with gold. Over the simple altar rises a gold canopy.

To the left is the golden pulpit. Plays are now performed in the church, such playwrights as the Italian Luigi Pirandello lending themselves well to the surroundings. Masses are held only in summer, as winter is too cold in the snow bound environs. The church is open for guided tours on Saturday afternoons at 3 p.m. and, judging by the groups queuing to get in, has its *aficionados*.

24 Karl-Marx Hof, Vienna

Modern architecture

Art nouveau architecture became the byword of Vienna, but after such structures as the Kirche am Steinhof were built other less edifying constructions began mushrooming between the two World Wars. Faceless communal housing blocks such as the Karl-Marx Hof, nevertheless, met with international recognition. Mercifully the city centre remained free of such atrocities, though the Vienna International Centre, headquarters of the UN, has also received a barrage of criticism.

Considering the fact that centuries earlier Vienna had formed a melting pot between east and west and thus was a nation of many peoples, it is hardly surprising that the visitor should find a multi-faceted city which is both traditionalist yet eclectic. If it had not been for the traditionalists, however, Vienna may well have fallen prey to ruthless city planners determined to tear up the old, supplanting it with the hideous concrete buildings seen so often today in other European cities.

The Ring

Despite the Viennese inherent dislike of demolition, the old walls of the city were torn down to make way for the Ring, which begins at Aspernplatz by the

Danube canal. Along this wide, tree-lined thoroughfare many new buildings sprang up during the nineteenth century. Today the city spreads out from the Ring, making it a simple matter to find your way to any of the many historic buildings *en route*. From the Votive Church, Universitätstrasse runs to the Renaissance building of Vienna University, which is expanding at such a rate that other buildings are having to be made available to accommodate all the student facilities.

City Hall

On Rathausplatz stands the City Hall. It is interesting to compare architectural styles of the Altes Rathaus (the old City Hall) and the Rathaus (New City Hall). The latter, built between 1872 and 1883, has a 330-ft (100-m) tall tower and seven inner courtyards, while the Altes Rathaus, owned by the city since the fourteenth century, has in its courtyard the eighteenth-century fountain of Andromeda, by George Raphaël Donner.

Kunsthistorisches Museum

Progressing down the Ringstrasse you reach the neo-classical style colonnades of the Parliament building, in front of which lies the Pallas Athene fountain and, shortly after, the Kunsthistorisches Museum (Museum of Fine Arts) on Maria Theresien Platz. Empress Maria Theresa's statue graces the square, surrounded by the equestrian statues of her most noted generals, the Prince of Liechtenstein (whose seventeenth-century palace now houses the Museum of Modern Art), Chancellor Kaunitz, and the musicians of her reign, Mozart, Haydn and Gluck.

The Habsburgs are responsible for the great collection of art seen today in the Kunsthistorisches Museum, which includes the works of Spanish, Italian, French, Flemish, Dutch and German masters, among them Pieter Brueghel the Elder, whose work completely fills one gallery; Van Dyck; Memling and Peter Paul Rubens. The Renaissance artist Albrecht Durer, Titian, Veronese, Rembrandt and Velasquez are all there, as well as Holbein, and some early works of the Danube School of painting. Before going to the Kunsthistorisches Museum make sure you have plenty of time to spare, for the collections, which include Egyptian, Greek and Roman art, are superlative.

The Hofburg

Continuing down the Ringstrasse, on the opposite side of the road from the Kunsthistorisches museum, lies the Hofburg, the Imperial palace of the Habsburgs. This amazing complex of buildings, part of which originates from the early thirteenth century, was updated when the Ring was constructed, and so extends into the twentieth century. It incorporates the Neue Burg (New Castle) which was constructed in Italian Renaissance style; the sixteenth-century Amalienhof; the Hofburgkapelle (chapel); Imperial Treasury; the National Library by Fischer von Erlach; the Spanish Riding School; the eighteenth-century Albertina; the church of the Augustinians, and the Schloss Lobkowitz.

As in the case of the Kunsthistorisches Museum you need time to explore the Hofburg. It is as well to start at the Imperial Treasury for there the powerful Habsburg dynasty is revealed. The Habsburgs may have been rapacious landowners, but in addition to territory they accumulated an abundance of treasures. Through carefully arranged marriages they acquired immense wealth. In the Imperial Treasury the symbols of their 640 year reign can be viewed, from the treasures of the Holy Roman Empire (which include the tenth-century imperial crown), to Rudolf II's crown made in the seventeenth century, and which subsequently became the Austrian imperial crown until the collapse of the monarchy.

The imperial apartments are resplendent with Flemish tapestries. Emperor Franz Josef spent some time in the Hofburg with the Empress Elizabeth, as did Napoleon's son, the Duke of Reichstadt. The Habsburgs were buried in the imperial crypt, with the exception of the assassinated Archduke Franz Ferdinand, and the last Habsburg monarch, Karl I who abdicated. Empress Maria Theresa lies in a sarcophagus beside her consort, François of Lorraine. The Kaisergruft (Capuchin's crypt) was built in the seventeenth century and contains the tombs of more than 100 archdukes, and 12 emperors. The Duke of Reichstadt's remains lay originally in the Capuchin crypt, but now rest in Paris.

The white marble mausoleum housing the tomb of Archduchess Marie-Christine, the Empress Maria Theresa's favourite daughter, is situated not in the crypt but in the fourteenth-century church of the Augustinians (Augustinerkirche) which lies within the confines of the Hofburg. This is the church in which her mother, Empress Maria Theresa, was married to François of Lorraine. The Kaisergruft and the Augustinerkirche are open to visitors daily, while in the Castle chapel (Hofburgkapelle) High Mass is performed on Sundays by the Vienna Boys Choir. If you can squeeze in, standing room is free. You enter by way of the Schweizerhof. If you book tickets by mail you should do so two months in advance. Write to the Hofmusikkapelle, Hofburg, Vienna 1010. In Vienna you can go to the box office at Burgkapelle the preceding Friday at 5 p.m.

The Spanish Riding School

One of the greatest modern day delights of the Hofburg is the Spanish Riding School (Spanische Reitschule) designed by Josef Fischer von Erlach on the orders of Emperor Karl VI, and where from March to December you can watch the magnificent white Lippizaner stallions going through their paces. The riders, dressed in brown coats, white breeches and black, cocked hats, enter the arena, and to the music of Lanner and Strauss waltzes the stallions parade, also performing to the gavotte and the polka. The Lippizaners are one of the true spectacles of Vienna. Tickets cost between 120–400 Schillings and are very difficult to obtain. If you are not bothered about the music and the lack of chandeliers, training sessions, though not so spectacular, are engaging. They last approximately half an hour and take place from mid-February to the end of

25 *Riding school*

June on weekdays, except Monday, from 10 a.m. until noon. Tickets are sold at the entrance: Gate 2, Josefsplatz, Vienna 1.

The Stallburg, a separate building, surrounds one of the courtyards. It comprises three floors of which the lower was used by Maximilian II to stable the horses of the palace guard, and is today used as stables by the Spanish Riding School.

Michaelerplatz, one of the entrances to the Hofburg, leads to the square known as In der Burg, with its statue of Emperor Franz Josef II, and into the Swiss Court (Schweitzerhof) beside the Imperial Treasury (Schatzkammer). As well as the remarkable possessions of the Schatzkammer and the Hofburg, the National Library, considered to be one of the finest baroque libraries in the world, contains priceless tomes, some of which came from the library of Prince Eugene of Savoy.

Neue Hofburg

The Neue Hofburg houses museums and art collections, including the collections of Court porcelain and silver which were used by the Habsburgs until the end of the monarchy. These include Sèvres and Chinese porcelain, and can be viewed from 9 a.m. until 1 p.m. daily. The Neue Hofburg is also the home of the Ethnographic Museum, the New Gallery with paintings by French and Austrian painters, and the Ephesus Museum where you can view the remarkable Ephesus reliefs which came from the mausoleum of Lucius Verus, co-regent of Emperor Marcus from AD 161–169. Two fascinating collections are those of musical instruments and armour. The former possesses instruments dating from the sixteenth century, and includes those played by some of the Habsburgs and by such eminent musicians as Mahler, Beethoven, Schubert, Liszt and Brahms.

The arms collection (Waffensammlung) in the Neue Burg enjoys a worldwide reputation and is of immense interest, containing swords, crossbows, guns, and helmets made by some of the finest Spanish, German, and Italian craftsmen from the Middle Ages to the seventeenth century. Also displayed are some of the spoils from the Turkish sieges. The Neue Burg houses an Ethnographic Museum, which is unusual in that it contains Montezuma's treasure, the feathered headdress said to have been given to Cortés, and some of the objects brought back from Australasia by Captain Cook.

The Albertina

Duke Albert of Saxe-Teschen married Empress Maria Theresa's daughter Marie-Christine, whose tomb lies in the Augustinerkirche, and gave his name to the Albertina, the collection of graphic art in the Neue Hofburg. In 1920 the Duke of Saxe-Teschen's personal collection received additions and some of those engravings date back to the sixteenth century. The Albertina also houses Rudolf II's collection, so altogether more than one million engravings, some of them architectural designs, repose in the Albertina and give a marvellous illustration of the graphic arts dating from the fourteenth century. Almost beside the Albertina lies the Burggarten, once the private garden of the Sovereign. In it stands the Mozart monument, and the statues of Emperor I and Emperor Franz Josef.

On the collapse of Napoleon's empire in 1814, Vienna was the place to which everyone gravitated. It welcomed princes, archdukes, and kings, and soon ousted Paris as the cultural mecca of Europe. Receptions and grand balls were the order of the day. It was the era of Metternich who had served as ambassador in Paris, and thus could observe Napoleon I at close quarters. Vienna glittered with diplomats, aristocrats and musicians. The waltz permeated the city. It was not only Emperor Ferdinand who strolled in the Prater, the scene of a daily fashion parade, but also the young Duke of Reichstadt, the son of Napoleon. Vienna was the stage for Europe's heroes, courtesans, and pleasure seekers. The Congress of Vienna had given back Austria's lost territories and it was a time of gaiety and self-indulgence.

Entertainment

Vienna has always been a city of music and dance and today it welcomes international performers to its Opera House. First erected in 1861-69 in French Renaissance style, the Staatsoper was inaugurated with the first public performance of Mozart's *Don Giovanni*. It suffered heavy damage during the Second World War and had to be rebuilt during the years of 1946-55. The Viennese are great opera lovers and swell the opera nightly. It is only with great effort and determination (and with the right connections) that you will obtain a ticket for a performance. When you do, you will find audiences attentive. Not an extraneous sound is heard. Only the singers and orchestra fill the auditorium. You will observe national dress at both the Opera and the well-patronised Burg

Theatre, Austria's national theatre, built in the late nineteenth century in Italian Renaissance style, and shattered by bombs during the Second World War. It reopened in 1956. The original Burg theatre dates from 1776 and was situated on Michaelerplatz.

Vienna has no fewer than 28 theatres, from traditional theatres like the Burg Theatre to modern theatres such as the Volkstheater and the Schauspielhaus where avant-garde plays are performed. There is also an English theatre which, as its name implies, shows plays in English. Extemporary theatres and street players add to the variety, and when you tire of theatre there are Vienna's 70 cinemas to visit. Pop artists perform at the Stadthalle. There are also jazz clubs, discotheques and a variety of updated distractions, but you are never quite allowed to forget that the première of Beethoven's *Fidelio* was performed in Vienna, and that it was also the city in which Franz Lehar's *Merry Widow* was first heard.

Museums

Vienna is also a museum city as much on account of its Baroque splendours as on its treasures laid up in countless city depositories. In Vienna there is a museum for everyone – in fact more than 50 of them – from the Imperial Coach collection at Schönbrunn Palace, which houses 60 coaches and sedan chairs dating from the seventeenth century, to the Museum of Modern History, open daily except on Fridays. There, in Vienna's arsenal, Austria's history is laid out before you, from weapons to the uniforms of the imperial army.

The Museum of Modern Art was established in 1979 in the seventeenth-century palace of the Prince of Liechtenstein, and possesses two important art collections: the Hahn collection from Cologne, and the Ludwig collection from Aachen. Austrian artists like Gustav Klimt, and Egon Schiele mingle with Max Ernst, Leger, Picasso and Magritte, and the modern works of Roy Lichtenstein, Christo, Rauschenberg and Warhol.

In addition to arts, Vienna has a plethora of special interest museums such as the Museum of Technology, which as well as steam engines (including the Pullman car of Empress Elizabeth), has a coal mine in the cellar and Siegfried Marcus' first car, constructed in Vienna in 1888. The Clock and Watch Museum includes a picture clock with a cascading waterfall, an astronomical clock and all kinds of watches, though the chiming of innumerable timepieces may prove too much for some. St Stephen's cathedral also has a museum full of reliquaries, Gothic sculptures and baroque art.

A real find is the amazing Tobacco Museum on Mariahilferstrasse which contains the oldest pipe in Europe, dated 1601, which once belonged to the Duke of Braunschweig. You will find all manner of oddities connected with smoking from cigarette holders to cigar cases.

As you might expect there is a Sigmund Freud Museum which was formerly the psychoanalyst's consulting room, and which is furnished with some of Freud's own furniture. It was at this house on the Berggasse that Freud wrote down some of his theories on dreams and psychic illnesses. Following the Anschluss of 1938, Freud left Austria for London.

26 Statue of Johann Strauss, Vienna

Another fascinating museum is the Museum of the History of Medicine, in the Josephinum on Wahringerstrasse. It was on those very premises that the doctors of the imperial army were trained. The museum traces the development in medicine of the Vienna School from Gerard van Swieten to Sigmund Freud.

Museums dedicated to some of the world's most famous composers are also found, not surprisingly, in Vienna. Franz Schubert's birthplace on Nussdorferstrasse has now been restored. At Kettenbruckengasse you will find the room in which he died. Haydn lived and died on the Haydngasse close to Mariahilferstrasse. Beethoven lived in Heiligenstadt and the Doblinger Hauptstrasse where he composed the *Eroica*. Johann Strauss lived at Paterstrasse, and Austria's great musical genius, Wolfgang Amadeus Mozart, lived for a time close to St Stephen's cathedral at the Figarohaus. There's another Mozart house on the Judenplatz.

More down to earth, but fun just the same, are the Old Bakery at Langegasse 34, open from noon, Tuesday to Saturday, and the Old Smithy at 1 Schonlaterngasse.

Travel

Horse drawn buggies (Fiakers) on Heldenplatz and Stephenasplatz will transport you from one end of the city to the other in romantic style, taking in the Am Hof, the biggest square in the Inner City and once the site of the Duke of Babenberg's castle, to the Ring.

The subway, built in 1970, is clean and swift with stations dotted all over the city. Tickets are stamped when you begin your journey and may be used for any journey in one direction. Red and white street cars are the alternative. These ply up, down and across the city, but take longer. Visitors to the city can buy a three day Vienna rover ticket which can be used on the subway, trams and buses. Taxi cab drivers can usually muster passable English if you get stuck with halting German. A map of the network of public transport, called a Netzplan, can be obtained from Information Centres. It lists underground routes and tramlines.

Shopping

Shopping is a big lure for most visitors and Vienna's street market, noted for its displays of vegetables, is a good place to wander. There's a Christmas market too, held in front of the City Hall, but it is the impromptu Saturday flea market on the Naschmarkt, with its stalls full of antiques, jumble, clothes, books and *objets d'art*, that is the sensation of the city. Open from 9 a.m., until 6 p.m., you will find all manner of quaint objects from exotic walking sticks and canes with silver handles, dog and snakes' head handles, all selling well despite the expensive price tags. Immigrant workers revel in the flea market where they sort through mountains of ancient ice skates to piles of avant-garde jumpers.

Traditional shopping is more usually done in the Mariahilferstrasse (Vienna's longest street), the Herrengasse, and the pedestrian areas of the Graben and Kärntnerstrasse with their narrow side-streets crammed with chic boutiques selling fashionable merchandise. As well as shops, the Herrengasse is lined with former palaces, many of them used as government offices. The eighteenth-century Wilczek palace adjoins a sixteenth-century castle, now occupied by the Ministry of the Interior. Just off the Landhausgasse lies Minoritenplatz with its fourteenth-century church, the Minoritenkirche, considered to be one of Vienna's most aristocratic squares. Two fine palaces can be found there, the Dietrichstein, and the Starhemberg, which is now the Ministry of Information.

Stretching from the Opera House to Stephansplatz is the Kärntnerstrasse, where just about anything from a Loden coat to a Gucci handbag can be bought. Café tables line the middle of the street, just as they do in the Graben, and in summer the area is awash with sunbronzed faces, as visitors and Austrians alike take their ease in the sunshine. It is interesting to note in this hive of rushed activity that seems to go on in the Kärntnerstrasse from morning until night, that squeezed between shops is the church of the Knights of Malta, the Malteserkirche, which was founded in the days of the Crusades. It is another world from the lively hustle of the Kärntnerstrasse, but that is what makes life enjoyable in Vienna, the old and new blending together in the most unlikely places.

You will find all kinds of souvenirs in Vienna from *petit point* to glass, porcelain – Augarten porcelain is world famous – and Biedermeier furniture. Vienna is also full of antique shops. The Dorotheum holds regular auction sales, where you can sometimes pick up a bargain. Furs in modish styles are also a speciality of Vienna, where winters can be harsh.

If it is Cerutti, Dior, Yves Saint Laurent and Fiorucci you are after, you can find them in Vienna alongside Austrian fashion designers. Old dolls are another Viennese speciality, and anything at all connected with art nouveau. Antique shops in the old part of the city are marvellous places to browse on a Saturday morning. You can wander at will, admiring the displays which all too often look as neatly arranged as museum pieces. At Vienna airport too you will find good shopping facilities, from liquor and cigarettes to duty free watches by Cartier. You can also find beautifully packaged Mozart chocolates from Salzburg and the famous *Sachertorte*.

Food

Vienna is the city of patisserie. On the Kohlmarkt, a chic shopping street leading from the Hofburg to the Graben, you will easily spot one of the finest pastry shops, Demel's. There in a relaxed, but traditional, atmosphere you can take your choice of coffees ranging from Brauner to Melange, together with a fantastic assortment of pastries. At L. Heiner's, another famous Viennese confectioner, you can take your choice between hot and cold pastries, from Milchrahm (a white cheesecake in hot vanilla sauce as smooth, light and airy as a summer's breeze) to a Mohr in Hemd (Negro in a shirt). Schlag (cream) is much in evidence and your Viennese hosts will raise eyebrows if you reject it and settle for the less ambitious Gugelhupf (dough cake) while they order Toffenknödel (white cheese dumplings) or Cremeschnitte.

Pastry makers came mainly from Bohemia to Vienna, making their dishes from flour as it was then a cheap commodity. As meat was both scarce and expensive, they settled for sweet ingredients, growing more daring as the years progressed so that today we have works of art served to us in the Konditorei of Vienna, and not mere pastries. The Aida Konditorei chain operates across the city, serving all kinds of patisserie at lesser prices than the likes of Demel, Heiner and Lehmann.

The Café Central at Freyung in the Old City, a lesser Deux Magots, with its plain upright chairs and stacks of newspapers to read, and where Stalin and Trotsky played chess, reopened in 1982 and is an interesting place, despite its initial austere ambience, but it is greatly enlivened by the clientele which varies from artists to visitors who have heard about its once illustrious patrons. The Café Hawelka on Dorotheergasse is usually crowded and is much beloved by artists and their associates.

There are endless cafés to choose from. Some have music, others do not. In some the coffee is better, at others the patisserie, or hot chocolate is the major attraction. One of my favourites is the Savoy café opposite the flea market. This sprawling café has a genuine art deco ambience and your hot chocolate is served in special china mugs. The service is friendly, efficient, but not rushed as you listen to tangos and old 1920s hits. From the windows, as you sip your Glühwein, you can watch shoppers braving the snow and ice as they pick over the last remnants of the day's bargains. Two Konditorei with fine reputations are Sluka, and the Sacher café on Philharmonikerstrasse.

Sachertorte

The *pièce de resistance*, however, is the Hotel Sacher. Over a century old it is more an institution than a hotel. Franz Sacher, in 1832 at the age of 16, invented his masterpiece, Sachertorte, for Prince Metternich. By 1857 Eduard, the son of the cake's inventor, was working for his father. Franz Josef I was on the throne, and in the year 1866 Eduard opened a restaurant and set up special rooms where the echelons of society could eat without being disturbed. With the opening of the new Opera House, the Sacher hotel went from strength to strength. Eduard was determined both to get his father's invention recognised, and to get the original Sachertorte patented. To that end he wrote to the influential editor of the chief Viennese newspaper of 1888. At that time Franz Sacher was 72 years old. As a young cook at Prince Metternich's court, he had created the cake and served it for the first time. It was enthusiastically received by everyone and highly praised by the Prince. 'Since then,' Eduard wrote in his letter, 'all efforts to reproduce the "original" Sachertorte have failed. The best proof I can offer is that only my father's cake is served daily to His Majesty and the Crown Prince. In fact our Sachertorte has become so popular I employ four people day and night all year round. Some 200–400 cakes, costing 1–6 florins each are sold and sent all over the world, to Paris, Berlin, London and even to overseas countries.'

The recipe continues to be a well kept secret. Over 70,000 'original Sachertorte' cakes, more than half the output, in their distinctive bitter chocolate coloured boxes are despatched all over the globe each year. At Christmas and in peak seasons the demand exceeds the Sacher hotel's maximum capacity of 1500 a day.

More than 600,000 eggs, 40 tons of chocolate, and 30 tons of sugar are used each year in the production of Sachertorte by the Sacher pastry chefs. The largest ever Sachertorte was a 15 layer cake which served 500 people. In the kitchens of the Sacher Hotel lie such dark chocolate confections. Does the original Sachertorte really taste so much different from other chocolate gateaux? Peter Gürtler, the present owner of the Sacher hotel and grandson of the founder, believes it does. In any event the recipe remains a closely guarded secret, and in no way does it appear that commercialism has made the Sachertorte any the less important. Like so much else in Vienna it is a tradition. As for the Hotel Sacher itself, that continues to be as much an institution as it ever was, where the rich and famous feel at home. The guest list is impressive. In a small room off the lobby hang the photographs of honoured patrons juxtaposed with international stars. Heads of State and diverse royalty stayed, and still stay at the Sacher as a matter of course.

Taverns and cafés

Restaurants in Vienna are not cheap, but while dinner in a four star restaurant may be expensive, quality and service are guaranteed. Many restaurants have lunch time specials which are a good way of trying out local specialities. Wine taverns are lively spots where you can eat simply but well, sampling the local wines into the bargain. The Viennese have their own special favourites, but even if you do not know the city well, there are plenty of Beisels to choose from, some more colourful than others. Outdoor cafés are favourite eating places in summer and there is always the pastry shop. In summer the Heurigen come into their own. Streetcar number 38 transports you to Grinzing and the wine taverns.

Nightspots

While you will find nightspots in Vienna most Viennese prefer the Opera, theatre or concerts. Since music is a byword in the city, you will never be short of concerts, most of which take place at the Wiener Konzerthaus or the Gesellschaft der Musikfreunde, better known as the Musikverein.

Fasching, the Carnival Season lasting from New Year's Eve to Lent, is a splendid time to be in the city since it is the season of grand balls and receptions. The season starts with the Kaiserball in the Hofburg on New Year's Eve, and sparks off a glittering season crowned by the opulent Opernball in the Opera House, a huge gala occasion. Other top social events are the Philharmoniker Ball and the Jägerball, a hunt ball at which you see the Styrian hunting costume well displayed. The Festival of Vienna takes place between May and June. Then music halls like the Musikverein and Konzerthaus come into their own. There are also concerts at Schönbrunn palace. December is the time to hear church music, and on Christmas Eve midnight mass in Austrian churches is well attended.

Vienna Woods

Those who want to get out of the city and see something of the surrounding area will find the Vienna Woods a delight. You can easily visit Kahlenberg and Klosterneuburg as well as Mayerling. Tour operators arrange daily sightseeing tours of the city and there's a 'Vienna by Night' tour too.

Parks

In addition Vienna has plenty of parks where visitors can ramble. The subway runs to Donaupark on an arm of the Danube. During summer this is a popular spot for swimmers and sunbathers. The Donauturm (Observation Tower) has a revolving café. Schönbrunn Park is magnificent, with gardens formally landscaped, while the Belvedere Park has interesting sculptures on its Italian style terraces.

Most popular of all is the Prater, which you can reach by subway from Karlsplatz. Once a hunting area it is now Vienna's Luna Park with a giant Ferris Wheel, the Riesenrad, roller coasters, ghost trains, and pinball machines. Open all year round it is also a sports centre with a race track, a stadium where Vienna's football fans can watch international matches, a swimming pool, and riding stables. In short, the Prater is to Vienna what the Bois de Boulogne is to Paris. You can ride a bicycle in it, or sit and gossip beneath an avenue of chestnut trees. But the days when Emperor Ferdinand strolled unescorted, and elegant carriages formed a stately procession in the late afternoon, have vanished forever. Like every other city, Vienna is undergoing change.

8
STYRIA

Iron mountains may sound forbidding but had it not been for the rich iron deposits in Styria, the Celts and Romans might never have settled there. Centuries later the iron was put to practical use, for it was from iron that the armour which clad the Christians in their battles against the Turks was made.

Erzberg (literally ore mountain), situated in the Eisenerz Alps, is known as the mountain of iron because of its iron ore which is quarried not mined. Picture the Celts and Illyrians hacking away at the huge massif which towered over the Eisenerz region and being staggered, not only by the quantity, but also by the quality of ore, which was 34 per cent pure. Today Styria remains a mining province, producing lignite and magnesium in addition to iron and steel; but it is also a huntsman's paradise, for game in the forests is abundant.

The Styrian adores his 'green province' and nowhere else in Austria, with the exception of Vienna and Salzburg, will you see national dress so proudly worn. The grey jackets with their green lapels, the Styrian suits with green stripes on the outside of the trousers like bandsmen, and the hunting hats, are virtually a uniform in Styria. In the country breeches are sported with thick woollen socks and sturdy mountain boots, for the Styrian is a hardy walker and climber. In the forests of the province, huntsmen like nothing better than a weekend's shooting.

Austria's second largest province extends some 6324 square miles (16,378sq. km), half of which are covered by forests. It has its vineyards, such as Ehrenhausen and Gamlitz in the south, which produce some of Austria's best white wines. The province also produces three excellent beers: Gosser, Reininghaus and Puntigamer. The Styrian landscape is one of dense woods, grasslands, vineyards and lakes, for the province shares the Salzkammergut with Upper Austria and Land Salzburg. The countryside is sprinkled with charming Gasthöfe and welcoming inns in which you can try the good Styrian wines and beers.

A major advantage is that Styria, like Burgenland, is less expensive as regards accommodation than some of Austria's other provinces. In Styria you can stay in an unpretentious Gasthof, a mountain chalet, or a traditional hotel. The Styrian cuisine is hale and hearty, with plenty of game and local specialities on the menu, and no self-respecting town would be without its coffee house and patisserie. Taverns are plentiful and if you are so inclined you may join in a song to accompany your glass of wine, for the Heurige is notorious for bringing out the best or worst in a person, according to his lights. Should you over-indulge it is handy to remember that Styria is also a province of spas, and should those fail, there are always outdoor activities to enliven your programme.

While Styria could benefit from more accommodation facilities in some of the ski areas, the skiing is good and, like the province itself, unpretentious. If you are searching for smart *après ski* to be found in some of Austria's upmarket resorts, Styria is not for you, but the sporting amenities are fine. You can ski the Dachstein glacier all year through. Styria can claim one of the biggest ski jumps at Kulm, Bad Mitterndorf, and the chair lift at Tauplitz is said to be the longest in the world. Tauplitz, 2 miles (3km) from Bad Mitterndorf, has two ski lifts and a ski school. Its major advantage is that it usually has snow throughout April.

As you might expect, mountain climbing is popular, with plenty of lodges scattered across the mountain ranges. Styria has produced some of the best climbers in the world, so if you decide to attempt it you will be in expert hands. Alpine flowers such as edelweiss and gentians dot the spring and summer landscape and make walking a pleasure rather than a chore. In summer, fishing is a favourite sport with Styria's rivers abundant with pike, carp and rainbow trout; and naturally enough hiking is equally popular. Spas like Bad Aussee, Bad Mitterndorf and the southern spa of Bad Gleichenberg – the most important in Styria – as well as treatments, prove restful, relaxing places. However, it is as well to remember that while Bad Gleichenberg holds concerts during its season from May to October, spas are primarily intended to provide rest and a healthy environment, so anyone interested in disco dancing had better look elsewhere.

Bad Aussee

Bad Aussee is the chief town of Styria's Salzkammergut. With most spas which have become fashionable, one usually finds a person of some charisma or special importance behind its sudden rise to popularity. Such is the case with Bad Aussee. Emperor Franz Josef was the man behind Bad Ischl; Archduke Johann, the son of Emperor Leopold II, was the power behind Bad Aussee. Although he lived in Graz he travelled often in Styria. At his hunting lodge at Brandhof on the Aflenzer Seeberg Pass, in 1827, he secretly married Anna Pochl, the postmaster's daughter. As a result of his romantic marriage, many tales were spread about Archduke Johann, who in some circles was dubbed the 'Prince of Styria'. The marriage, however, had been brought about only after endless negotiations and innumerable obstacles to the path of true love.

Anna Pochl was born at Bad Aussee, the first of 13 children. Archduke Johann had first seen her at a dance at Grundlsee in 1816 when he was already 34 years old, and Anna a girl of 12. Some years later Strechau castle, some miles distant, featured in the romantic tale. The eleventh-century Burg Strechau is one of the oldest castles in Styria and it was there that Archduke Johann, a true Habsburg who permitted nothing to stand in his way, met Anna Pochl in 1823 to make plans for their secret marriage, for his father, the Emperor Leopold II, would never have countenanced his son marrying a commoner. Eventually, after much deliberation, the couple were married in the presence of two witnesses at the Brandhof hunting lodge. By that time the Archduke was 47 years old and Anna 29. They lived in a country house in Brandhof, and ten years later their son Franz was born. Archduke Johann died in 1859 at Graz, while his widow Anna, lived to be 81, dying at Bad Aussee.

In the Kurpark stands the statue of the spa's best known patron, Archduke Johann. It is touching to think that although the archduke attracts most of the attention, the Pochl family is also remembered in the former post office on Meranplatz, where Anna's father was once the postmaster.

The town of Bad Aussee is notable for its fine parks and gardens. Like all spas it has promenades to stroll along to admire the views. Of particular interest is the Kammerhof (Salt Office) where the controller of the mines lived. Over its portals are depicted the coats of arms of Styria (Steiermark) and the Habsburgs. In the Kammerhof is the local museum where the history of Bad Aussee's mining unfolds. The town also has its plague column.

In the general region of Strechau castle, close to the town of Admont, lies the picturesque pilgrims' church of Frauenberg, with its twin spires rebuilt in the seventeenth century by the Abbots of Admont. Thousands of pilgrims left their votive offerings there in the form of hearts, limbs, eyes and so on, but instead of being made out of the customary wax the votive offerings at Frauenberg were remarkable in that they were made of silver.

The monastery of Admont

Even more amazing is the Benedictine monastery of Admont, founded in the eleventh century by Gebhard, Archbishop of Salzburg, and a saint, Emma of Gurk, who was canonised in 1938. Emma, a Countess in Carinthia, had founded the first convent in Gurk. The spires of Admont Abbey, which was gutted by fire in 1865 and rebuilt in neo-Gothic style, vie with the domes of Frauenberg to the west, but it is Admont's library, with its ceiling frescoes by Altomonte, which is the greatest source of pride, for it is reputed to possess the most important collection of manuscripts in Austria. In the late fourteenth century, Admont had in its possession over 600 Latin manuscripts, and a century later was outstripped only by the Vatican which could claim 800. During the sixteenth century Admont acquired volumes of natural sciences which were beginning to attract attention, partly as a result of the fine illustrations which were being done at the time, some of them by monks and nuns who proved themselves dedicated artists. Today Admont Abbey displays some of the manuscripts from its vast collection of over 2500 volumes, preserved by the Benedictines.

It is nothing short of a miracle that the manuscripts survived, for in 1939 the Nazis confiscated the monastery and its priceless possessions. At least 2000 of the manuscripts were sent to Dachau and were considered lost, but Admont could not let the matter rest there. At the end of the war, with the Nazis defeated, the librarian of Admont journeyed to Dachau and heroically retrieved the books, which today bear the stamp of that notorious camp.

Purgg

Between Admont and Liezen flows the river Enns. In the other direction lies the breathtaking Gesäuse, a wild gorge between limestone cliffs. From Liezen, the Enns valley leads to Purgg, an ancient village in a lovely mountain location. It is assumed that the name originates from Burg, meaning a castle, for the town was

27 Grundlsee

built on a medieval site, and the Traungau family, once the foremost family of the province, built their castle there. The castle no longer exists, but the Gothic church of St John still preserves its twelfth-century frescoes. From Purgg the road leads directly back to Bad Aussee.

From Bad Aussee excursions can be taken to nearby Grundlsee, 3 miles (5km) to the north-east, and Altausee, 2½ miles (4km) north. Grundlsee is hemmed in by the jagged Totes Gebirge cliffs which, as well as its lake, makes Grundlsee a good climbing area. Altaussee too is shielded by the Totes Gebirge, the Loser and the Tristelwand mountains. The lake is marvellously blue and if you want a more comprehensive view you can hire a boat. Altaussee has a salt mine at nearby Sandling which can claim a historic footnote, for it was there that the Germans stowed their art collection for safe keeping during the Second World War. Further off lie the Toplitzsee and Kammersee. Bad Aussee can be reached easily by rail from Graz and Vienna.

The Dachstein massif which straddles Salzburg, Styria and Upper Austria contains, on its north face, the fabulous ice caves, while on the south wall the glaciers reach the Hunerkögel. The Dachstein glaciers are a world away from the Styrian lakes, but provide some of the finest mountain climbing in Austria.

To the east lies Rottenmann in the Enns Valley, an unprepossessing name for one of Styria's oldest towns. As it lay on the old salt road, Rottenmann quickly looked to its industry, which grew rapidly due to the salt trade. The town retains traces of its ancient walls, but the castle of Strechau attracts more attention than the town, not only for its connections with Archduke Johann, but also because it once acted as a refuge for Protestants in Upper Styria.

The road continues to Hohentauern with a population of just over 600, down to Möderbrugg with its raging torrent, and onwards to Oberzeiring whose population numbers close on 1500. Oberzeiring, once a mining village, is no longer operative but an old silver mine can be visited. Almost opposite Oberzeiring lies Unterzeiring. When the Benedictine Abbey of Admont needed

28 Ramsau am Dachstein

to expand, a priory was built at Unterzeiring, and formed an attachment to Admont. The village of Unterzeiring is pretty enough, but its ruined Hanfelden castle is its main tourist attraction.

Judenburg, a Jewish settlement, lies on the Mur river. It was known in Roman times and the castle is thought to be connected with the Liechtenstein family. The road continues to Köflach, a mining centre noted for its lignite – the richest deposits in Austria – and for textiles, before turning left to the village of Pack. From there it is a mere mile (1.6km) to the Carinthian border. Alpine flowers grace the meadows around the village, making it a hiker's delight. As you travel south you reach the Packsattel or Four Gate Pass which ascends to almost 4000ft (1220m). The countryside between the Packsattel and Wolfsberg in Carinthia is thickly forested, but be careful of the sharp bends in the road!

From Judenburg the Mur valley continues to Leoben. An interesting detour is to the Benedictine abbey at Seckau. Founded in the twelfth century, it was the centre of the diocese of Styria from the thirteenth to the late eighteenth century, and thus the bishop of Seckau, who has his dwelling at Graz, is known as the bishop of Graz and Seckau. The abbey is famous for its architectural styles which range from the original Romanesque to the Renaissance. The mausoleum of Archduke Karl II, constructed in the Renaissance style, lies in the abbey.

There is a sharp contrast between Köflach's lignite and the village of Pibier, 2 miles (3km) to the north-east, a village which no rider, nor animal lover would ever miss. Situated in southern Styria, Piber is the noted stud of the pure white Lippizaner horses, which can trace their ancestry back to 1580 when Archduke Karl of Styria established a stud at Lippiza, near Trieste, then part of the Austro–Hungarian empire. In 1920, when Austria lost Lippiza to Yugoslavia, the stud was transferred to Piber, near Köflach. The stallions, whose lineage is Spanish, Berber and Arabian, are born in various colours from grey to black, and turn white only between the ages of two to seven years. They are not tall, measuring about 15 hands, but are noted for their equable temperament and alertness, which make them such a delight to watch during their performances at the Spanish Riding School in Vienna. In 1983 30 Lippizaner stallions died at the stud due to a viral infection, but the breed, although depleted, is flourishing once again.

Farther south, almost on the Yugoslavian border, lies Ehrenhausen, with its castle and mausoleum of the Eggenbergs constructed by Fischer von Erlach. From Ehrenhausen the road continues east to Radkersburg on the Mur, an ancient frontier town which controlled one of the approaches to Croatia. The Dukes of Styria built their castle on high ground. It suffered a series of attacks from the Turks and little remains of its thirteenth-century aspect. Radkersburg is today a divided town with that part of town in which the castle is situated being, since 1918, in Yugoslavian hands, the rest belonging to Austria.

As Radkersburg is also a spa it is often referred to as Bad Radkersburg. Like many spas it specialises in the treatment of rheumatism, but is best known for its kidney cures. Radkersburg has a Pestsäule and can boast the remains of its sixteenth-century fortifications which comprise city walls and towers. The Town Hall is chiefly noted for its octagonal tower which reaches 156ft (47m).

From the spa town the road takes us back to Bad Gleichenberg and on to Riegersburg castle, once one of the greatest and most powerful of the castles of Styria, which dominated the town and which the Turks thought the greatest in Christendom. West of Riegersburg is Fürstenfeld, once an imposing and strategic fortress built in the twelfth century as a link in Austria's defence. You would not expect to find the Knights of Malta in Fürstenfeld, but the fortress town did, in fact, become one of their Austrian seats. The thirteenth-century Schloss Herberstein, home of the Herbersteins since that time, is considered one of the most lovely of Styrian castles and was rebuilt in the seventeenth century.

The Lafnitz valley winds its way upwards to Vorau with its Augustinian Abbey, founded in the twelfth century, and its overloaded, baroque monastery church. Like many abbeys of its time, Vorau was rich, and in addition to land – nearby Festenburg castle belonged to Vorau – contained fine paintings and frescoes.

Graz

To reach Graz, capital of Styria and Austria's second largest city with a population of over 245,000, we must return to the Mur valley, the home of Austria's iron, steel and engineering industries, where Stiftrein claims to be the country's oldest Cistercian monastery.

Graz boasts a fine baroque castle – Schloss Eggenburg – on its outskirts. Its history is neatly preserved in its Zeughaus (armoury) built in the mid-seventeenth century, where, in one of the finest collections of armoury anywhere, are 2000 complete sets of armour, 8000 assorted firearms, and 7300 combat weapons including arquebuses, crossbows and swords dating from the sixteenth to the eighteenth century. The collection also includes jousting and hunting weaponry. The Styrian nobility is also well represented in a miscellany of castles and mansions from Herberstein, Attems, Stubenberg, Galler and Dietrichstein. The Renaissance castle of the Stubenbergs conjures up visions of medieval Styria, and the Stubenberg name is still alive today.

Spread out on both banks of the Mur river, Graz developed around a ninth-century Celtic settlement, but documentary evidence does not appear until three centuries later. By the thirteenth century Graz had become an official town, marked by city walls, and was the capital of Styria as well as Istria, which formed part of the Austro–Hungarian empire. After the Treaty of Neuberg in 1379, Graz became the residence of one of the Habsburg lines. The river Mur divides the city into the old town on the left bank, and the new business area on the right bank. Napoleon thought it charming, but that was presumably before the Napoleonic Wars which destroyed much of the city, with the exception of the Uhrturm (clock tower) which comprised part of the city's fortifications; that survived because the citizens of Graz paid the French not to destroy it. Today this famous clock tower on the Schlossberg is Graz's most famous landmark.

Thanks to its iron ore, which lent itself to the making of swords, armour and firearms, Styria was able to ward off several attacks, for everyone who could handle a weapon did so in defence of the empire. An arsenal was soon built next to the Landhaus which ensured a ready supply of arms. Even the Archduke Johann personally played an active role in the campaigns against Napoleon I.

The Archduke made his home in Graz and it was not long before the former capital of Central Austria, with its ready supplies of iron, was soon in the vanguard of industrial development. A railway was built from Graz to Köflach, an industrial centre in the making, and soon the Eisenerz district with its iron mountain was opening up its mines, which in the Middle Ages had consisted of mere quarries. One can imagine what Napoleon, who had romantic visions of the city, would have thought of its industrial suburbs today with their car and motorcycle plants, electrical, paper and cellulose industries.

Graz is a town for walking, so leave your car and explore the town on foot, for there is a wealth of things to do and see. The first thing most visitors do is take the funicular railway to the Schlossberg, the 400ft (122m) high hill from which they can get the best overall view of the town. During the Napoleonic War of 1809 the Schlossberg was badly damaged (with the exception of the clock tower). Today you can take a leisurely stroll in the Schlossberg gardens before descending by way of St Paul's Gate, once part of the town's fortifications, to the Hauptplatz. Graz's main square, the Sackstrasse, leads off it, and is notable for its old palaces which give a clue to Styria's aristocratic connections. Palaces of the noblest families are to be found on the Sackstrasse, including the Khuenburg, where Archduke Franz Ferdinand was born in 1863, and the baroque styled Palace Attems with its stucco decorations.

Two interesting streets, the Sporgasse and Herrengasse, lead off the Hauptplatz. The former, which merges with the Paulustorgasse, is full of old houses. The sixteenth-century palace of Saurau stands there. On the corner of the Hauptplatz and Sporgasse is the Luegg House, of interest chiefly for its stucco façade.

The Herrengasse, which runs towards the Am Eisernen Tor, is notable for its fine houses, among them the fifteenth-century Herzogshof, or painted house, as well as for its shops which are among the most elegant in Graz. The Landhaus, in earlier times the seat of the Diet of Styria, is today the seat of the Landtag, or the provincial diet, whose members are elected every four years. Depending on the size of the province, the number of members varies between 35 to 60, with Vienna the only exception with 100 members.

The Landhaus was built in Renaissance style by the Swiss–Italian architect Domenico dell'Allio, and the façade on the Herrengasse may seem plain by comparison with its arcaded courtyard and loggia. When you have gazed for a while at the three tiered arcades, the old well in the corner made by Styrian craftsmen, with its charmingly wrought bronze canopy decorated with cherubs, is a nice contrast. Next to the Landhaus is the seventeenth-century Zeughaus considered to be one of the largest in the world. It is interesting to note that Empress Maria Theresa permitted the arsenal to be preserved long after the Turks had been routed, and it is to the advantage of future generations that she did, for the Zeughaus with its fabulous collection gives an excellent idea of how a country defended itself against wars, sieges, and invasions. As one strolls in the arcaded courtyard of the Landhaus, it is not difficult to imagine the knights and volunteers lining up to collect their arms before going to war.

The Herrengasse also has some of the best patisseries in Graz. Most of the main shopping streets emanate from the Hauptplatz, the Herrengasse and its side streets being one of the best. There are all kinds of things to tempt you in the shop windows from Styrian national dress to dirndls, hats, leatherware and handicrafts. Hunting rifles are an excellent buy. Graz's pedestrian areas make shopping a pleasure as you are not always having to dodge the traffic.

Like most Austrian cities, Graz enjoys both opera and drama, the former taking place in the Operhaus at the Opernring, just off Am Eisernen Tor, and drama at the Schauspielhaus. A delightful setting for theatre in the open is the Schlossberg where you can watch performances in summer. The Landhaus and Schloss Eggenberg are also put to good use, where in the courtyards you can hear concerts in summer as well as in the city park, while the Styrian autumn festival is acknowledged to be decidedly avant-garde.

Graz's city museum, the Joanneum Landesmuseum on Räubergasse, is one of the oldest museums in Europe. The old buildings house the natural history exhibits and the prehistoric museum, while the new building contains the picture galleries. The museum is of special interest to devotees of medieval art for it possesses works by Lukas Cranach the Elder, Jan Brueghel, and the Gothic Admont madonna carved in wood in the early fourteenth century.

The Styrian Folklore Museum on the Paulustorgasse was formerly a Capuchin monastery and is open from April to October. If your speciality is native arts and folk costume this Steirisches Volkskundemuseum will be of great interest, for alongside old Styrian costumes there are costumes worn in Celtic times, and those from the Hallstatt period. Spinning wheels, farm implements and hand embroidery give an insight into life in Styria during the sixteenth century.

Not far from the Paulustorgasse is the Domkirche (cathedral) and the mausoleum of Emperor Ferdinand II. Emperor Ferdinand III's coat of arms is depicted over the main entrance of the cathedral, which was built at his command during the fifteenth century. Of particular interest is the baroque altar and the fifteenth-century fresco *Divine Torments* in which some of the world's scourges are depicted, while the two reliquaries, carved in the same century and placed at the entrance to the chancel, were the marriage chests of Paola of Gonzaga, the daughter of Ludwig II of Mantua.

Adjoining the cathedral is the baroque mausoleum of Ferdinand II, which dates from the early seventeenth century. Fischer von Erlach, born in Graz in a house by the Parish church, was partially responsible for the mausoleum's interior and, in particular, the frescoes. The parish church dates from the sixteenth century and has Tintoretto's *Assumption of the Virgin* decorating the altar.

Across the river on Mariahilferstrasse stands the twin-towered Mariahilfkirche, an early seventeenth-century church devoted to Our Lady of Succour, patron of Graz. Her painting hangs over the high altar, framed in silver. The church is of interest for its baroque façade and its Renaissance interior.

Schloss Eggenberg

The right bank is the business area of the city, as you might guess from its modern buildings, but it does possess some old edifices. If you go westward from the right bank for 2 miles (3km) you reach one of Graz's best-known residences, the Schloss Eggenberg. From the centre of town a streetcar will

29 *View of Stadtpark church, Eggenberg*

drop you there, for Eggenberg should be on any visitor's list. Reconstructed by Italian architects in the early seventeenth century, Eggenberg castle has been the residence of the Eggenberg family since the Middle Ages. Its baroque apartments and Jagdmuseum (Hunting Museum) are much admired. You will not be altogether surprised to notice that some of the apartments are decorated in the Chinese style which, at the time, enjoyed something of a vogue in Austria, as you will have observed already in the Chinese chambers with their lacquer and porcelain in Vienna's Schönbrunn palace.

The Hunting Museum contains not only the usual assembly of hunting trophies, but also collections of ancient weapons and complete records in great technical detail of aspects of game hunting. The Jagdmuseum is open from Tuesday to Friday and at weekends from 9 a.m. until noon. There is also a collection of Styrian antiquities including a votive chariot from the Hallstatt period on the ground floor of the south wing. Also at Eggenberg is a department of the Joanneum Landesmuseum known as the Gallery of Ancient Art, containing a fabulous collection of medieval art and stained glass by Styrian artists dating from the twelfth to sixteenth century.

In addition to Eggenberg there is a variety of trips you can take from Graz, including the health resort of St Radegund – Schöckel, a 20 minute ride from the city and well known by Graz citizens for its fine walks – and Gratwein, where in nearby Rein, in a fine old monastic church known as Stift Rein, you will find an altar painting by Master Schmidt of Krems. Graz holds a spring trade fair in April and an autumn fair at the end of September or early October. The city and its surroundings offer skiing in winter at several locations including the Schöeckel, known as the ski mountain of Graz, from where you will have superb views over the Alps. There is good skiing too both at Plabursch and Platte. Golfers can try the nine hole course at Murhof in Frohnleiten about 12 miles (19km) north of Graz, while enthusiasts of the increasingly popular sport of gliding can enjoy using Graz airport for takeoffs and landings. If you are interested in stalactites you should make the 14 mile (22km) journey to Peggau which can claim the largest stalactite and stalagmite cave in the country, with an underground lake and 3 miles (5km) of caverns.

Mixnitz

From Graz the Mur valley winds on to the town of Bruck an der Mur, which lies right at the confluence of the Mur and the Mürz in the Styrian Alps. On the way you pass through Mixnitz where, according to old legends, dragons existed. Looking at the wild scenery and cascading waterfalls it does not surprise me. Mixnitz, at an altitude of close on 1500ft (460m), is the place for those adventurous people who like to pit themselves against the elements, and at Bärenschutzklamm they have the opportunity of negotiating the precipitous gorge by ladders.

Bruck an der Mur

Leaving behind mythical dragons and prehistoric cave bears, Bruck an der Mur jolts one back to the present, for this is an industrial city where factories hum as they process the rich iron ore deposits. One thing Bruck an der Mur is not short of is iron, so it is no surprise that the town's focal point is its Eisener Brunnen or iron well, a magnificent piece of seventeenth-century craftsmanship by Graz ironsmith Hans Prasser, its simple elegance enhanced by Renaissance decoration.

Due to its industrial connections many visitors hurry on to their next destination, but Bruck an der Mur possesses some historic buildings worth seeing, among them the Kornmesserhaus, named after its owner, a wealthy citizen of the town Pankraz Kornmess. Built in the early fifteenth century the style is Gothic, with later additions of Italian Renaissance. It would be nice to know Herr Pankraz Kornmess's opinion of his ornate dwelling which is now one of the wonders of Bruck an der Mer.

Several other old houses dating from the fifteenth and sixteenth centuries can be observed, and like Graz's Landhaus, the courtyard of Bruck an der Mur's town hall is built with three tiered arcades adding a touch of elegance to the often forbidding façades of town halls in many other cities. Bruck an der Mur's restaurants serve Styrian dishes, so after taking a look at the parish church, famous for its knocker on the wrought iron sacristy door which is believed to have been taken from the Kornmesserhaus, you might decide to sample Styrian cuisine.

Leoben

Linked on account of its industrial communications with Bruck an der Mur is the steel town of Leoben, to the west of the city. Leoben is an ancient town, which has held the status of a market town since the Middle Ages. It is remembered historically because Napoleon Bonaparte, after his Italian campaign of 1796, signed a peace treaty at Leoben in 1797. Under the terms of the treaty, the Emperor of Austria received Istria and Venetia, but was obliged to relinquish Lombardy.

These days Leoben has forgotten all about Napoleon and concentrates on heavy industry and mining. As it is so close to Eisenerz with its iron ore, visitors tend to overlook the fact that Leoben has not entirely neglected other aspects of its past. For instance, the church of Maria Waasen with its fifteenth-century Gothic windows is worth more than a glance; so too is the main square with its plague column and, as no town hall should ever be bypassed, the Rathaus. But in Leoben one cannot avoid industry. On the road from there to Donawitz you pass iron and steelworks and blast furnaces preparing you for entry into Eisenerz. The iron road, the Eisenstrasse, leads through the Eisenerz Alps and should you wish to break your journey temporarily, Prabichl gives you a good view of the Erzberg. The iron mountain towers like a bulkhead, its rust colour

30 Eisenerz

contrasting with the Alpine meadows. If you want a closer view of the iron mountain, you should take the chair lift up the Polster, which takes about 15 minutes.

Eisenerz

Eisenerz at the foot of the Erzberg is an old mining town, which today forms the largest open cast mine in Europe, from which ore is transported to the blast furnaces at Donawitz and Linz. Like the mining communities of Wales with their chapels, so the Eisenerz has its old Gothic church of St Oswald, with its defensive walls built to ward off Turkish attacks. In the valley, the bell of the Schichtturm (shift tower) no longer rings to herald the change of shifts in the mines. If you wish, you can make a tour of the mines from May to October, and if claustrophobia is not a problem it's a fascinating experience.

Ore has been mined in the Eisenerz Alps since Roman times and, during the days of the Austrian empire, heralded the foundation of industrial power. From quarries developed the great open cast mines of modern times with their complicated systems of tunnels. Surface mining is the format today with terraces forming tiers up the mine – a distant cry from the improvised chipping of the rock face of earlier days. Surface mining continues all year round, and accounts for a third of Austria's iron ore production.

In contrast to the mines, at a distance of less than a mile (1½km) is the lovely Leopoldsteinersee, enclosed by its walls of rock which form part of the Hochschwab and Seemauer range. Although small, the greenish waters of the lake must have proved idyllic to the miners after working on the iron mountain.

From the Leopoldsteinersee the road winds through the Erzbach valley with its spectacular gorges, but from Hieflau the road is uneven and care should be taken on the steeper descents.

The Salza valley, which leads through Weichselboden to Mariazell, is a tributary of the Upper Enns. Massive limestone Alps dispel would-be strangers, and are hardly conducive to habitation, with their forested ravines and swift currents below. Until you reach Presceniklause with its dam there is little of abiding interest, and even at the next village of Weichselboden the church is the salient point of the village. So steep are the valleys on this stretch of the Salza that they have been given ominous names like 'In Hell'. After Weichselboden the valley widens as the road climbs on to Mariazell, one of the chief places of pilgrimage in Austria. The Habsburgs were big patrons of Mariazell and today it is a place of inspiration and worship with its candlelight processions flickering through the village to the basilica.

Mariazell

In the twelfth century a group of Benedictine monks founded a priory. The Madonna of Mariazell, the object of veneration believed to possess miraculous powers, stands on a silver altar designed by Fischer von Erlach. In the days of the Austrian empire, many triumphs were attributed to the Gothic Madonna, but even in the fourteenth century, pilgrims who strongly believed in miracles were arriving at the church. Victories on the battlefield, as well as the solution of more mundane problems, were credited to the Madonna, with the result that a cult developed and quickly spread, so that in no time at all Mariazell was hailed as one of the most sacred places in the country.

During the seventeenth century so great was the volume of pilgrims arriving in Mariazell that the church had to be enlarged. An Italian architect, Domenico Sciassa, undertook the work of increasing the size of the original Gothic building, and to his credit he kept the Gothic porch intact. The church's dome-shaped towers which he designed symbolise Mariazell and all it stands for. Most visitors head at once for the Chapel of Miracles with its Virgin of Mariazell always clothed. In the treasury one can see some of the costumes in which she is decorated, together with some votive objects.

Emperors, kings, and commoners came to Mariazell, including Archduke Ferdinand II and Leopold I, who made several pilgrimages. Charles VI was another monarch who set great store by the Madonna's powers. Many pilgrims went on foot; other penitents carried heavy crosses. During the Second World War, Mariazell was a British Occupation zone. These days it is a pleasant summer resort with hotels and restaurants catering to the influx of tourists, and pilgrims who arrive for the Saturday evening candlelight processions, held throughout the year.

Mariazell is also a ski area with a big sports centre. It has ten ski lifts, toboggan runs and a skating rink, but the pilgrims' church which was instrumental in attracting visitors is never forgotten. Hotel space can be limited, especially during the carnival procession in February which marks the

31 Pilgrimage church at Mariazell

end of Fasching, and during public holidays, but the town is easy to reach by rail from Vienna, Linz and Graz.

A cable car ride to the Bürgeralpe gives one an overall impression of the region and there are various excursions around Mariazell ranging from Alpine panoramas over the Ötscher massif to the Erlaufsee. If you take the road south over the Seeberg Pass you can enjoy some breathtaking mountain scenery *en route* to Aflenz Kurort, a mountain climbing centre and medium altitude resort standing at 2500ft (762m). Its highest mountain, the Bürgeralm, reaches over 5000ft (1525m). Aflenz is a noted skiing and walking area with hotels, restaurants, and a Gasthof on the Bürgeralm. The heart of Austrian skiing in Styria once lay in the Mürz valley at Mürzzuschlag, which was the venue of the 1904 Winter Olympics, and there is still a Winter Sports Museum there displaying old glories.

Neuberg

At Neuberg, Emperor Franz Josef had a hunting lodge and, once the Emperor was known to favour the place, Neuberg became the summer residence of

Austrian presidents. The town has a fourteenth-century monastery founded by the Cistercians which is famous for its cloisters – some would argue the finest in Styria.

We have digressed into the Mürz valley and must now return to Thorl by way of Kapfenberg, an industrial centre with a late Renaissance town hall, and twelfth-century Oberkapfenberg castle, which, as its name implies, overlooks the town. Less than half a mile away (0.8km) is seventeenth-century Krottendorf castle. Thörl can also claim a castle, that of Schachenstein, now in ruins.

We have come full circle back to Bruck an der Mur. On the way to Carinthia many visitors like to take a look at the Austrian Open Air Museum in the Mur valley, easily reached from Bruck an der Mur and Graz. If one is interested in domestic architecture the museum will prove fascinating, as it represents homes from the nine Austrian provinces set in 100 acres (40ha), each dwelling reposing in the nearest equivalent to its own natural landscape so that Tirolean chalets are set against mountain backdrops and the Appenzell-type houses of the Vorarlberg are set in rural surroundings. Nor is the Styrian farm neglected; there is a beautiful example in the Open Air Museum, with its typical kitchen and hearth.

From spas to pilgrimage churches, any number of sporting events and entertainments, the 'green province' offers the visitor a variety of choice.

9
CARINTHIA

Whereas still blue lakes and age-old forests once symbolised Austria's southernmost province of Carinthia, today it represents the destination of the universal package tour. With Italy and Yugoslavia on its borders, it is not altogether surprising that Carinthia has come to be known as Austria's riviera. What the Tirol is to ski enthusiasts, so the Carinthian lakes are to summer package tour devotees.

Southern Carinthia was the place where Slovene ethnic groups settled, continuing to speak German and the Slovak languages. Today four per cent of Carinthia's inhabitants speak Slovene. In 1920 these Slovenes voted in a referendum to remain part of Austria, and confirmed it in 1945 when they petitioned to prevent part of Carinthia from being swallowed up by Yugoslavia. After the Second World War, Carinthia formed part of the British Occupied Zone and since the early seventies has been highly popular with both Austrian and foreign vacationers. The British are especially fond of it.

Over 200 shimmering blue lakes are part of Carinthia's landscape, and the more popular ones such as the Worthersee are crowded with holidaymakers in summer. Surrounded as it is by mountains, Carinthia seems a very compact province, its land area about half that of Styria, its population bordering on 550,000. It is possible to ignore the hydroelectric plants in the mountains and concentrate instead on Carinthia's natural beauty, which varies from lakes to snowy peaks, wooded slopes and church steeples.

Carinthia is an old province which has yielded Bronze Age graves and historic findings. The Illyrians and Celts first inhabited the area, followed by the Romans. When they left in the sixth century, the early descendants of the Slovenes arrived in the area. It is thought that their centre was Zollfeld, which has revealed over 20 prehistoric sites, castles, Roman ruins and a ducal throne. Later medieval documents referred to Carinthia and its Celtic tribes as Caranti, *car* originating from the Illyrian word for rock.

From the eighth century Carinthia had its own independent dukes. The first Duke of Carinthia to live in sovereign state in his capital was Bernard of Spondheim, and the last Duke of Carinthia was invested in 1615. Bavarians arrived some time during the ninth century to assist the Carinthians in repelling invasions, and an alliance was formed. A century later, the Slovenes had been overruled by the Franks, and Carinthia became an imperial Duchy. In the fourteenth century the Habsburgs incorporated Carinthia into their territory and ruled it for the next 600 years. When the Austrian Empire crumbled in 1918 it became one of the nine federal provinces of the Republic. By the late sixteenth century gold mining was at an end and many Austrians emigrated. Powerful families like the Spondheims and Eppinsteins remained in Carinthia and their descendants are extant today.

If crowds do not spoil your pleasure, a good time to visit Carinthia is the months of July and August, admittedly a peak period when Carinthia receives most of its tourists, but ideal for water sports or for relaxing by the lakes, for those with less ambitious projects in mind. Warm sunlight is virtually guaranteed, but as these two months represent the height of the tourist season, hotel accommodation can be limited for last minute bookings. Tour operators have usually reserved well in advance and one look at the Tourist Pullmans will convince you there will be little room for latecomers. However, the spring and autumn months can be delightful especially if you are not particularly interested in getting a suntan, and with lakeside resorts less crowded one can see much more. Another advantage is that Carinthia generally attracts a quieter kind of holidaymaker out of season – one who is prepared to formulate his own sightseeing programme.

One of the best ways of seeing the province is to hire a car, although if you happen to enjoy railways, you can take a train from Klagenfurt to the chief cities of the provinces. In summer you can ride the Europabus to Vienna, Salzburg, and on to Italy and Yugoslavia, but a trip on one of the lakes can prove more enjoyable than being confined to a bus. Lake boats ply between towns on the Wörthersee and Ossiachersee, and it is interesting to compare the differences between eastern and western shores. As well as swimming, sunbathing and strolling, the lakes offer a wide range of fish for the keen angler, from grayling to perch, carp to trout. In the river Drau you will find excellent fishing, but don't try it without a licence. This can be obtained locally, so ask at the local Tourist Information Office.

Lavant valley road

If you are arriving in Carinthia from Styria, you will, in all probability, head for Friesach. Alternatively, if you are coming from Graz, opt for the Lavant valley road which runs to Klagenfurt. The Abbey of St Paul im Lavanttal is a Romanesque church which has always been connected with the Benedictines. The monastery is impressive, not only for its magnificent library (which contains over 50,000 manuscripts including a Gutenberg bible), but also on account of its situation, high on a rock above the Lavant valley. It had, prior to its consecration in the thirteenth century, been the castle of the Counts of Spondheim and had become connected with ecclesiastical matters since the eleventh century when the Duke of Carinthia and a member of the Spondheim family requested the monks to serve in the castle chapel. The Count subsequently founded a monastery and granted the castle and its lands to the Abbott. The monastery was dissolved in the late eighteenth century. It seemed the service of the monks was at an end, but a group of Benedictines settled there soon after. Beneath the altar in the crypt which once formed part of the Spondheim castle lie 13 Habsburgs.

The bishops of Lavant had their residence at St Andra im Lavanttal and the town still boasts monastic buildings and a cathedral church. Five miles (8km) further on, Wolfsberg is southern Carinthia's fruit-producing area. Its land is particularly fertile. The castle of the Henckel-Donnersmark has been given a nineteenth-century appearance while the parish church has a painting on its baroque altar by Master Schmidt of Krems.

To continue along the road is to arrive in Styria's Packsattel, so now is the time to consider what would have happened had we taken the route from Styria to Friesach.

Friesach

Friesach in the Metnitz valley is an old Roman town where most of the prehistoric finds in Carinthia have been unearthed. The first castles were built there and the first churches founded. These days you can still see traces of Friesach's fortifications. Its ramparts and moat give some idea how this town, which received its charter in the eleventh century, must have looked in its heyday.

As it lay on the road between Vienna and Venice it was of military importance, and during the Middle Ages was the scene of jousting tournaments. The Carinthian Knights were a popular attraction in the area, and as Friesach belonged to the Prince-Archbishops of Salzburg, it seems likely that they may have watched the occasional bout.

The town has three castles: St Petersberg, Geiersburg and Virgilienburg, and at least six old churches, one of them, Peterskirche, dating from the ninth century, and two Gothic churches dating from the twelfth and thirteenth centuries. The thirteenth-century Dominikanerkirche was originally the Dominican Order's first monastery in a German-speaking country. The church has the longest nave in Carinthia and contains medieval sculptures and an ancient crucifix. St Thomas Aquinas once preached there. Richard Wagner also had connections with Friesach. Members of his family had worked in the town as Salzburg administrators and it is thought he may have used this family link when he composed *Tannhäuser*.

Gurk

From Friesach the road divides, one branch leading on to Klagenfurt, the other onto the Gurk valley. The latter takes us to the town of Gurk, bypassing on the way the ruins of the Renaissance castle of Strassburg where the Prince-Bishops of Gurk once resided. Gurk is a market town and remained a Bishopric until the late eighteenth century when the Prince-Bishops took up residence in Klagenfurt.

Gurk cathedral was constructed between the late twelfth and early thirteenth centuries and is today considered one of the finest Romanesque churches in central Europe. It was built on the site of a church which had been founded by Countess Emma of Friesach-Zeltschach, who was canonised in 1938. When her husband and son were both killed in battle, St Emma devoted her life to religion, giving her money to the building of churches. She was extremely pious

The Renaissance
Landhaus at Linz

Wotruba's church in
Vienna

Sunset over Kleinwalsertal

Alpine scene

and founded no less than ten churches, the monastery of Admont in Styria and the convent at Gurk in which she died in 1045. Her body lies in the cathedral crypt which is supported by 100 columns. It was specially constructed to contain her sarcophagus.

The building of the twelfth-century cathedral spanned 40 years from its beginnings in 1140. Baroque decorations were added later. It is an impressive building with its three naves, gothic windows and Romanesque doorway, yet the overall effect is one of strict severity, as is so often the case with Gothic churches. Gurk cathedral, while at the height of ecclesiastical power throughout the Middle Ages, dropped from favour during the early nineteenth century, but has been revived so that today few visitors to Carinthia pass it by. It contains a wealth of treasures from thirteenth-century frescoes to the fine Samson doorway, with its carvings of Samson killing a lion, which dates from 1180, a Renaissance winged altar, a rococo pulpit, and the oldest Carinthian Fastentuch (the cloth used to cover the altar during Lent and painted with biblical scenes from the Old and New Testaments), which dates from 1458. The Bishop's chapel contains a series of Romanesque murals. Gurk cathedral is open to visitors from April to November; the crypt and Bishop's chapel may be visited by guided tour.

As well as splendid architecture and interior decorations of such cathedrals as Gurk, it is intriguing to see the dwellings of the monks or the church canons themselves and to ponder on how they lived and what were their thoughts in those far-distant days. You can satisfy your curiosity by just one glance at the priory buildings in which those venerable canons lived during the fifteenth and sixteenth centuries.

St Veit an der Glan

Continuing on through the Metnitz valley the next large town is that of St Veit an der Glan, named after the patron saint, St Veit. The town itself is of medieval origin and its environs are crowded with old castles. St Veit an der Glan was the seat of the Dukes of Carinthia from the thirteenth century until 1518, when the duchy of Carinthia was administered from Klagenfurt. Many of the old buildings in the town have been destroyed but the main square, the Hauptplatz, can at least claim an early eighteenth-century Pestsäule and fountain, the Schüsselbrunnen, whose basin is thought to have originated from the Roman settlement Virunum, the capital of Noricum.

The sixteenth-century bronze statue, the Schüsselbrunnbartele surmounting it, is the town's mascot. Also in the Hauptplatz are the Rathaus, a typical municipal building which was given a baroque appearance in 1754 and on whose pediment is embossed the double-headed eagle symbolising the Holy Roman Empire, and the military headquarters built in the late eighteenth century.

St Veit is the ideal base for exploring the castles and medieval strongholds of the region, which range from the eleventh-century Hochkraig, to fourteenth-century Niederkraig.

Hochosterwitz castle

In the opposite direction, east of St Veit an der Glan, lies the castle of Hochosterwitz situated off the main road to Launsdorf. Hochosterwitz sits on the edge of the Zollfeld and has been in the hands of the Khevenhuller family since the sixteenth century.

From 1534 to 1587 Georg Khevenhuller was the governor of Carinthia. Clearly he was a kindly man for the castle fortress became a refuge for Protestants. On one of the fourteenth-century tower gates to the estate sits his bust. The fine collection of arms belonging to the Khevenhuller family is of interest, but not all of the rooms of the castle are open to the public. The Hochosterwitz is thought to be one of Austria's most romantic castles. Built on a hill it has all the trappings of a make-believe world, so it is fun to explode the myth at close quarters.

At Launsdorf the church is noted mainly for its mixed styles of architecture, leaving you to guess which is Romanesque, and which Gothic. Is that really a pomegranate the Virgin in the chancel is holding? And could it be Gothic?

St Georgen am Langsee holds no such secrets. Its Benedictine Abbey has stuck to its original design although its church did succumb to the baroque style in the early eighteenth century, and its arched inner court is worthy of mention.

Magdalensberg

Taking the road to Klagenfurt from St Veit an der Glan, it is worth taking an upward turn to Magdalensberg, noted for its archaeological excavations as well as for its view over the Klagenfurt basin, the Saualpe range and the Karawanken. Excavations have revealed traces of a town inhabited by the Romans as early as the first century BC. Although excavations had started in the latter part of the nineteenth century, they were interrupted by the First World War and after the Second World War, they began again. A sixteenth-century farmer had started it all off by unearthing, while tilling his land, a small statue, which came to be known as the Youth of Magdalensberg, now reposing in the Kunsthistorisches museum in Vienna. The statue was thought to have been brought as a gift by the Roman traders who later settled in the area, to the then Celtic town of Magdalensberg.

Vierberglauf

The town has another claim to fame, the ancient Vierberglauf which is an Easter Pilgrimage. The pilgrims gather on the hillside at the Gothic Pilgrims' church dedicated to St Mary Magdalene. Then begins the ancient ritual of lighting bonfires and the reading of the midnight mass, after which everyone descends the hill carrying their flaming torches. The participants then begin the walk over the four hills after which this special pilgrimage is named. To an untrained eye they look more like a group of hikers who have come together for a celebration, as they troop over the Zollfeld plain, following a solitary cross in front. Having negotiated the first mount, the second hill is the 3350ft (1020m) Ulrichsberg known, during the Celtic period, as one of the sacred mountains of Carinthia. Onward march the pilgrims up the mountain, down the mountain and back again to the Glan valley where they begin to ascend the even higher Veitsberg at 3850ft (1173m). Those who are able to continue pass through the village of Sörg to the last mountain, the 3200ft (975m) high Lorenziberg. The rule is that the pilgrimage must be completed in 24 hours and, considering the distance – approximately 25 miles (40km) much of it uphill – and bearing in mind that masses are said on each of the four hillsides and often elsewhere, the pilgrimage resembles a penance more than an act of worship. In fact originally it had little to do with Christianity as it was based on pagan rituals which included worshipping the sun, the coming of day (on the Vierberglauf the sun's movement is from Magdalensberg in the east to Veitsberg in the west, the pilgrimage ending after dark at Lorenziberg in the north), along with special rites and acts of veneration for the cultivation of crops.

The Zollfeld plain

Over the Zollfeld plain, which runs from St Veit nearly to Klagenfurt, the Roman legions marched, and founded the province of Noricum, with Virunum as its capital. Remains of their civilisation can be seen in Carinthia, particularly in the Landesmuseum at Klagenfurt. The Roman province of Noricum extended from St Pölten (Cetium) in Lower Austria, incorporating Salzburg (Juvavum), Lienz (Aguntum), to Virunum. Some ancient documents survive which testify to Roman habitation.

The church of Maria Saal

In earlier times the church of Maria Saal was known as Sancta Maria, and the city of Maria Saal was the first centre of reconversion of Carantania (Carinthia). In the mid-eighth century, the Carantanian Duke, Cheitmar, who had been converted to Christianity, desired that the Carantanians also acquired the faith, and thus spoke to the Bishop of Salzburg, who sent Bishop Modestus to found the church of Maria Saal.

Maria Saal's present church building dates from the fifteenth century. Its twin towers are constructed from volcanic stone and its green coloured roof has been variously described, but perhaps the closest description is that of a baroque helmet. Lying in the barren plain it is not difficult to imagine how vulnerable the church was to the Turkish invasions of the sixteenth century. Inside the church the late Gothic vaulting of the central nave depicts Christ's genealogy.

Another point of interest is that the Roman sarcophagus beneath the ninth-century altar is said to contain the body of St Modestus, the original church's founder. In the church's annexe lies an octagonal charnel house built in the fifteenth century after the fashion of the Holy Sepulchre in Jerusalem.

The Ducal throne

The Ducal throne, the Herzogstuhl, still lies on the Zollfeld plain. This was the investiture chair of the Carinthian Dukes who had been entrusted with sovereign power to rule their territory of Carinthia. Another similar stone chair is the Furstenstein or Prince's stone which, like the Herzogstuhl, was made from the last vestiges of Virunum, and now rests in the Landesmuseum at Klagenfurt.

Klagenfurt

To the south lies Klagenfurt, founded in the twelfth century. It has been the capital of the province since 1518 and today the city's population is estimated at around 85,000. When you note its geographical position you see how far south it is – a mere 18 miles (30km) from the Yugoslavian frontier, and 37 miles (59km) from the Italian border. It is a city of Romanesque and Gothic architecture, whose walls were destroyed during the Napoleonic campaigns in 1809. In the latter part of the nineteenth century there was a brief economic revival.

Klagenfurt is one of the easiest towns to explore, for its streets are neatly interlaced, and once you arrive in the centre, the four 'Ring' streets – the wide Viktringer Ring, Villacher Ring, St Veiter Ring, and Volkermerkter Ring – enclose a simple pattern of cross streets. In summer the city is hot, as it lies in an Alpine basin, but the big advantage is that it is an easy drive to the Wörthersee; so while the city shimmers you can take a dip in the 10 mile (16km) long lake and return in time to enjoy a concert at the Konzerthaus on Viktringer Ring or an opera at the Stadttheater.

Klagenfurt is not so dragon-orientated as Styria's Mixnitz but the Neuer Platz does have as its emblem the dragon fountain which is hard to miss since the crouching open-mouthed dragon looks pretty lethal. This square is the pulse of Klagenfurt. It boasts a statue of Empress Maria Theresa to remind us that Klagenfurt is not just Lindwürm (dragon) folklore. From the Neuer Platz the Alter Platz is just a street away, forming the oldest part of the city. It was destroyed by fire during the early sixteenth century and was then rebuilt. Grand baroque houses grace the wide street and square upon which the sixteenth-century Landhaus stands. The Landhaus, whose arcaded courtyard, designed by Johann Antonio Verda, is lovelier than the façade on the Alter Platz, is the provincial seat of the Diet and was originally an arsenal. Its great hall contains 665 Carinthian coats of arms. Josef Ferdinand Fromiller, the Carinthian artist born in 1693, decorated the ceiling of the state hall and his painting of the Fürstenstein investiture is of special interest to Carinthians.

You may be surprised to learn in a staunchly Catholic country like Austria that Klagenfurt's sixteenth-century cathedral was built as a Protestant church. (In 1604 every Protestant inhabitant of Klagenfurt had to renounce his beliefs or leave the city.) It stands on Lidmanskygasse and is easily reached from the Viktringer Ring. Even closer is the Landesmuseum which is situated between Miesstalerstrasse and the Ring. Objects of interest therein are the already-

32 Landhaus in snow, Klagenfurt

mentioned Furstenstein, the youth statue from Magdalensberg believed to date from the fifth century BC, and the mosaic floor found at Virunum. There is also a display of Carinthian folk costume. The Bishop's Palace on Mariannengasse contains some excellent examples of medieval ecclesiastical art in its Diocesan museum.

The Wörthersee

From Klagenfurt you can reach St Veit an der Glan, Villach and Velden. Two main railway lines connect Klagenfurt with other parts of Austria. From Klagenfurt to Vienna takes about four and a half hours. The city's bus station is not far from the railway station. The city bus line will take you to Krumpendorf on the northern shore of the Wörthersee which extends from Klagenfurt to Velden. Its major advantage is its warm waters which can reach a maximum temperature of 28°C (82°F) in summer, and the lake's charming surroundings. The Wörthersee is sufficiently warm for some hardy types to swim in in May and as a result has caused a multitude of vacationers to invade Krumpendorf, a more family-orientated spot.

Pörtschach

Pörtschach is considered chic and has become one of the best-known resorts of the Wörthersee. Situated on a peninsula its smart private villas are discreetly screened by foliage and flowering shrubs. Its promenade along the lake is reminiscent of Switzerland's Ticino canton with its masses of flowers.

Velden

At the western end of the lake is Velden, the most popular spot on the lakeside, notable for its Mediterranean atmosphere rather than the quieter, Carinthian charm of the southern shore. Velden, like Pörtschach, attracts a fashionable crowd who appreciate its more cosmopolitan atmosphere and the chance to play baccarat, blackjack and roulette at the casino which opens daily at 5 p.m.

The original castle at Velden belonged to the Khevenhuller family, and when it was transformed into a hotel in 1894 the baroque main doorway and the pediment displaying the family coat of arms remained, as did their castle at Hochosterwitz. At Pörtschach you can stay in the converted Schloss Leonstein and dine in its courtyard. Velden can match it with Schloss Velden, though this is a much larger, less intimate hotel. The original baroque castle dates from 1603 and has antique decor in the public rooms to add a historical note. This luxury hotel has a private beach, tennis court and dancing during the high season. If you are not seeking such luxury, there are plenty of Gasthofe in and around Velden and rooms in private houses.

Velden has water ski schools, a sailing school and riding facilities. It holds a sailing regatta in June and a parade of historical floats in August. Pörtschach has a yacht club and holds regular water ski jump competitions. It also prides itself on skeet shooting, for to retain that 'exclusive' tag it has to be different.

Maria Wörth

On the southern shore of the lake is a golf course at Dellach, the only one in the area, where golfers can improve their drives less than a mile (1.5km) from the delightful peninsula of Maria Wörth. Considering its romantic situation – it is almost cut off by water – it is perhaps surprising that an enterprising property developer has not built groups of holiday villas there, but, thankfully, Maria Wörth remains unspoiled in its tranquil lakeside setting. Its two pilgrimage churches, one dating originally from the ninth century, the other from the twelfth, are of interest for their Romanesque architecture, but the larger of the two displays other architectural styles, including Gothic and baroque in its interior. Maria Wörth's Ascension Day parade with its boat procession on the Wörthersee is a big event. At Dellach there is the Golfhotel near the golf course which is open from mid-April to the end of October. You can also stay at Reifnitz, a smaller lake resort close to Maria Wörth, and at Sekirn.

Pyramidenkögel

From Reifnitz a good road leads to the aptly-named pyramidenkögel, which has its own viewing tower. If you are a person who cannot resist observation towers and panoramic views, Pyramidenkögel is the place for you, for once there you have an uninterrupted view of Carinthia. You might even pick out Ulrichsberg, celebrated at Eastertide by the Vierberglauf (Four Hill Walk), and the peninsula of Maria Wörth in the foreground.

Leaving behind the Pyramidenkögel and the bathing resorts of Reifnitz and Sekirn, the Cistercian abbey of Viktring is well worth a detour. Its architecture served as a model for several Cistercian monasteries. Viktring is built around two arcaded courtyards and originated in the twelfth century but was altered in the fourteenth century. However, its three beautiful Gothic stained glass windows remain.

From Viktring the road leads to Hollenburg castle whose fortress overlooks the Drava Valley. In this region, known as the Rosental, lies Ferlach, a village famous for its gunsmiths. Shotguns and sporting rifles made over the centuries by its craftsmen can be seen in the Gun Museum. During the Napoleonic wars· Ferlach gunsmiths turned out 20,000 guns a year. These days the handmade hunting guns of Ferlach are still much in demand.

Across the Drau river is the town of Völkermarkt which received its status as a town during the Middle Ages. Its Town Hall forms part of the castle. Volkermarkt is interesting for its Biedermeier houses which line the main square and for the frescoes of its Gothic church. The Biedermeier houses date from the early nineteenth century; their typically bourgeois style was a welcome change after so much baroque architecture. If you follow the main road you will arrive once more in the Lavant valley, so it is as well to turn back to Klagenfurt and from there take the road which runs along the Wörthersee, to Moosburg, which lies inland from Pörtschach. Moosburg's now ruined castle was the birthplace of Arnulf, a ninth-century German Emperor. Schloss Moosburg, a fifteenth-century castle in a large park, has been converted into a hotel. Feldkirchen, the seat of the Bishops of Bamberg, has Biedermeier houses and a defence tower.

Ossiachersee

On the way from Moosburg to Feldkirchen we skirted the Ossiachersee, which is exactly what other tourists often do, as they know the Wörthersee much better and are only too ready to crowd its already jam-packed lakeside rather than investigate the lesser-known and wilder-looking Ossiach Lake, Carinthia's third largest lake after the Wörthersee and Milstättersee. Innumerable legends have sprung up around the lake, probably due to its wooded setting— mists and forests being the customary location of myths and dragons. One of the legends, which grew up about the eleventh century, concerns Polish King Boleslaw II, who, after murdering the Bishop of Cracow, fled to Ossiach where he disguised himself as a Benedictine monk and continued as a penitent for eight years. The weight of his conscience finally caused him to confess to the murder on his deathbed. Legend or not, the king merited a tombstone.

From the eleventh century the Benedictine Abbey of Ossiach had seen the re-Christianisation of Carinthia and had also witnessed much visiting by prelates and royal guests, including Charles V of Austria. Its frescoes are the work of Joseph Ferdinand Fromiller, the Carinthian artist whose work decorates Klagenfurt's State Hall. The old abbey is now the Stiftshotel, and should you stay there your room is likely to be a former monk's cell, and might even be that of King Boleslaw II.

At Ossiach you can sail on the lake where once Charles V, in the sixteenth century, watched a fleet of sailing ships, a performance which was put on especially for the royal visitor. The first sailing regatta each year is held in June. Although it cannot match Salzburg for patronage at an international level, Ossiachersee's Carinthian summer festival has begun to attract large audiences.

Landskron

The ruins of Landskron castle do indeed crown the land from their strategic position, just as the Austrian name implies. Landskron lies at the southern end of the Ossiachersee and during the Middle Ages belonged to the Carinthian branch of the Habsburgs. In the sixteenth century it became the property of the Khevenhuller family, who already owned the castle at Velden. The Khevenhullers favoured the Reformation and during the Thirty Years' War were instrumental in protecting Protestants.

Many such castles have been transformed by entrepreneurs into hotels or restaurants where their historical associations add charm to the surroundings, for such fortresses were usually situated in fine positions and surrounded by pleasant landscapes. Landskron, though not transformed into a hotel, does have an excellent restaurant and a café terrace where you can reflect upon Carinthian history, as you survey the view. After the seventeenth century the castle fell into disuse, and is viewed now as another landmark in Austria's past.

The Dobratsch mountain

From Landskron you can pick out the town of Villach and the Dobratsch mountain in the Villacher Alps. Even if you dread heights you must still visit the Dobratsch, for the view it affords is stunning. You can reach the mountain by road, take a chairlift to the highest platform and then climb the rest of the way. The Dobratsch is about 7000ft (2130m) high and affords unsurpassable views over the Karawanken, the Tauern and the Carinthian lakes.

Villach

From the mountainside the road leads back to Villach. Although it may not seem so big, (Villach has a population of around 40,000) – it is Carinthia's second city. As well as being a holiday centre, Villach is a railway junction, as you will notice if you have occasion to arrive by train. Its spa of Warmbad Villach, long before it became what it is today with its hotel, restaurant and radioactive waters, was used by the Romans. The Salzburg doctor and philosopher Theophrastus Paracelsus lived, for a while, in Villach as his father was the doctor there, and doubtless Paracelsus tried the thermal waters of the spa.

Villach's noble families were the Widmanns and Neumanns. Anna Neumann was not only beautiful and rich, she was clearly an unusual woman. She married on six occasions and was widowed four times. Her possessions and wealth accumulated as Anna had no heirs. She deliberated what to do. Whenever she married it was always to immensely rich men and, even at the age of 82 and still without a child, Anna decided in 1677 to marry the 28-year-old Count Georg von Schwarzenberg. When she died she left her lands in Carinthia to him, thus swelling the already full coffers of the Schwarzenbergs still more.

It is probably true to say that were it not for the Ossiachersee, Villach would be virtually neglected by tourists. As it is the town offers hotel facilities, restaurants and taverns. If you drive into the countryside only a few miles from the town you will discover some fine restaurants like that at Landskron castle, a mile (1.6km) north of Villach. Sixteenth-century Schloss Wernberg, just over a mile (1.6km) east of the city, houses a small pension operated by nuns who live in the convent.

Villach, damaged by fire in 1524, can today boast a baroque Trinity column, some delightful Renaissance houses, including the Paracelsushaus, where the philosopher Theophrastus Paracelsus lived, and a museum. The Schiller park is open from May to October and there a relief model of Carinthia measuring 65ft (20m) long is displayed. The relief enables first-time visitors to pick out places of interest in the town and surrounding countryside. It always intrigues me how many people are fascinated by it. The Fasching festival in February is the highlight of Villach in winter, the Carinthian festival in summer, and for gourmands there is a culinary festival in Carinthia in autumn.

The church of Maria Gail

Before going on to Spittal an der Drau it would be a shame not to cross the Gail river to take a brief glance at the pilgrimage church of Maria Gail, which has retained its rural simplicity and, on that account, is a pleasant change from some of the all too ornate baroque churches which can appear gaudy. The little church of Maria Gail possesses some Romanesque frescoes. Another interesting fact is that some of the inscriptions are in Slovene, thus illustrating that the Slovene minority was also catered for in Carinthia.

Spittal an der Drau

In the opposite direction from Maria Gail, heading westwards, you follow the Drava river to Spittal an der Drau, 25 miles (40km) from Villach. Spittal an der Drau is the chief town of Upper Carinthia and is especially noted for its magnificent Italianate palace, the Schloss Porcia, with its arcaded courtyard.

33 Porcia castle, Spittal an der Drau

Built in the mid-sixteenth century for the Count of Salamanca, and considered to be one of the finest examples of Renaissance buildings in Austria, the castle stands in the centre of the town. Classical plays are performed at the Schloss in July and August, and Spittal an der Drau also has a landing site for gliders. For winter sports enthusiasts there are toboggan runs, skating and curling rinks, so most tastes are catered for in Spittal an der Drau.

An interesting excursion from the town is the Roman settlement of Teurnia about 3 miles (5km) away, which was believed to have been converted to Christianity during the fifth century when it was part of the Roman province of Noricum. Excavations revealed a cemetery church whose mosaic floor appeared to be decorated with Christian symbols. Teurnia was destroyed by Slav invaders during the sixth century.

Millstatt

Carinthia's second largest lake, the Milstattersee, lies at a short distance from Spittal an der Drau. It measures about 8 miles (13km) in length and its waters are warm in summer with temperatures rising to 26°C (79°F). Millstatt lies on the north shore and is the chief resort of the lakeside area. The abbey of Millstatt originated as a Benedictine monastery, founded in the eleventh century by two Bavarian Counts. It flourished until the late fifteenth century when it became a priory of the Knights of St George. These knights constituted a Chivalry or

Military Order founded by Emperor Friedrich III to defend Carinthia and, effectively, Christianity against the Turks, but the Order eventually foundered due to lack of recruits. In 1598 the priory became a Jesuit House which survived until 1773. Statues commemorating the Jesuits can be seen in the main nave of the church. It was the Knights of St George who were responsible for the Gothic vaulting of the cloisters, and these are fittingly commemorated. The abbey is now a hotel.

Carinthia was re-Christianised several times, with each successive overlord trying to surpass the last in building monasteries and churches. Soon Millstatt was to become the chief cultural centre in Carinthia, and the renowned Millstatt manuscript has been in the safe-keeping of the Historical Society since 1845. Millstatt can also claim to be famous for its dumpling festival held in June each year, and its international organ festival in August.

The 1000-year-old Linden tree has lent its name to the fifteenth-century Hotel Lindenhof, housed in a wing of the old abbey. Most hotels are open in summer only. Some are situated right on Lake Millstatt where a skindiving school is an added attraction.

Gmünd

Up the Drava valley leading to Katschberg is situated the picturesque town of Gmünd. Gmünd lies at the junction of the Malta and Lieser valleys at an altitude of 2400ft (730m) and is both a winter and summer resort. The Malta valley, which possesses no less than 30 waterfalls which cascade to the valley bottom, is a noted area for climbers with its peaks of Hochalm at 11,000ft (3350m) (the highest by about 1000ft [300m]), the Sauleck, Reitereck, and Reisseck. The Malta-Hochalm toll road leads to Austria's highest dam, situated at 6000ft (1830m). Though not a smart winter sports resort, Gmünd nevertheless has a ski school, ski jumps and toboggan runs. At Malta you will find the Sporthotel on the toll road. Situated at over 6000ft (1830m) it has wonderful views over Austria's highest artificial lake.

The town of Gmünd was of strategic importance to the Archbishops of Salzburg as it was situated on the trade route from Nuremberg to Venice, which led to Katschberg higher up the valley. Fortified towns in Carinthia, such as Gmünd, revealed a special kind of town planning with the town square shaped in a rectangle and sandwiched between the town's gateways.

Two castles dominate Gmünd. The older ruined castle, which dates from the fifteenth century, overlooks the city's rooftops, while the mid-seventeenth-century Neues Schloss with its twin towers was built by Christoph Lodron, the brother of Paris Lodron who was born in 1619, and was the architect of Salzburg's Residenz. A fascinating and unusual feature of Gmünd is a chapel in which mass is celebrated only twice a year, at Whitsun and Easter. Furthermore the chapel is divided by a footpath – the altar being on one side, the congregation on the other!

Those wishing to reach Salzburg fast can make use of the Katschberg tunnel, open from April to September. Otherwise the climb over the Katschberg Pass is the normal route. From Katschberg, two roads lead to Radstadt in Land Salzburg, while the Möll valley extends to East Tirol. The Drava river flows on past Greifenburg, bypassing the Weissensee (the fourth largest of Carinthia's lakes). A few villages huddle on its shores and are slowly beginning to attract holidaymakers. From Winklern the road ascends to Döllach where gold and silver were once mined, to Heiligenblut, a winter sports centre over 4000ft (1220m) high and noted for its mountain climbing school. As well as a few small hotels Heiligenblut has a camp site and a Youth Hostel. In the distance you can now pick out the Grossglockner, and shortly you will be at the tollgate where the road leads to the Franz-Josefs-Höhe, ascending to close on 8000ft (2440m). In the days when the Emperor Franz Josef explored the Grossglockner there were no roads, so it is to his credit that he got as far as he did, and to commemorate his journey, the Höhe (height) was named in his honour.

SALZBURG

Most of Europe's major cities have undergone change in one way or another, but Salzburg would seem to be the exception. If Mozart were to return to his city today he would recognise much of it, for Salzburg has remained Austria's showpiece. Few countries have a finer one. The nineteenth-century traveller Alexander von Humboldt, who was born in Salzburg, described it as 'One of the three most beautiful cities on earth'.

The city of about 140,000 people built its reputation on salt which gave both city and province, Land Salzburg, their name. Salt had been mined for centuries and was as precious to the Salzburgers as was the gold to the prospectors of the Klondike rush. Today it comes as no surprise to find them as chauvinistic about their city as the Viennese are about theirs.

Land Salzburg extends for 2762 square miles (7150sq. km) across the lakes of the western Salzkammergut, the eastern part of the Kitzbühler Alps, the northern sector of the Höhe Tauern range, and the western region of the Niedere Tauern. Apart from the city of Salzburg itself, the province has five administrative districts including Hallein, Zell-am-Zee, and St Johann, all of which you pass on the main railway line from Salzburg to Kitzbühel, a journey of two and a half hours.

Salzburg

The city of Salzburg is the headquarters of the provincial government and the seat of the Archbishop of Salzburg. The Prince-Archbishops once dominated this Alpine city which lies at the centre of Austria, but once the boy prodigy Wolfgang Amadeus Mozart began to be talked about, even they with all their power paled into insignificance, for if anyone ever left his imprint on a city it was that particular Salzburger. Born in a house on the Getreidegasse on 27 January 1756, the child prodigy was the son of Leopold Mozart, a violinist and printer from Augsburg and his Austrian-born wife Anna Maria. Today the house where the Mozart family lived, the third floor of a merchant's house, is a museum where Mozart's piano reposes in the study where he embarked upon an unstoppable career which was a thorn in the side of the less dazzling court musician Antonio Salieri. By the age of 14, Mozart had volumes of music to his credit. Until 1777 he lived in Salzburg, when he went to Vienna, but returned to his native city a year later and remained there until 1781. Upon his marriage to Konstanze Weber he settled in Vienna, but while he is buried in St Mark's cemetery there, his wife's remains lie in Salzburg.

To be in Salzburg is to be reminded of its most illustrious son. Everywhere you walk you stumble across Mozart from St Peter's Abbey where his *Mass in C Minor* was heard for the first time on 25 October 1783 and where his *Requiem* is performed annually on the eve of 5 December, the day he died in Vienna, to the Ritter Saal of the Residenz where the ten year old Mozart played some of his own compositions.

What would Mozart's reaction be if he could return for a fleeting moment to his city? Perhaps he would be flattered by the crowds of tourists turning in at that merchant's house on Getreidegasse to gaze upon his memorabilia which includes, as well as music scores and letters in his hand, a lock of his brown hair and several oil paintings of the Mozart family, of Mozart himself decorated as a Knight of the Golden Spur – an honour which had been bestowed on him – of Konstanze, his sister Nannerl, and his two sons Carl and Wolfgang (the former of whom set out for Poland and became a composer, while Wolfgang moved to Milan and became a minor official).

Like all old cities Salzburg has a long history. A Bronze Age settlement had been discovered long before the Celts moved into the area in the eighth century. During the Roman occupation Salzburg was known as Juvavum. It flourished as an administrative centre, but when the Germanic tribes arrived, led by their general Ottokar, they routed the Romans, who left the territory a decade later. Little more was heard until the seventh century when Bishop Hruodbert (Rupert) was sent from Worms as a missionary, and on the ruins of Juvavum he founded St Peter's monastery. He died in 718, by that time having founded the convent of Nonnberg, where he had installed his niece as Abbess.

By 754 an Irishman by the name of Virgil, who was the builder of Salzburg's original cathedral, had been initiated as Bishop of Salzburg, and in 803 Charlemagne arrived in the city and is reputed to have dined in the Keller adjoining St Peter's, which was founded in that same year and which today rates as one of the oldest existing restaurants in Europe. The name Salzburg first appeared in documents as early as 755, but the founding of the diocese of St Boniface had already taken place 16 years earlier.

After Virgil's three-aisled cathedral was destroyed by fire in 845, the ninth century saw much coming and going in Salzburg. Monasteries and convents were being consecrated, engendering visits by neighbouring dignitaries. It was the Prince-Archbishops who commanded the building of the fortress, the cathedral and many of the city's fine churches – 46 of them Roman Catholic, two Protestant.

In the twelfth century, a century after the construction of the Hohensalzburg fortress was begun, the rebuilding of St Peter's Abbey was started as well as the reconstruction of the town.

By the thirteenth century the Bishops had been endowed with the title Princes of the Holy Roman Empire, which meant that their influence extended from Austria into parts of Italy. Salt mining had become profitable, and in addition to running the state they were able to build with the money that was flooding into the church coffers from the salt-mining in the Salzkammergut.

By the fifteenth century, Salzburg had become an imperial city and a succession of Prince-Archbishops one by one took the helm. They commissioned great numbers of buildings, conceiving fantastic ideas of turning Salzburg into another Rome. It was Wolf Dietrich von Raitenau, appointed bishop at 28 years of age, who established himself as a force in the city – a man who created during his tenure the Residenz, the Capuchin Monastery and, in 1606, the Mirabell Palace, formerly called Altenau. With Wolf Dietrich von Raitenau at the helm, the city expanded. When the former cathedral burned down, the ambitious and energetic Wolf Dietrich seized his chance, and commissioned an Italian architect, Scamozzi, to build a much more grandiose edifice which, he hoped, would outshine St Peter's in Rome.

Before Wolf Dietrich von Raitenau could put his plans into effect, however, it was necessary to pull down much of the old town. It was a bold move that was successful. But then Wolf Dietrich von Raitenau, who hailed from the Vorarlberg, was nothing if not controversial. Although Archbishop he contracted a marriage (though most considered his 'wife' to be his mistress) with the alluring Salome Alt, the daughter of a Salzburg merchant, and installed her in his palace.

The salt trade proved almost too profitable for it had made Wolf Dietrich von Raitenau too ambitious, and his clash with the Dukes of Bavaria ended in his incarceration in the Hohensalzburg, where he remained until he died.

His successor, Marcus Sitticus, saw the founding of Salzburg University in 1623. The Prince-Archbishops were subordinate only to the Emperor and thus continued to wield excessive power. Archbishop Paris Lodron, however, was farseeing and, in 1620, began erecting fortificiations in preparation for the Thirty Years' War. Lodron completed the cathedral and the Residenz, both of which were begun by Wolf Dietrich von Raitenau, the latter having been the residence of the Prince-Archbishops since the twelfth century.

By the year 1656, when one of Austria's most celebrated baroque architects, Johann Bernhard Fischer von Erlach, was born, much had happened to Salzburg. A university had been founded and the cathedral consecrated. By the turn of the eighteenth century, Fischer von Erlach, who had returned from five years of study in Italy, was finding commissions in Salzburg as well as Vienna. By 1705 he had designed four churches: the Holy Trinity, University Church, St John's church and St Mark's Ursuline church.

Mirabell

It was on Salome's account that the fabulous Mirabell came to be built, for Wolf Dietrich von Raitenau had it constructed for her, and the gardens laid out by Fischer von Erlach, with their fine statues depicting figures from Greek mythology, for her 15 children to play in. The Pegasus fountain was moved from the Makartplatz and now graces the Mirabell gardens.

The Mirabell, grandiose though it was, with its baroque cherub staircase and sumptuous Marmorsaal (marble room), where today concerts are held for international audiences, was not the only palace of note in the Salzburg of those times. Hellbrunn, the summer residence of Archbishop Marcus Sitticus, with its trick fountains, was just one of them. Families like the Kinskys and the Schwarzenbergs all wanted homes in the fashionable, art-loving city. Composers and musicians all gravitated there, since the arts were patronised by a long line of influential Prince-Archbishops.

If you climb to the top of the Mönchsberg to the Café Winkler, with its casino adding a modern touch, you have the best view of the city, for it lies in a valley, sheltered by mountains, the whole of its Old Quarter intact. From there the domes and spires of the city glitter in sunlight, for another of Salzburg's advantages is that it has many fine, clear days.

The Hohensalzburg

Archbishop Wolf Dietrich von Raitenau's fortress, the Hohensalzburg, is the city's landmark. It is one of the best-preserved medieval fortresses and is well worth the climb to the top, though it can also be reached by a funicular railway. Once the residence of the Prince-Archbishops, it was begun in 1077 when Gebhard, Heinrich IV's chancellor, became Archbishop, but it is the powerful presence of Wolf Dietrich von Raitenau, whose individuality you sense as you enter the rooms, that prevails. The fortress was enlarged during the twelfth century and underwent further structural alterations during the fifteenth and sixteenth centuries, when it was strengthened still further, so that two centuries later it was considered to be impregnable. However, by the nineteenth century it was no longer used for its original purpose and stands today as a reminder of its past.

It is fascinating to step back into the Middle Ages as you wander through the fortress, observing the torture chamber and grand ducal apartments. As in Schönbrunn Palace, the stoves are of particular interest, each room possessing a different, and seemingly more ornate one, until you reach the amazing construction known as the majolica stove in the Golden Chamber.

Before ascending to the Hohensalzburg, visitors are generally informed about the fortress's open-air organ. As you stand in the town square below you can see it jutting from the castle wall. This surprising mechanical organ was built in 1502 and is known as the Salzburg Stier because it is jokingly said to bellow like a bull. In fact the organ is very much part of Salzburg and had chorales written for it by Leopold Mozart, and composer and organist Paul Hofhaymer. It still plays three times a day, usually following the Glockenspiel chimes.

Glockenspiel tower

The Glockenspiel tower overlooking the Residenz-Neugebäude adds a lighthearted touch to the busy goings on of the town. At 7 a.m., noon and 6 p.m. each day, visitors begin to gather to hear the performance. The 35 bell chime, cast in the seventeenth century by Melchior de Haze, was intended for a belfry in Breda, Netherlands, but before the glockenspiel could be set up, the church was burned down, and so it arrived in Salzburg where its musical recitals are enjoyed by everyone.

34 Nonnberg convent at the foot of the Zintersberg mountain

The Nonnberg convent

Below the Hohensalzburg lies the Nonnberg convent where Bishop Hruodbert installed his niece Erentrudis as abbess in the year 700, and which can claim to be the oldest existing religious community for women. It is interesting to speculate on what Erentrudis might have thought about the nunnery today with its community of 50 sisters. The present Benedictine abbey was built on the early foundations during the fifteenth century. If you intend to visit the abbey it is best to check visiting times in advance as they can be somewhat haphazard, especially in winter.

At the foot of the road leading from the Nonnberg and the Hohensalzburg you will notice a wall plaque on one of the houses indicating that Michael Haydn, composer of church music and brother of Josef Haydn, once lived in the shadow of the convent. Archbishop Wolf Dietrich resigned in the sacristy of Nonnberg in 1612 and was henceforth kept as a prisoner in the Hohensalzburg. He was succeeded by Marcus Sitticus who commissioned the court architect, the Italian Santino Solari, to re-design the cathedral. Sitticus's coat of arms, alongside that of Paris Lodron, adorns the pediment between the two towers. By the time the Hellbrunn Palace was completed in 1619 Archbishop Wolf

Dietrich von Raitenau was dead, and the first opera north of the Alps was performed in the Rock Theatre of the palace. It was Monteverdi's *Orfeo* and this opera set the scene for the future musical development of the city.

The cathedral

Churches began to be built right across the city, but few would compete in splendour and magnificence with two of the best-known today – the cathedral and St Peter's Abbey. The cathedral (Dom) stands in the Domplatz and is a mix of several architectural styles dating from its original conception in the eighth century through to the twelfth, when it was reconstructed under Konrad III from a three-aisled church to a five-aisled Romanesque basilica. Prince-Archbishop Wolf von Raitenau laid the foundation stone of the present baroque cathedral, with its twin towers of Salzburg marble, in 1610.

During the Second World War the dome was damaged by a bomb dropped by the US Air Force on the cathedral in October 1944. Restoration of both the dome and the cathedral's interior was completed in 1959. The wrought iron gates show the dates of each major building period – 774, 1628, and 1959. Stucco and marble decorate the interior which, if nothing else, is impressive on account of its sheer size. The crypt contains the tombs of the Prince-Archbishops, while the cathedral museum reveals many of the Dom's treasures, including Hruodbert's crosier, tapestries dating from Archbishop Paris Lodron's time, and a valuable collection of mitres, monstrances and vestments.

The cathedral itself is a virtual feast for visitors with its huge bronze doors symbolising Faith, Hope and Charity, each designed by a different creator. Giacomo Manzu, designer of the door of St Peter's in Rome, was the designer of the Charity Door, so in a sense Wolf Dietrich von Raitenau's desire to make Salzburg's cathedral as great, if not greater, than St Peter's was fulfilled. The German sculptor Ewald Matare, who had designed the door of the Church of Peace in Hiroshima, was the designer of the Hope door, while Toni Schneider-Manzell (Austrian) designed the Faith door in neo-Romanesque style and also designed the pulpit which replaced the old wooden one, and the front cover. Each door is believed to have cost 1,500,000 Austrian schillings.

As befits a musical city, the cathedral's organ was built by the court organ builder Christopher Egedacher in 1702, but has been re-built and enlarged until today it is the proud possessor of 120 registers and 10,000 pipes.

The abbey of St Peter's

Older than the cathedral by almost 80 years is the abbey of St Peter's, Salzburg's only Romanesque church, which was re-constructed in the seventeenth century. Its rococo interior is considered by some Salzburgers to be overloaded and yet the overall effect is stunning. Kremser Schmidt was responsible for some of the fine altar paintings. Frescoes depict the life of St Peter, while paintings tell the life story of St Rupert and St Benedict. Its baroque statues and decoration perfectly represent a city noted for its spectacular churches. Archbishop Wolf Dietrich von Raitenau commissioned the marble tomb of his

35 San Franciscan church, and cathedral, Salzburg

father, Hans Werner von Raitenau, who died in battle in Croatia, which lies in one of the chapels. In St Peter's you will also find plaques to the memory of Nannerl, Mozart's sister who was four years older than Mozart, and a monument to Michael Haydn. It is fortunate that the Prince-Archbishops were not like the sixteenth-century Abbott Martin Hattinger who had had the original frescoes, dating from the twelfth century, whitewashed over.

St Peter's churchyard with its array of wrought iron and gilt tombstones dates from the early seventeenth century and is still in use. It has become a place of pilgrimage for those wishing to see the last surviving examples of Christian catacombs north of the Alps, where Christians fleeing from religious persecution hid out in the rock face. Buried in the graveyard are Michael Haydn and the court painter Andreas Nesselthaler, as well as an American General, Harry Collins, who had commanded a division during the Second World War, and had fallen in love with Salzburg. His tombstone is on the main pathway and catches attention in what must be one of the world's most distinctive resting places.

Guided tours from May to September show you the catacombs in detail. There are three chapels: St Gertrude's, St Maximus', and St Margaret's, which stands in the centre of the churchyard. St Margaret's, built in late Gothic style, is open only on occasions. St Gertrude's chapel dates from the late twelfth century and contains a fifteenth-century fresco of the martyrdom of St Thomas à Becket. The chapel throws an interesting light on religious practices of the times, revealing a clearly marked-off area in the chapel where heathen converts to Christianity were permitted to hear only the first part of the mass. A marble tablet in St Maximus' chapel proclaims that the saint, together with 50 of his disciples, was martyred there, but this claim is now open to speculation.

St Peter's churchyard is noted for its arcades which house family vaults and you can have a fascinating time identifying the occupants, which include the Italian architect Santino Solari (the designer of Hellbrunn palace), the historian Franz Thaddeus Kleinmayrn, and Lorenz Hagenauer (the merchant in whose house the Mozart family lived).

The Franciscan church

One could go on recounting the splendours of Salzburg's churches, but one that really should not be missed is the Franciscan church on Franziskanergasse, just off the Domplatz. The church was built to replace the old St Mary's church which had been burned down in the twelfth century. The nuns of St Peter had obtained permission to hold prayers there while the building was extended. It was completed in the fifteenth century when a spire was added, but a century later, when the church was given over to the Franciscans, the nuns of St Peter were disbanded.

Michael Pacher designed the original high altar, but the one visitors see today is that of Fischer von Erlach which replaced it in 1710, although it incorporated Pacher's original Madonna. Archbishop Wolf Dietrich von Raitenau was also partially responsible for the Franciscan church, for he commissioned the Archbishop's oratory, which was built in Renaissance style in 1606.

Residenzplatz

A few steps from the Franciscan church is Residenzplatz which, until the sixteenth century, had served as a cemetery. With the building of the Dom, however, everything was swept away to make room for a new beginning. A seventeenth-century fountain, made of Untersberg marble and designed by Tommaso di Garona, is the focal point of the square, while the two chief buildings are the baroque cathedral and the Residenz, initiated by Wolf Dietrich von Raitenau, which replaced the original twelfth-century building where the Prince-Archbishops had resided.

The Residenz was the scene of Wolfgang Amadeus Mozart's early symphonies (he conducted them himself) and his first opera, *La Finta Semplice*. It was the palace in which Emperor Franz Josef received Napoleon III, and later Kaiser Wilhelm I. There are more than 170 rooms, of which 15 are state rooms full of tapestries and frescoes. You can make guided tours of these state apartments, which include the Throne Room, the Conference Room where Mozart played, the Audience Room and the Kaisersaal, with its portraits of the Habsburgs.

The Residenzgalerie (art gallery) was also established by the Prince-Archbishops. Open from 10 a.m. to 5 p.m., the gallery contains European paintings from the seventeenth to nineteenth centuries including Rembrandts,

Brueghels, Titians and Rubens, the Residenz-Neugebaude (new building) across the square from the Residenz was commissioned by Wolf Dietrich von Raitenau and was originally intended for the Archbishop's residence. Today it is used as offices by the provincial government. The mighty Prince-Archbishops even had their own pharmacy in town, and this ancient apothecary's shop, the Hofapotheke across the square from the Tomaselli restaurant founded by the Italian opera singer of that name, is one of the oldest surviving pharmacies in Austria.

Mozartplatz

In the Mozartplatz, adjoining the Residenzplatz, stands the Mozart monument sculpted by Ludwig von Schwanthaler. Modern Salzburgers are very disparaging about it, for they can see little likeness between the statue and the real person. The monument was unveiled in 1842 in the presence of Mozart's two sons. Konstanze had died in March, a few months earlier, and it would have been interesting to know what her opinion would have been.

The Mozart house at 8 Makartplatz, where the family was in residence from 1773–87, was damaged during the Second World War and only the original entrance remains.

The right bank

The river Salzach neatly divides the city, the preserved old city clustered on the left bank. Most hotels are situated on the right bank and each day hordes of walkers set off over the bridges to the old city. It is on the right bank, however, that the massive St Sebastian's church, built in late Gothic style and enlarged in the eighteenth century, can add another aspect to the Mozart history; for there, in the cemetery commissioned by Archbishop Wolf Dietrich von Raitenau, lie the tombs of the Mozart and Weber families. Konstanze Weber, Mozart's widow, married Danish diplomat von Nissen, who subsequently wrote Mozart's biography. When Mozart's sister Nannerl died, Konstanze refused to permit her burial in the Mozart family grave, and consequently Nannerl's grave is to be found in St Peter's cemetery. In St Sebastian's graveyard lies the tomb of another celebrated Salzburg character, the physician Paracelsus.

One of the right bank's distinctions is that it has the Mirabell palace, as well as the Capuchin monastery, on the lower slopes of the Kapuzinerberg, from which the mountain takes its name, and the fine Loreto church built by Paris Lodron during the Thirty Years' War as a sanctuary for refugee nuns. At the foot of the Kapuzinerberg lies the Old City Gate, the Inneres Steintor. Also on the right side of the river lies the Mozarteum Music Academy, the Marionette Theatre and the Landestheater. The Salzburg Marionetteres have been active for the past 60 years and, as one would expect in the city of Mozart, they devote themselves, in the main, to his operas, such as *Le Nozze di Figaro*, *Die Zauberflöte*, *Die Entführung aus dem Serail*, as well as Johann Strauss's *Die Fledermaus*, Rossini's *Il Barbiere di Siviglia*, and Tchaikovsky's *Nutcracker Suite*.

On the corner of Makartsteg bridge, which links the right bank with the left, lies the Landestheater. Built as a ballroom by Paris Lodron it has been used as a theatre since the eighteenth century. The new theatre, built a century later, was called the Stadttheater, but was renamed Landestheater.

No one had given a thought to a music festival until 22 August 1920 when the first performance of *Jedermann* (whose origin had been the old English morality play *Everyman* which tells the story of the life and death of a rich man) was staged in the cathedral square and marked the beginning of what was to become known as the Salzburg Festival.

Festspielhaus

In the shadow of the Mönchsberg, which stretches the length of the south side of the Hofstallgasse on a site which was once the stables of the Prince-Archbishops, lies the Festspielhaus (Festival Hall), comprising one Small Festival Hall re-designed in 1962/3, and the Large Festival Hall begun in 1956. Once more Fischer von Erlach appears, for in 1693 he was responsible for building the Rocky Riding School, so called because it is hewn out of the rockface just as the galleries of the large Festspielhaus are.

The first festival performance to be staged was Max Reinhardt's production of *Das Grosse Salzburger Welttheater* by Hugo von Hofmannsthal. While the Small Festival Hall stages smaller productions of plays and concerts, the Large Festival Hall is concerned with much more ornate displays. Although Clemens Holzmeister, architect of the Large Festival Hall, had planned his theatre to seat 2400, it was still not large enough, and a part of the steep rocks forming the Mönschberg had to be blasted to make more space. These days the technical installations are considered to be amongst the best of their kind, so much so that the Festspielhaus was used as a model when the Sydney Opera House, the largest opera house in the world, was being constructed.

Today the Salzburg Music Festival has as its participants orchestras from all over the world, including the Berlin Philharmonic and the Boston Symphony Orchestras. It also attracts the Vienna State Opera and some of the world's greatest conductors, among them Claudio Abbado, Ricardo Muti, Lorin Maazel and Neville Marriner. From the last week of July to the end of August more than 160,000 visitors, 60 per cent of them from abroad, flood the city. What started as an idea soon after the First World War, has ended up being one of the most popular events of our time.

Not only is the summer festival a major event but the Easter and Whitsun Festivals, pioneered by Herbert von Karajan, are popular too. Never has there been so much music-making, so much choice or so many venues. From concerts to ballet and opera the annual Salzburg Festival, mounted by the Salzburg provincial government, is a money-spinner for the city. It has firmly established Salzburg as a musical phenomenon. Concerts are held in the two Festival Halls, the Felsenreitschule (renovated in 1970), Cathedral Square, the University Church, the Salzburg Fortress, the Marmorsaal of the Mirabell Palace where winter concerts are also held (it was there that Leopold Mozart gave concerts with his son Wolfgang and daughter Nannerl), the Landestheater, and the Mozarteum.

Since 1970 the Salzburg street theatre has joined in performing, free of charge, plays across the city, in squares and courtyards. The Hellbrunn summer festival also has its devotees rating about 16,000 visitors each year. The setting could not be better – formal gardens, extensive parkland, an open-air theatre, and lively audiences.

The Getreidegasse

The Getreidegasse is Salzburg's picturesque main shopping street, with delightful alleys, each of them with a charm of its own, leading into hidden courtyards containing upmarket boutiques. Arcades are full of merchandise ranging from ultra chic international designer clothes to porcelain, glass, candles and the dried flower and spice bouquets that are a speciality of Salzburg. Above are the wrought iron and gilt shingles based on the original Middle Ages trade signs hung for the benefit of illiterates, so that they could identify specific trades by the painted symbols.

Off the Getreidegasse lies the Judengasse, where the Jewish ghetto flourished until 1404 when the Jews were hounded from the city. This narrow, medieval street was the home of Franz Schubert during August 1825. (He spent that month at no. 8.) In addition to Judengasse and Getreidegasse the best shopping streets are the Griesgasse, Linzergasse and Schwarzgasse, and squares like the Residenzplatz which are full of typically Austrian merchandise. You can spend your schillings on exquisite jewellery, leather, ski clothing and a host of such luxury items.

To make things even simpler the historic centre has been turned into a huge pedestrian area where you can stroll at will. The city fathers, determined to keep out traffic, have instituted four underground car parks comprising 2600 parking places. In the centre of Salzburg the car stays unseen while ancient monuments can be thoroughly inspected. The historic city has been preserved as a living museumpiece, bearing out Hugo von Hofmannsthal's belief that 'Salzburg is the place, more than anywhere else on earth, one would wish to be born'.

Restaurants

But Salzburg is a vibrant museum and not a dusty timepiece, as can be judged by its wide variety of restaurants which range from the ancient Peter's Keller of the Abbey, where you can sample all kinds of game, to the Goldener Hirsch, the best hotel restaurant in town, to the smart, yet rustic K & K (Kaiser und König). Such restaurants as these usually require advance bookings, but in more moderate spots, like the Brasserie serving French and Austrian cuisine, it is not imperative. There are plenty of inexpensive restaurants around, such as the well-established Sternbräu, a great brewery restaurant with its entrance on the Getreidegasse and an ideal spot to try the local Salzburg beer. At the foot of the Hohensalzburg lies another popular place, the Stieglkeller, which serves local beer, and is popular with just about everyone, although open only from May to September.

Like most Austrian towns, Salzburg has its share of cafés and patisseries, such as the Schatz Konditorei in an alley off the Getreidegasse, and the café Tomaselli whose outdoor tables in summer are full to capacity, and where in winter it is difficult to find a seat inside, with everyone catching up on the international newsheets which you take yourself from the wicker stands in the corner.

Art galleries

As well as museums, such as the Rupertinum where the latest modern paintings can be viewed or the Carolino Augusteum which outlines the city's development from prehistoric to modern times, Salzburg has plenty of art galleries, like the well-known Galerie Weltz at Sigmund Haffnergasse. Of interest are the Bürgerspital Almshouses, built in the sixteenth century, in which the pensioners' cells were cut out of rock, one row above the other. Sadly the building suffered war damage and had to be rebuilt in 1790. A building that did survive is the original fifteenth-century bakery on the Schleifertor, whose medieval shopfront still attracts interest.

Entertainment

It is logical to assume that most visitors arrive in Salzburg for musical entertainment rather than night clubs, and as well as concerts and theatres, a variety of wine taverns often put on musical entertainments. There are discotheques, however, and the Salzburg Tourist Information Office can inform you about what's new in town. In fact, you need not be shy about making outlandish requests. They will be kindly and efficiently dealt with, as in the case of the American tourist who wanted to get married in Salzburg and was anxious to find someone to play *Edelweiss* on a violin at the ceremony. The town was searched for a violinist, and the lady got her wish. She was duly married in the city of Mozart to the strains of a melody from *The Sound of Music*.

Hellbrunn Palace

One could easily imagine that Salzburg is a festival city all year round, as one event merges into another, but the rest of the province is worthy of much more than a glance or quick excursion. Within the city area alone there are several palaces, one of the finest being the Schloss Leopoldskron, a rococo mansion built for Prince Archbishop Firmian in the eighteenth century, and another is the Hellbrunn Palace, built during the early seventeenth century at the command of Prince-Archbishop Marcus Sitticus. You can reach Hellbrunn by taking the Hellbrunnerstrasse from the Rudolfsplatz, a distance of 3 miles (5km). It has come to be known in modern times for its trick fountains, which have the habit of showering the unsuspecting visitor, but the palace (which was Marcus Sitticus' hunting lodge and summer residence) is of interest for its eighteenth-century interior, the dining room of which contains a majolica stove, and the domed Octagon which was used as a music room. In the grounds of the palace are fishponds and ancient trees, some of them more than 300 years old. The fountains prove particularly popular with children, due to their unpredictability, as does the Alpine zoo with its deer herds and free-flying vultures.

Robinighof

An interesting house is the eighteenth-century Robinighof in a suburb of Gnigl, where Wolfgang and his sister Nannerl used to stay with the Robinig family who were family friends of the Mozarts. Hills, woods, and lakes border the city. Still in the footsteps of Mozart it is worth looking at the Maria Plain church to the north of the city where the composer wrote his *Coronation Mass* in 1779.

If you are searching for a cure, the Paracelsus Kurhaus, named after the Salzburg physician Paracelsus, has been recognised as a cure resort since 1968. There you can try the brine baths, mineral waters and mud treatments. The complex includes a Roman bath, indoor swimming pool and two saunas. Should you be an admirer of *The Sound of Music* (the film was shot in Salzburg and its environs) there is a *Sound of Music* tour which delivers you to some of the locations, and where you may listen again to the sound track against the background of the Pegasus fountain in the Mirabell gardens, the Nonnberg Abbey where Maria was a novice, and the Salzkammergut countryside.

Salzkammergut

The Salzkammergut is the province's lakeside area and is easily reached by local bus. Schloss Fuschl, once a hunting lodge used by the archbishops, is now a hotel but in the village of Fuschl you can see Emperor Franz Josef's hunting lodge. Wolfgangsee, Mondsee, Traunsee and Attersee, the largest of the Salzkammergut lakes, are all accessible from the city. The Wolfgangsee, which Land Salzburg shares with Upper Austria, stretches for nearly 8 miles (13km). Today St Wolfgang is besieged by tourists due to the popularity of the *White Horse Inn* operetta by Ralph Benatzky. In the twelfth century it was a place of pilgrimage for religious reasons, but those days are long gone.

The Wolfgang lake

At the end of the Wolfgang lake, and much used by the Prince-Archbishops, lies St Gilgen, one of the most delightful in the Salzkammergut, not just because of its shimmering landscapes, but for its connections with the Mozarts. Wolfgang's mother, Anna Maria Pertl, was born there in 1720. His sister Nannerl married the governor of the district, Baron Berchtold zu Sonnenburg, and lived there for some years. A fountain to Mozart's memory was erected in 1927 in front of the Town Hall, and is known as the Mozartbrunnen.

The lakes are the breeding ground of romantic tales when long lazy summer days make the setting ideal for the occasional flash of fantasy. But one must not forget the salt which was so important both to the city of Salzburg and to the province, providing not only economic growth but brine for spas like Bad

36 Krimml waterfall

Ischl, Badgastein and Bad Hofgastein. Hallein developed during the thirteenth
century around the salt pans of an island in the Salzach and was a much prized
possession of the Prince-Archbishops of Salzburg. The Dürrnberg mines date
from Neolithic times, and today guided tours are in operation lasting about an
hour and a half, during which you will discover how salt was extracted and
utilised.

Spas

The spas of Badgastein and Bad Hofgastein are noted for what used to be called
the 'taking of the waters'. Such waters have been imbibed since the nineteenth
century. Today hotels and shops are a feature of the resort of Badgastein, whose
cure centres on the thermal and radioactive springs of the area, which have been
used since the thirteenth century. The mineral content of the waters is low, but I

am reliably informed that the mountain climate greatly assists. At Bad Hofgastein you can take identical cures to those at Badgastein. This resort has a swimming pool filled with spring water and any number of hotels where you can relax while undergoing treatment. You can ski, too, on the Schlossalm slopes.

The Salzach valley

Salzburg's answer to the Tirol's Stuiben Falls is the Krimml waterfalls of the Salzach valley, which cascade some 1250ft (380m) and are believed to be the finest falls in the Alps. The Salzach valley comprises the Pinzgau (which incorporates the regions of Zell-am-Zee, Saalfelden), the Pongau, the Tennengau and the Flachgau. The lake and the mountains of Zell-am-Zee, in addition to its easy access from Kitzbühel – a 45 minute train ride – make it an area of tourist interest, for it ranks as one of Land Salzburg's top winter sports centres. There are hotels in all categories and plenty of sports in which to participate. Gliding is a major event in Austria, and a big draw in Zell-am-Zee is its gliding school where you can fly from March to December. Alpine gliding is offered to advanced gliders. Whatever else, they can rely on stupendous scenery below while airborne.

Salfelden is a large market town noted for its Noric houses. Cross-country skiing is popular in Saalfelden as is the *après ski*. You can reach Saalfelden by the Salzburg–Innsbruck rail line. East of the town is Bischofshofen, which can lay

37 Zell am See

claim to a fine Gothic church. During the festivals of June to August, wooden staves, measuring up to 23ft (7m) high and decorated with flowers, are born in procession through the streets before being placed in the town's churches.

Salzburg province

Valleys like the Saalach and Salzach, ravines, cataracts, lakes, and flower-filled Alpine pastures make up the landscape of Salzburg province. Caves are less usual and so the Eisriesenwelt caves in the Tennengebirge above the Salzach valley, with their 25 mile (40km) long galleries, merit attention. The ice formations, which in places measure 65ft (20m) thick, are as spectacular as a lunar landscape. The caves can be visited from May to October, but remember to take a jacket or you will freeze, especially at the Eistor (Ice Gate) which reaches 5500ft (1675m) at its highest point, or at the aptly named Ice Palace which ends the amazing subterranean tour.

The Grossglockner road

The region is also noted for its tunnels and mountain passes. None could be more spectacular than the Grossglockner road, opened in 1935, which paved the way for a series of Alpine routes right across Europe. You pay a toll to use the Grossglockner, but the views are stunning, ranging from mountain passes to wooded valleys and corniches. There are plenty of lookouts, such as Edelweisspitze, from which you can glimpse the summit of the Grossglockner, and the Schönek, from which you can see Heiligenblut. Shimmering glaciers and icecaps make this an unforgettable ride.

The Felbertauern road

The Felbertauern road changed the face of the eastern Alps with its 3 mile (5km) tunnel passing between the Grossglockner and Grossvenediger mountain ranges, opening the way between Lienz in the eastern Tirol and Innsbruck in the northern Tirol. The Felbertauern road is open all year round, but the Grossglockner is passable in summer only. Drivers pay a toll on the Felbertauer, which starts at Lienz. The return ticket is valid for the Arlberg tunnel and the Brenner motorway.

As with the Grossglockner, the scenic views from the Felbertauern can be awe-inspiring. On the southern slopes of the Tauern mountains you can spot Weisenstein castle, which once belonged to the Bishops of Salzburg. The Katschberg Pass, which links Salzburg province to Carinthia, over which marched the Roman legions of Septimus Severus, is bypassed by those anxious to reach the Katschberg tunnel despite the toll required. The Radstädter Tauern road was also used by the Romans, while the town of Radstadt, built in the thirteenth century by the Archbishops of Salzburg, still maintains its medieval aura, with well-preserved city walls.

Spas like Badgastein with its six indoor swimming pools, Bad Hofgastein, and the winter sports area of Kaprun with its mountain hotels and lodges are ensuring that visitors no longer go to Land Salzburg just to spend their time in the city of Salzburg, despite its many cultural attractions. The Grossglockner mountain road is one of the loveliest routes over the Alps as well as being the most important. The Rädstadtertauern is the proud possessor of some of the most stunning scenery in the Austrian Alps, but another advantage of Land Salzburg, from a visitor's point of view, is its proximity to Bavaria.

Berchtesgaden, where Adolf Hitler used to stay, is a mere 15 miles (24km) from Salzburg, and still arouses morbid interest. Once an independent principality, it was incorporated into Austria in 1805, and returned to Bavaria in 1809. Hitler's mountain lodge, the Berghof at Obersalzberg no longer exists, but such memories die hard.

TIROL

The last wild mountain ibex was shot in the Tirol in 1708. Although the animal was not a sacred cow, it was nevertheless endowed with similar spiritual values, and was respected due to the superstitious belief that certain extractions from the ibex had curative properties. Today ibex are once again bred in Austria. However, with or without the ibex, the Tirol concentrates on its priorities, although it does have an intriguing number of apothecaries.

Before the First World War, the Tirol extended over a much greater area and included the wine-growing region of the Alto Adige in the South Tirol; but under the terms of the Peace Treaty, the southern part was ceded to Italy. The Tirolese still entertain vague hopes of regaining the territory, but meanwhile have no choice but to accept the situation. These days the Tirol covers an area of 4822 square miles (12,485sq. km) and is divided into two sections – the central Tirol, which is the larger area adjoining the Vorarlberg, and the East Tirol adjoining Carinthia, which tucks part of itself neatly beneath the province of Salzburg.

The British came to regard the Tirol as their discovery, and indeed before the Second World War it proved to be one of Austria's most popular areas for them until they were overshadowed by the influx of German tourists. The British insisted upon spelling the word as 'Tyrol', and the spelling stuck. They liked the stunning scenery of the province, its healthy air, and it quickly became one of the most favoured winter sports areas of Europe, bringing in more foreign currency than any other province.

The Tirol fits the tourist's concept of Austria: chalets and old farmhouses set beneath soaring Alps; and the people themselves decked out in colourful national costume. These are the factors which immediately endeared it to the British who still continue to favour ski resorts such as Söll, Kitzbühel and Igls. While the chirping of cuckoo clocks may not assail your ears, the Tirol, with a population of over 585,000, does maintain its old folk customs and you will hear plenty of brass bands and folkloric music, which apparently appealed both to Goethe and Sir Walter Scott.

Two-thirds of the Tirol is Alpine and the Kitzbüheler Alps and the Arlberg are big tourist attractions. Tour operators are only too eager to send British tourists to the Tirol and every year finds more and more visitors from Britain on the pistes, and in the many good hotels of the region.

Innsbruck

Innsbruck is the Tirol's capital, with a population of 116,000; and as well as being a good ski area there is plenty of sightseeing to do in town. Its name means 'bridge over the Inn'. The town is situated at the junction of several trans-continental communications links – the Inn valley motorway, the Brenner highway, opened in 1969, and the 9 mile (14km) Arlberg road tunnel which provides the first all-weather road link between the Tirol and Vorarlberg, while the Felbertauern motorway links the east and northern Tirol. The Brenner Pass, opened in 1864, is the lowest crossing of the Alps by main rail line.

The Goldenes Dachl

The Tirol became a state in the twelfth century and two centuries later came under the jurisdiction of the Habsburgs, who liked to be near their family seat, Habichtsburg. It was Emperor Maximilian I who, during the fifteenth century, married his second wife, Bianca Maria Sforza, at St James's Church, Innsbruck, and who gave instructions for the Goldenes Dachl (Little Golden Roof) to be built with its balcony covered by a golden canopy, from which he could watch such dances as the Morisken, representing the battle between Christians and Saracens, in the square below. He had ordered the construction as a reminder of his royal wedding and today the Goldenes Dachl is one of the major attractions in Innsbruck, with its ornate carvings of Maximilian I, his two wives, and its gilded wooden tiles. The gilding of copper was a much practised art during the Middle Ages, but the Goldenes Dachl was more resplendent than any gilded church steeple. Completed in 1500, it was Friedrich, Duke of Tirol, who ordered that the roof be covered with gold coins to dispel rumours that he was penniless. It was customary in the Middle Ages to attach such tags to monarchs as 'fearless', 'bold', and the like, but poor Friedrich was lumbered with 'penniless', so he went to great lengths to prove otherwise.

The Hofkirche

Maximilian was determined to be buried, as well as married, in Innsbruck, and decided that his mausoleum should lie in the Hofkirche; but it was never to be, for Maximilian died in 1519 at Wels in Upper Austria, and was buried at Wiener Neustadt. Nevertheless, work on his tomb continued for a further 40 years.

The Hofkirche, open from May to September, was built by Ferdinand I and constructed with three aisles so that it would be large enough to house Maximilian's mausoleum. The style is Gothic with later additions of baroque and the church is of interest for its statuettes of the saints who protected the mighty Habsburgs.

Emperor Maximilian had entertained ambitious plans for his mausoleum. It was to have enormous statues guarding it, as well as the busts of Roman Emperors. It was also to have a kneeling statue of Maximilian himself, at its head. In fact the empty tomb, fenced in by a wrought iron grille, is surmounted by the kneeling figure of Maximilian, with four statues carved by the Belgian craftsman, Alexandre Colin, at each corner. The Hofkirche also contains the tomb of Andreas Hofer, the hero of the Tirolean resistance against Napoleon in 1809, while Archduke Ferdinand II lies in the Silver Chapel, built so he could rest beside his morganatic wife, Philippine Welser. Her tomb was designed by Alexandre Colin, who also carved the statues guarding Maximilian's tomb.

Philippine Welser, who descended from a family of Augsburg merchants, had secretly married Ferdinand when she was 28 years old, and he 30. The Archduke's father, upon hearing that his son had married a commoner, ordered the marriage to remain secret. Any children of the union would automatically be barred from succession. Thus Ferdinand founded Ambras castle and went to live there with Philippine.

During the reign of Empress Maria Theresa, Innsbruck prospered. The Hofburg palace was built and it was there that the Empresses's husband died in 1765, the year in which another dynastic union was formed between Leopold, Duke of Tuscany, and the Infanta of Spain. The state rooms of the Hofburg are open daily from 9 a.m. to 4 p.m. The Riesensaal (Giant's Hall) is noted for its ceiling painted by one of the most outstanding painters of his time, Franz Anton Maulpertsch.

Two other buildings of note are the Helbinghaus, with its eighteenth-century rococo façade, and St James' cathedral, with its baroque interior. It contains a devotional painting, the Mariahilf (Our Lady of Succour) painted by Lukas Cranach the Elder, which Archduke Leopold is thought to have taken with him on his travels.

Innsbruck has its Triumphpforte (Triumphal Arch) which is a reminder both of the marriage of Archduke Leopold and of the death of Emperor Franz I in that same year of 1765. A further example of baroque architecture can be seen in the Landhaus constructed in 1725 for the provincial government. Innsbruck's museums have good displays of Tirolean arts and crafts, and in the Museum of Popular Art you will find a collection of mangers. Other museums to look out for are the Armoury on Zeughausgasse, built by Maximilian I, and the Kaiserjäger Museum at Bergisel which tells the history of the Tirolean Imperial Mountain Regiment. It is open in summer from 8 a.m. to 6 p.m.

The historic quarter of Innsbruck becomes a pedestrian precinct after 10 a.m. each day. Since it played host to the Winter Olympic Games in 1964, Innsbruck added to its tourist facilities by building an airport, an ice stadium (with an indoor ice rink) and a ski jump. For the Winter Olympics of 1976 further equipment was installed, including a speed skating track.

Innsbruck is one of Austria's chief winter sports centres with skiing country which ranges from city suburbs to the Patscherkofel mountain. The New Olympic ice stadium is usually packed with skaters. You can hire horse sleighs, watch ice hockey, go mountain climbing, ride, play golf at the 18 hole course in Rinn, and watch soccer at the Tivoli stadium.

The town itself has plenty to offer, from hotels in all categories to inexpensive Gasthöfe. Restaurants come in many varieties, and during the Innsbruck fair in autumn there is a Tirolean Culinary Week when several restaurants offer gourmet dishes. In the best Austrian tradition there are several patisserie shops, the best known being Munding, on Kiebachgasse, which has been making pastries for over a century. For shopping, the Maria-Theresienstrasse and the arcades of Herzog-Friedrichstrasse are best. There you can find Tirolean hats, loden coats, dirndls, glass and woodcarvings. On the Meranerstrasse can be found *petit point*, handicrafts, gifts and souvenirs, as well as wrought iron, and wood carvings.

Brass bands often perform, especially during festivals, right outside the Goldenes Dachl, and folkloric performances are commonplace through the peak months of July and August. Don't miss a trip to the Stubai Valley (the Stubaital), a beautiful region containing no less than 80 glaciers and 40 Alpine peaks. As well as mountain climbing and skiing on glaciers, the Stubai region is a popular summer resort.

Although winter sports are the major earning power of the Tirol, historic castles and abbeys, such as twelfth-century Wilten monastery, the oldest in the northern Tirol, or Ambras and Stams castles give the province an added dimension.

Wilten

Wilten in the southern part of Innsbruck was known in Roman times as Veldidena, but is today chiefly renowned for its monastery, which was known to exist in 1138 although there was a monastery on the site as early as the eighth century. The present baroque abbey church dates from the seventeenth century and was partly destroyed during the Second World War. Wilten parish church was restored in the mid-eighteenth century and was raised to the stature of a basilica in 1957 to perpetuate the worship of Our Lady of the Four Columns who had drawn pilgrims to Innsbruck in the Middle Ages.

Bergisel

South of Wilten lies Bergisel, which in 1809 was the scene of the battle between the Tirolean Liberation fighters led by Andreas Hofer, and the French. Hofer's memory is perpetuated by a bronze statue, known as the Andreas Hofer monument, while the Tirolean riflemen who died in the First World War are commemorated by a monument to the Imperial Tirolean Riflemen. Ski jumps were built at Bergisel for the Winter Olympics of 1964 and 1976 and since then the wooded slopes have been a big draw both for skiers and walkers who enjoy strolling along the laid-out walkways.

Ambras castle

Since the sixteenth century Ambras castle has been divided into the lower and upper sections. The upper part, once a medieval fortress, comprises the castle in which the Archduke Ferdinand, Regent of the Tirol, resided with Philippine Welser. It was the Archduke's favourite residence, and he proved to be something of an art collector, accumulating various *objets d'art*. His wife's bathroom housed a copper-lined bath of impressive dimensions, measuring 10ft (3m) in length, and must have taken hours to fill. In the lower gallery of Ambras, is a collection of armour and weapons, which include medieval jousting equipment; and in the upper part of the castle can be seen Habsburg portraits dating from the fifteenth century.

The abbey of Stams

Between Silz and Telfs stands the Cistercian abbey of Stams, founded in the thirteenth century by Elizabeth of Bavaria in memory of her son who died in Naples. Stams is situated in a delightful fourteenth-century village. The abbey church is a mix of baroque and Romanesque and contains the rose grille, considered a masterpiece in ironwork, dating from the eighteenth century. Stams Abbey was the burial place of the princes of the Tirol until 1600.

The Inn valley

The Inn valley motorway has made the region considerably easier to explore. It is in the Inn valley that people remark upon that Austrian curiosity, the Föhn, a wind which is particularly prevalent north of the Alps, and especially in the Inn. As well as its aggravating effect on some, its also melts the snow so that sheep can graze in their Alpine pastures; but even so, many use it as an excuse for their bad humour. In the mountains, however, the Föhn puts climbers on the alert, for it can trigger avalanches.

During the Middle Ages, the town of Hall in the Inn valley ranked with Salzburg for its salt, on which the city's economic prosperity relied, and thus it was of special interest to the princes of the Tirol. Today the Oberstadt (Old Quarter) looks much as it did in the sixteenth century. The Fugger family of Augsburg, Europe's first millionaires, made their money in the Austrian mining boom. After Innsbruck, Schwaz, also an important mining town dating back to the twelfth century, was the second most populated city, with its silver and copper mines working at full strength. The Fuggers played a prominent part in the town where, at its height, it was said to be so prosperous miners could afford to have their boots shod with silver nails.

Three miles (5km) from Hall lies Volders, on the river Inn. The Servite church there is of importance due to its fine example of Tirolean baroque. The Servites, founded in Florence in 1233, were a mendicant order of the Servants of the Virgin. Those in Hall dedicate themselves to maintaining pilgrimage sanctuaries throughout Austria.

The Upper Inn valley is a beautiful wooded area of valleys and gorges. Parts of the Imst valley are densely wooded as well as narrow, so its best not to make too many impromptu stops to admire the view. The town of Imst is noted for its houses with rounded grilles, and for its carnival procession, the Schemenlaufen, an event symbolising the battle between evil spirits and the spirits of fertility, which takes place every five years.

Kufstein

Kufstein, about an hour from Innsbruck by fast train, is the last town in the Inn valley and is noted for its awe inspiring fortress, which provided the ideal lookout over Bavaria in time of fraught relationships between Austria and its neighbour. The fortress is the chief tourist attraction of the town, which now gets its share of visitors due mainly to its limestone massif, the Kaisergebirge, which towers above it. You can see one of its crests, the Kaiser, from Kitzbühel, while the Kaisertal, which separates the southern and northern sectors of the Kaisergebirge, runs between Kufstein and the Stripsenjoch. Kufstein can boast a truly picturesque wine tavern, the Batzenhäusl, on Römerhofgasse. The town also has castle plays during July and August.

Mariastein

Eight miles (13km) east of Kufstein lies the castle of Mariastein, with its huge fourteenth-century tower, built on a rock. Originally built for military and defence purposes, Mariastein eventually became noted for its pilgrimages during which pilgrims climbed the Alpine slopes to the chapel of miracles, the Gnadenkapelle.

Achensee

Travelling towards the Tirol's largest lake, the Achensee, brings you to another limestone massif, the Karwendl, which stretches into Bavaria. Its grey cliffs are much loved by climbers, and can be seen to advantage from the Bavarian side of the range. The Achensee was greatly admired by the Tirolean Archdukes, many of whom, including Ferdinand II, established their hunting grounds there. Together with his morganatic wife Philippine Welser, Ferdinand built a shooting lodge near Pertisau. The Achensee, cut off from the upper Inn valley by a dam, was one of the loveliest of Austrian lakes until it was marred by the largest hydroelectric installation in Europe.

While the Archdukes preferred the Achensee, the Duke of Coburg-Gotha had a hunting lodge built during the nineteenth century at Hinteriss, west of Achensee. Pertisau, however, is a great spot for watersports, with a bathing lido. You can hire sailing boats, swim and go rowing. For walkers Pertisau is ideal for it has delightful forest walks and nearby mountains like the Karwendel for hikers and climbers.

Rattenburg

In the Inn valley between Achensee and the Kaisergebirge lies the small and picturesque town of Rattenberg, interesting because of its distinctive sloping roofs camouflaged skilfully by horizontal ledges. In the Hauptstrasse, or main street, you will see some stucco and plenty of pink marble, both in churches and on the door frames of houses. Close by, the ruined castle on the Schlossberg once belonged to the Dukes of Bavaria. It became part of the Tirol in 1505, coming under the jurisdiction of Emperor Maximilian I. During the sixteenth century the Tirol and Bavaria fought over Rattenberg until Emperor Maximilian finally annexed the Lower Inn valley. Today the little town is noted for its glassware made in the local workshops, but during the sixteenth century, Rattenberg, like Schwaz, was noted for its mining of silver and copper.

Kitzbühel

East of Rattenberg lie the Kitzbüheler Alps, between the Wörgl-Saalfelden gap and the Upper Salzach valley, reaching an altitude of 7750 (25,425m) at the Grosser Rettenstein. The chief town is the international ski resort of Kitzbühel, which was settled in prehistoric times, and with a present population of 8000. The earliest mention of Kitzbühel was in the twelfth century when it was written as 'Chizbuhel'. In 1271, Ludwig II of Bavaria granted the town civil rights and, in the early sixteenth century, Kitzbühel became part of the Tirol. From the seventeenth to nineteenth centuries the Counts of Lamberg, who owned Schloss Kaps, ruled the town. As in Schwaz, silver and copper mining brought prosperity to the area, with the Fugger and Rosenberger mines being among the more notable. During the nineteenth century, with the extension of road building, Kitzhühel began to attract foreigners who could enjoy the stunning scenery, mountain views and good clean air. Those who looked for cures in health centres found the mud from Lake Schwarzee ideal for rheumatic complaints.

In 35 minutes you can reach the Kitzbühler Horn, which rises to 6550ft (2000m); from there you can view the summit of the Grossglockner, take the cable car to the Hahnenkamm or drive the 12 miles (19km) to Pass Thurn, whose slopes in winter form the ski pistes of Mittersill. Winter sports enthusiasts have been skiing in Kitzhühel since 1892. With the construction of the Hahnenkamm cable car in 1928, the first cable car in Austria, the Kitzbühel area began to develop as one of the best ski areas in the country. Each ski area is reached by lifts and all lifts are guaranteed free of avalanches, providing you stick to the marked pistes. The Kitzbühel ski circus, which is especially appreciated by expert skiers, contains six major ski areas in the Kitzbüheler Alps: the Hahnenkamm, Kitzbüheler Horn, Pass Thurn, Kirchenberg, Jochberg and Bichlalm.

Whether you ski or not, a ski pass will enable you to ride the cable cars to the mountain tops (all descents are gratis) so that you can get a suntan on the restaurant terraces before the skiers arrive for lunch. Restaurants serve all kinds of food from Austrian specialities like goulasch, to pizzas, crusty ham rolls, local wines and beer. The lower areas beneath the restaurants provide sundecks for lounging. Kitzbühel has over 35 ski runs covering a diversity of terrain. The Hahnenkamm run is one of the most popular, so expect it to be crowded. Although new installations have eased the queuing you can still anticipate 20 minute waits.

Ski buses quickly take skiers out to the chairlift stations, and the ski school operated by the 'Red Devils' is one of the best in Austria. Sixty cable cars and chairlifts operate regularly, and with a ski pass you are entitled to use the indoor swimming pool, Aquarena, as well as having free use of the ski buses. Cross country skiing follows over 19 miles (30km) of trails branching out in a variety of directions. You can try ice skating and curling at the Lebenberg rink. Sleigh riding, tobogganing and ice hockey are just some of the diversions. If you are more of a spectator than a participant then the Hahnenkamm International ski race, which forms part of the World Cup series, is the great event. The downhill

38 Kitzbühel

race starts at 5510ft (1680m) and ends at 2820ft (860m), while the Koasalauf is one of the most important international cross country ski races.

The town of Kitzbühel in its Alpine setting, rising from 2625 to 6560ft (800 to 2000m), has preserved an old world charm. The houses are built in the Bavarian style with sharp sloping roofs and gables. Several old houses are reminders of the mining era, such as the town granary – now the local museum – and three other houses on the Hinterstadt, which were originally the mining Law Courts, the trading office of the Miners Guild, and the erstwhile Mining Authorities Office (now the Forestry Office).

From being one of the world's best-known ski areas, Kitzbühel has developed into a summer resort too. The Kitzbühel Guest Card enables visitors to take part in mountain walking tours, as well as entitling them to reductions at the Schwarzee (the indoor swimming pool), riding and at the tennis centre at Castle Kaps. You can walk to the Schwarzee from the centre of Kitzbühel in no more than 20 minutes, and if you want to enjoy a safe mountain hike, you can do no better than the Hahnenkamm Panorama Walk, designed for novices in the mountains. As for *après ski*, Kitzbühel is full of all kinds of distractions, from café bars to discotheques. It also has a casino where you can chance your luck at roulette, baccarat and blackjack. Restaurants with smart upmarket ambiences, like the Goldener Greif to the popular Londoner – billed as an English pub – cater for all tastes. Streets lined with cafés, bars and restaurant chains, such as the ubiquitous Wienerwald, satisfy all needs. Hotels, pensions and chalets offer all kinds of accommodation, from the homely Tiroler Gasthof, where the proprietor often acts as receptionist and general factotum, to the de luxe establishments like Schloss Lebenberg, a castle hotel with an indoor pool and tennis courts.

The Kitzbühel Tourist Information Office, at Südtirolerplatz 4, next to the cinema, lists every kind of accommodation from rooms to let to pensions and hotels. It can also assist you with ski passes and everything you need to know about winter sports, from where to buy or hire equipment, to ski buses and chair lifts. The ski season starts in December and continues through until April. On New Year's Day everyone gathers for the torchlight ski run, followed by a lively firework display.

The Kitzbühel Heimat museum is well worth a visit and gives an insight into the history of the town, which was Bavarian for nearly 1000 years. There you will encounter the first ski relics to be found, and trace the fascinating history of the mines which, in their time, were the deepest in Europe, thus enabling astute citizens to build their houses from the profits. The museum is situated at 34 Hinterstadt, and comprises three floors which display exhibits of prehistoric mining in Europe, and the northern Alpine Bronze Age. The winter sports section exhibits trophies of Kitzbühel ski racers like Toni Sailer, the triple Olympic champion in the 1956 games, who was born in Kitzbühel, as well as pictures showing the development of winter sports. You can spend a fascinating morning there, as the museum is heated in winter, and opens weekdays from 9 a.m. until noon.

Churches and monasteries are also a feature of Kitzbühel, their spires spiking the backdrop of the Alps. The fourteenth-century church of Our Lady was renovated in baroque style in the mid-eighteenth century, as was the parish church dating from the fifteenth century which was further restored in 1951. Two monasteries are of interest, the Pfarrhof (Parsonage), which was a Dominican monastery between the years 1640–1784 and has been a parish church only since the mid-nineteenth century, and outside the town, the Kapuzinerkloster (Capuchin Monastery), whose founder was one of the Dukes of Lamberg. The Lambergs' castles still stand: Lebenberg dating from 1670 and now a hotel, and Münichau near Reith bei Seefeld which has also been converted to a hotel.

The Zirlerberg lies between Reith bei Seefeld – as steep as 1 : 7 in places – and is a hazardous place to stop. There is a lookout on the only hairpin bend where you can gaze at the jagged Kalkkogel mountain.

Ten miles (16km) away, and situated above Kitzbühel, lies St Johann, sometimes known as Kitzbühel's satellite resort, which in effect has a traditional Tirolean flavour with delightful old inns and a lively atmosphere. The main funicular railway, the Angerer Alm, starts at the town centre and climbs to an altitude of 5250ft (1600m). North of Kitzbühel is Klobenstein on the Ache, noted for its ravine and its two chapels built in the rockface, one of which contains yet another of those ubiquitous Black Virgins. Like Kitzbühel, Seefeld enjoys a fine reputation as an international ski resort, more especially since the Olympic Games were held there. The Princes of the Tirol had the Gothic parish church built in the fifteenth century to keep alive the memory of a host dating from the late fourteenth century, which was believed to work miracles.

From a practical point of view Seefeld has over 75 miles (120km) of trails and provides excellent ski conditions for beginners, intermediates and advanced skiers. Situated at an altitude of 3870ft (1180m), it is a mere half-an-hour by fast train from Innsbruck. Most hotels insist on full or half-board, but there are plenty of pensions if you are just looking for a room. Seefeld has an 18 hole golf course, and swimming in the Wildsee is popular in summer. *Après ski*, like most popular resorts, is fine with a good choice of night clubs and discotheques. Seefeld also has a casino.

Ever since the 1976 Winter Olympics, Igls has taken on a new lease of life, with Olympic bobsled and toboggan runs. Right in the heart of the Tirol, Igls forms part of the Innsbruck winter sports area with a cable car connecting skiers with the Patscherkofel mountain. Igls is a resort much favoured by the British, for as well as the usual winter sports facilities it is close enough to the city for a sophisticated nightlife.

In the Zillertal Alps the resorts of Mayrhofen, and the quiet mountain village of Alpbach, offer contrasting ambiences. The former consists of two main ski areas, the Ahorn and Penken, on opposite sides of the valley. Mayrhofen is a mountaineering and skiing resort with two cable cars, 11 ski lifts and two ski schools. Like most of the hotels in the Zillertal, Mayrhofen's Gasthöfe, hotels and inns have cosy wine taverns and often feature the ever popular Zillertal music at weekends. You can even find *thés dansants* as part of the *après ski* programme, if you are interested in a departure from nine pin bowling.

Alpbach, on the other hand, with its typical wooden chalets, lies in a tranquil valley between the Kitzbüheler Alps and the Zillertal. Unlike some of the up-and-coming resorts it has not sacrificed its individuality to stake its claim, preferring to maintain its peaceful village charm. Its houses are decorated by belfries while the upper storeys have wooden balconies running the length of the building, giving them a genuine Tirolean touch.

The Zillertal

Until 1805, when it became part of the Tirol, the Zillertal region came under the jurisdiction of the Archbishops of Salzburg. The Gerlospass today links the region with the Oberpinzgau in Salzburg province. The Zillertal was noted for its musicians who played harps and zithers and were expert yodellers, said to have excited even the staid Queen Victoria on one of their visits to London. Today a similar Gemütlichkeit exists in the region, with the people of the Zillertal only too pleased for an excuse to celebrate with music and song.

Zell-am-Ziller is the chief town, and on the first Sunday in May the Gauderfest, the Zillertal's answer to Munich's Oktoberfest, takes place when huge amounts of specially brewed Gauderbier, a beverage of high alcoholic content, said to be the strongest between Syracuse and Hammerfest, and brewed specially for the occasion, are consumed. But all is hilarity and mirth,

39 Festival at Zell am Ziller

just as it is in the town of Brixlegg in the Inn valley, noted for its two fine castles – the twelfth-century Schloss Matzen, reposing on a mountainside, and Schloss Kropfsberg, built to defend the Ziller valley – as well as for its collection of unusual tombstones whose inscriptions make strange reading. Maybe the folk of Brixlegg had been sampling Gauderbier, for one of the epitaphs reads, 'Here lies my cantankerous wife, who was the plague of my life'.

The Ötz valley

The mountain villages of Obergurgl and Sölden in the Ötz valley can guarantee snow, for Obergurgl has one of the highest altitudes in the Tirol at 6320ft (1925m). Lower down the slopes is Hochgurgl, the custom-built satellite resort offering a very different atmosphere. Such resorts have not been greeted so enthusiastically in Austria as their equivalents in France, but maybe, given time, they will.

The Ötztal region, with the town of Ötz at its centre, is an area of valleys and ravines. In the valleys, apricot orchards, chestnuts and maize proliferate. The valley region benefits from the Föhn which brings warm conditions to fruit and vegetables which could not otherwise grow in such northerly climes. But the Ötztal with its total surface area of 67 square miles (173sq. km), 31 miles (50km) of which comprise ravines, is an area of glaciers in its upper reaches. The Ötztal Alps include the Wildspitze, the highest mountain in the northern Tirol, which rises to 12,382ft (3774m).

The people of the region are closely linked with those of the Alto Adige. The wild and differing landscape gives rise to tourist attractions like the Stuiben Falls, in a high, wooded ravine by the fast-flowing Otztaler Ache, on whose upper slopes there is a restaurant in case you should wish to linger. As a result of the rushing water the Ötztaler Ache has been worn into deep fissures. The valley is picturesque with its pinewoods and views, and the village inns are pleasant places to stop for refreshment.

Landeck

Landeck lies where the Inn valley and the Arlberg road meet. The town, which is not particularly attractive, is 17 miles (27km) from Imst and is notable chiefly for its thirteenth-century fortified castle. Once an important stronghold, most visitors now pass through on their way elsewhere, taking in as they go the typically Tirolean villages. However, Landeck's parish church at the foot of the castle is one of the best examples of Gothic architecture in the Tirol. Such churches often exhibit finely worked altarpieces, and Landeck's Pfarrkirche is no exception. Dating from the sixteenth century, it represents the Adoration of the Magi. The town is associated with an unusual rite which takes place at Christmas time each year. It is a tradition with the young men of the town to climb the crags surrounding Landeck. Once they reach the top they light circles of wood and roll them down the mountainside. They then try to race the fireballs to see who finishes first. Apart from that, the usually demure town offers mountain ski tours and toboggan runs.

The Arlberg region

The Arlberg region between the Tirol and Vorarlberg contains the road to the Arlberg Pass upon which wheeled traffic travelled for the first time in 1825. It also has the 6 mile (9km) long Arlberg tunnel, completed in 1884, providing the essential link between the Tirol and Vorarlberg. It was at St Anton am Arlberg, one of the best known of Tirolean ski resorts, that Hannes Schneider, born in the Arlberg in 1890, gave his first ski lessons to tourists. He had developed a new style which took the hard work out of learning to ski. It was dubbed 'the swing', but unlike that of a new dance craze which lasts a season, Schneider's ski method endured. He developed not only the theory of a new ski style, but also a way of controlling speed. The Arlberg period lasted ten years from 1920–1930 and in some ski areas you will still find it practised today. In St Anton, with its ski trails and runs, the Hannes Schneider technique is still taught, as well as the latest methods of ski instruction.

In 1927 Hannes Schneider, together with Alfred Lunn, formed the Kandahar Ski Club and today the downhill race named after it is a feature of St Anton, attracting worldwide attention. Like Kitzbühel, the town of St Anton is sufficiently diverting for visitors to enjoy strolling around. The *après ski*, with more than 12 discotheques and night clubs, is lively enough for all age groups. If you are a romantic you can try a moonlight sleigh ride. If not, you could do worse than sample one popular haunt, the Post Bar.

The Arlberg region has 70 ski lifts, and over 125 miles (200km) of pistes, the longest runs being 4 miles (7km). Most hotels are built in the traditional chalet style and offer a high degree of comfort. Hoteliers advise you to book rooms well in advance to avoid disappointment. With the arrival of the last cable car down the mountains at 6 p.m., most of the Tirol's ski resorts resound to the clatter of ski boots as weary skiers trudge back to their hotels and pensions in preparation for the evening's revelries. A dip in the heated indoor swimming pools eases the aches and pains.

An optimistic note is that doctors in the Tirol are used to all kinds of ski accidents and can quickly get you back on the pistes. While the bars of ski resorts are not exactly full of the walking wounded, recounting their suitably embellished tales of Alpine spills, it would be untrue to say accidents don't happen. Mountain rescue teams, however, are just about the fastest in the world, and if you do have an accident, you will elicit much sympathy, for the after-dark atmosphere of Tirolean ski resorts of any size is very sympathetic.

The Zugspitze

High above St Anton lies the mighty Zugspitze. Ehrwald at the western foothills of the Zugspitze cliffs has developed into a resort area from which you can ascend the mountain by the Zugspitze cable car. The Zugspitzkamm, the main cable car station, is situated in a steep ravine. If you are a good enough skier you can ski the Zugspitze from the top, back to Ehrwald. The run is known as the *Gatterlabfahrt* and covers a distance of 14 miles (22km). Adventurous though it is, it's wiser to take a guide, as any mountain rescue team will tell you. If you are simply concerned with the view, the panorama is magnificent. Spread out around you are the Zillertal Alps, and the Ötztal range, the Kaisergebirge, Karwendel and Dachstein, the Arlberg and Grossglockner. You can also look into Bavaria, just as the commander of the Kufstein fortress did in the eighteenth century when repelling Bavarian attacks.

Lienz

At the other end of the spectrum, East Tirol shelters beneath the jagged Dolomites. Before the 1967 opening of the Felbertauern tunnel, it was virtually truncated from the central Tirol. Its frontier with Carinthia, which has remained unchanged since the sixteenth century, is the Tiroler Tor, or City Gate, which consists of a small ravine of the Drava river. Lienz is the East Tirol's chief town, which looks modern on account of the new constructions which had to be made as a result of six major fires in the fifteenth, sixteenth and eighteenth centuries, the last occurring in 1825.

The Counts of Görz selected Lienz as their place of residence and built Bruck castle in the thirteenth century. It was rebuilt three centuries later. The Habsburgs inherited their estates which stretched from the Tauern into Istria. The Rittersaal (Knight's Hall) is of particular interest, as it illustrates how a castle looked in those times. Today Bruck castle houses the Museum of East Tirol with exhibits of Tirolean folklore and handicrafts. In the church of St Andrew's, with its nave dating from the late Gothic period, the sixteenth-century Salzburg marble tombstone of Count Leonard, the last of the Gorz line, can be seen, and in the chapel is the tomb of Albin Egger-Lienz.

The Albin Egger-Lienz Gallery, named after the nineteenth-century painter, some of whose works reflected the Tirol and its inhabitants, exhibits many of his paintings alongside those of contemporary artists. The section devoted to Roman archaeology mostly comprises objects found during the diggings south-east of Lienz at Aguntum. During the Hallstaff period Aguntum, originally an Illyrian settlement, had been a flourishing trading post under the Romans. Objects found during the excavation of Aguntum now lie in the Lienz museum. Slavs, Huns and Avars had, by the end of the sixth century, penetrated the Drava valley, and the bishopric of Aguntum became extinct.

Lienz, lying at an altitude of over 2000ft (610m) in a wooded valley, is a pretty little town with a funicular railway, and has become part of most visitors' itineraries, due to its delightful surroundings. It is within easy reach of the Italian Dolomites, Salzburg and Carinthia. It is a three hour drive from Munich if you go by the Felbertauern highway.

In the restaurants of Lienz, especially at weekends, you are sometimes lucky enough to hear Tirolean music as you sample game and fish specialities, and some hotels have dancing. Lienz has a mountain climbing school, and eight curling rinks as well as chair and ski lifts and a ski school. It also has a gliding field for glider pilots. You can swim in the nearby Tristachersee, and in summer, camping is popular. The East Tirol is full of surprises, not least the village of Obertillach which has a nightwatchman to take care of the villagers.

These days the Tirol produces hydroclectric power in the Zillertal and Kaunertal regions, and at Jenbach in the Inn valley is an electrical power station which utilises the waters of the Achensee. It also produces diesel engines at the Jenbacher Werke, and optical instruments; but it is a cultural centre, too, holding festivals of ancient music and concerts at Ambras Palace, from June to mid-August. Ambras, under the Habsburgs, became a music centre, and

40 Hauptplatz, Lienz

Emperor Ferdinand II selected musicians from all over Europe to make up his court orchestra. These days you can hear fine Renaissance music in the Spanish Hall and listen to international ensembles. Festivals and processions are a major feature of the Tirol, from the Feast of St John on the eve of the summer solstice, when mountains are bathed in floodlights, to the Gauderfest at Zell-am-Ziller, and the Schellerlaufen at Telfs.

    Wherever you are in the Tirol you can be sure of a warm welcome, for Tiroleans like nothing better than a celebration. They are especially skilful at home decorations, and in the autumn you will see wonderful displays of fir cones, dried flowers and sweet-smelling decorative bouquets of dried spices, all tied up with ribbon.

Above all the Tirol is a province for all seasons: from winter, when the sun shines on the glistening glaciers and the winter sports season gets underway, lasting until late spring, when the green pastures take over from snowy scenes, to summer, when clear, blue skies are reflected in lakes, and finally to autumn, when the tourists have packed up and gone home; then, once again, the Tiroleans can briefly have the landscape to themselves.

VORARLBERG

If a visitor arrives from Switzerland in the Vorarlberg, Austria's most westerly province, he could be forgiven for thinking he had never crossed a frontier, for the Vorarlberg, which covers just over 1000 square miles (2590sq. km), and is the smallest of the nine federal provinces, seems much more like eastern Switzerland, not only in landscape but also in language. The Vorarlbergers speak with a distinct Alemannic dialect which sounds quite unlike the language of the rest of Austria.

The Vorarlberg, with its population of over 305,000, of which 26,000 live in the capital city of Bregenz, was an independent state until it joined the Austrian Federal Republic of its own volition. For most of its history it was separated from the rest of Austria, and as a result the Vorarlbergers developed a high degree of self-sufficiency, running their own affairs and expecting little interference.

Long before Empress Maria Theresa introduced her enlightened education policies, through which primary school education spread throughout Austria, the Vorarlberg had its own primary schools. It was in the Vorarlberg that the first telephone call in Austria was made in Dörnbirn, which today is the province's commercial centre with a bigger population – 40,000 more – than Bregenz; while the first electric light was switched on in Kennelbach. Emperor Franz Josef hated speaking on the telephone and so the thrill of being the first to use the instrument fell to an ordinary citizen of the Vorarlberg. It so happened that a chemist in the same town was the first Austrian to drive his own motorcar.

Industry developed rapidly, especially in regard to textiles and lace making, with equipment keeping abreast of the times, so that today's textile factories between Bregenz and Bludenz are as modern as any in Europe. Moreover, you can still find family firms which have withstood all kinds of changes and kept going. If the Vorarlbergers are accused, as they sometimes are, of Kantonligeist, a provincialism that seems outmoded in today's competitive world, it is because for years they lived independent of the rest of Austria, and give the decided impression that they could do so today if necessary. It is perhaps on that account, and also because the province does not altogether typify what people expect of Austria, that the Vorarlberg is less well known than such provinces as Salzburg and the Tirol, which have more than their fair share of tourists.

Vorarlberg, literally meaning 'before the Alps', is well named. It is a land of marshes and Alpine massifs which might almost have become a Swiss canton on the collapse of the Habsburg monarchy in 1918. However, the Treaty of St

Germain decreed that it should be part of the newly formed Austrian Republic. Whether the Vorarlbergers regretted the decision or not, their homeland reflects its Swiss neighbour in its landscape dotted with picturesque houses with sloping roofs, their façades covered in shingles, with shutters at every window.

Bus services connect towns and villages. As for accommodation, apart from the winter ski resorts of Lech and Zürs, most hotels offer reasonable rates, and you will find all kinds of hotels from international ones to small regional ones.

Despite its size – only the province of Vienna which covers 160 square miles (414sq. km) is smaller – the Vorarlberg has an impressive history. Many of its churches date from the ninth and tenth centuries. The castles are connected with powerful landowners like the Montforts, who also built roads and encouraged trade links, and their cousins, the Werdenbergs, who lost out as a result of the ill-advised division of their territories.

The Habsburgs were also eager to become involved, and eventually took possession of the Montfort estates. The Habsburgs were nothing if not avaricious landseekers, enlarging their territory from Switzerland and Alsace and swallowing up vast tracts of Austria. Many families were only too willing to enter the service of the Habsburgs, but by the end of the fourteenth century they were ready to become independent Landesburgers. Even now small castles are as much part of the Vorarlberg as the peasant houses built in the Swiss Appenzell style.

St Columbus arrived in Bregenz around AD 600 and found a ruined township. Germanic tribes had flourished in the Vorarlberg during the third century BC, and, being a good missionary, the saint soon found a church which bore traces of Alemannic idols, so he set about founding a monastery.

It was during the Middle Ages that Bregenz began to assert itself. The Montforts, one of the most feudal families in the Vorarlberg, built their castle at Feldkirch. It is interesting to note that although Bregenz is today the seat of the State government, Feldkirch is the headquarters of the Chamber of Commerce, the highest court, and the financial administration of the province. By the end of the thirteenth century the Montforts had taken over whole areas from the Arlberg to the Rhine. Having gained their new estates they set about cultivating the area. It was necessary, if they wished to encourage trade and persuade people to venture into Alpine regions, to build access routes, and this they did, even to the extent of making a track over the Arlberg massif.

For more than four centuries the Montforts and Werdenbergs dominated the Arlberg, repelling invasions and maintaining their castles of Schattenburg, Neuburg and Hohenbregenz. After the Montforts and Werdenbergs came the Hohenems. By that time, however, serfdom had ceased and the citizens of the Vorarlberg had become true Landesburgers in charge of their own future. Ever since that time the Vorarlbergers were known for their fierce independence and their abhorrence of servility.

From the tourist's point of view the Vorarlberg offers a wealth of changing vistas from the Arlberg massif to Lake Constance. While its winter sports facilities at such international resorts as Zürs and Lech are well known, the lesser-known areas of the Montafon and the Bregenz forest have seen considerable changes, and there is a range of amenities for sports and entertainments available. Bregenz is notable for its summer festival. The New Congress and Festival Hall were opened in 1980.

While centres such as Zürs and Lech, which now have international followings, may charge higher prices during peak months, there are plenty of less-fashionable ski areas to hand, if you are interested only in skiing. You can ski from December to April in most ski centres, where you can hire boots and equipment. The ski areas are also popular in summer for climbers and hikers and look totally different in the cheaper 'green season' when you will find warm sunshine, marvellous views and Alpine meadows full of wild flowers.

You can reach Bregenz directly by train from Vienna and Innsbruck through the Arlberg tunnel. Once in the Vorarlberg, buses link the main towns. If you are driving you can choose your own route and plan your own itinerary. Even if you have arrived by air and are staying in a ski resort, there is no reason why you should not explore further afield. The local Tourist Information Centres are extremely helpful regarding hotel accommodation and transportation. The countryside of the Vorarlberg is well worth investigating, and out of the peak seasons you will find the roads reasonably empty.

Hotel accommodation throughout the Vorarlberg is adequate, and whether you stay in five star hotels or more modest ones, you can be sure of finding your room spotless and the service helpful.

Bregenz, situated on Lake Constance (the Bodensee), is a good place to start your trip. If you're the type who likes to survey a town from a strategic point, be it a castle, hill or mountain, the funicular railway from the centre of town will transport you to Pfander mountain. At over 3000ft (915m) you have a marvellous, panoramic view, and a general idea in which part of town your hotel is located. To your right is the German frontier, in front, a shimmering blue lake.

The Bodensee takes its name from the waters of the lake which were known to the Swiss during the Middle Ages as *bodan*. Today the Bodensee brings tourists to the lake shore for bathing, strolling along the flower-decorated promenades, and sightseeing. In fact the lake shore in particular reminds me of the Swiss lakes, with its strollers, and clear, tranquil views across the water. Sailing regattas are held on the Bodensee in June, while a most unusual festival takes place in Bregenz on Ash Wednesday. At dusk residents of the Old Town don white paper hats and carry their purses to the fountain of the main square. They then proceed to wash their purses to the strains of a funeral march. When this is done a firework display is put on to celebrate.

Across the quay from the Festspiel und Kongresshaus you will see the Vorarlberg museum (Vorarlberger Landesmuseum). Those with a penchant for Austrian arts will find it of special interest, as the eighteenth-century Swiss artist Angelica Kauffmann's paintings are on view. Although she lived both in England and Italy – she was one of the first members of the Royal Academy in 1768 – Angelica Kauffmann is associated especially with the Bregenzerwald. Born in Chur, and daughter of a painter, she showed a precocious talent for art and you can see some of her work at Schwarzenberg.

Like many modern towns, Bregenz has its pedestrian shopping area situated at the foot of the Altstadt (old town), which makes it simpler to get around. From the Innerstadt or lower town, where the Vorarlberg Museum stands, you can walk via the Martinstor to the Pfarrkirche, or parish church of St Gall, first mentioned in an eleventh-century document, in the Oberstadt (upper town) which, with its old town gate, the sixteenth-century Stadttor, and remains of the old thirteenth-century walls, is a world away from the hustle of the lake shore.

Bregenz was first a Celtic settlement which, during the time of Roman occupation, was known as Brigantium. During the Middle Ages it was, for a while, under the domination of the Counts of Bregenz who had previously been known under their Alemannic titles of Aargau, the town where the Habsburgs had their estates. In the early sixteenth century the Counts of Montfort, who then owned Bregenz, passed it over to the Habsburgs, and during the Thirty Years' War it was captured by the Swedes who had attacked the town in 1647. From the mid-thirteenth century, Bregenz had been mentioned in documents as a market town and, despite living under the domination of a succession of noblemen, finally emerged in the nineteenth century as a holiday and winter sports resort which could offer the visitor something different from the other federal provinces.

The title of the Counts of Bregenz had originated from Hohenbregenz castle on the Gebhardsberg where today you can see the ruins of Hohenbregenz. Other places of interest in Bregenz's environs are the already-mentioned Pfander, with its views over Lake Constance, and the winter sports resort of Lochau. In Bregenz itself you will find good, modern hotels and, as the town lies on the Bodensee at an altitude of 1300ft (396m), some fine views. The Zoll restaurant on the Albergstrasse has an excellent reputation. It is expensive but the local specialities and fish dishes are well worth it. Backhendl (fried chicken) can be found in more rustic places, and although there might be a touch of provincial rivalry, is much enjoyed in Bregenz. If you enjoy fishing you might try your luck in landing a pike, carp, or tench in the Bodensee, while Bregenz itself offers plenty of watersports, and riding facilities.

From Bregenz there are regular boat services on Lake Constance to the nearby villages of Lindau and north-westerly Friedrichshafen. If you are driving it is easy to reach both Germany and Switzerland. Regular rail services connect Bregenz with Vienna, Innsbruck, Munich, Berne and Zurich. You can tour the Rhine valley by bus or go just as far as the Bregenzerwald, an area the Bregenz folk like to relax in. There, more than anywhere else in the Vorarlberg, you will get the sensation that you are in Switzerland. The gentle landscape and Appenzell-style farmhouses do not deserve to have hydroelectric power stations which supply Austria as well as West Germany and the Benelux countries, built on their territory.

However, the sunny meadows dappled with mountain flowers manage to vie with the national costumes of the province, for the Vorarlbergers' dress is equally colourful. You will observe folk dress worn by brass bandsmen and also, on special occasions, by the women, who sport a variety of headgear from black straw to pointed hats.

Villages of the Bregenzerwald like Krumbach and Riefensberg are charming.

Schwarzenberg is the birthplace of Angelica Kauffmann's father, and from there you can easily reach Dornbirn where the first telephone was spoken into during the reign of Emperor Franz Josef. Today Dornbirn is the economic capital of the Vorarlberg and the most highly populated of all the province's towns, with a much visited textile fair held every July. Industry has not completely ruined Dornbirn, and the tranquillity of the Bregenzerwald's quaint architecture and old traditions make this part of the province particularly pleasant.

Should you arrive from Liechtenstein, the fortified town of Feldkirch, the oldest in the province, will be your first entrance to the Vorarlberg, for it is only a few miles from the principality's frontier. First known as Veldkirich, it was recorded as such in the ninth century, and parts of the town date from the Middle Ages. It is impossible to ignore the ghosts of the Montforts in Feldkirch, for their main stronghold, the castle of Schattenburg, the largest castle in the province, dominates the town. You arrive at the castle by a steep ascent if you are arriving by car, and up the Schlosssteig steps if you are on foot. The Schattenburg castle reveals a fascinating history. The Montfort family took possession of it in the early thirteenth century, and during its long history Schattenburg has endured sieges and wars such as the Appenzell peasant uprising in the fifteenth century, the Napoleonic invasions of 1790–1800, and, a century earlier, a fire which almost destroyed it.

These days the castle's original appearance has to be imagined from the tower's 12ft (4m) thick walls and conical roof, for it has been refitted as a restaurant. On the death of the last of the Montforts in the fourteenth century, the county was sold to Austria and has remained an Austrian possession ever after.

Feldkirch has conserved its medieval character in its ancient traditions, its enchanting squares and buildings. Interestingly, the Vorarlberg, in keeping with its independent attitude, did not place all its administration at Bregenz, but allowed Feldkirch to handle financial and legal matters. It also had grammar schools where Latin could be learned, enabling the Feldkirch citizens to enter the field of higher education.

Architecturally, the town's plan traces its history back to the thirteenth century, and is well illustrated in the Marktplatz with its solid arcades bordering the square. St John's church was once the monastery of the Knights of St John of Jerusalem who had undertaken to protect the passage through the Arlberg. On the route from Bludenz to Langen in the Arlberg you pass the Klostertal valley named after the refuge, the Klösterle (little monastery), built during the Middle Ages by these Knights to provide assistance to travellers in the Alps.

In the old town of Feldkirch, the cathedral is an excellent example of the late Gothic style with its paired naves, a style which was high fashion in the Alps. (You will have noticed that the parish church at Schwaz in the Tirol has four aisles and two chancels, in contrast to the late Gothic style in France.)

The Marktplatz brings you to the Johanneskirche founded by Count Hugo I of Montfort at the turn of the thirteenth century, while the Kazenturm on Barnhofstrasse, one of the town's old preserved towers dating from the end of the fifteenth century, can claim the largest bell in the Vorarlberg, cast in the mid-seventeenth century.

The Neustadt to the north-east has become the tourist area, with hotels and restaurants contrasting sharply with the lifestyle of the Middle Ages when towns like Rankweil (whose old name was Vinomna), on the road from Feldkirch to Dornbirn, was the chief place of pilgrimage in the Vorarlberg, strongly associated with the Virgin Mary. Before reaching Rankweil, however, you might decide to explore the environs of Feldkirch. Sixteenth-century Schloss Amberg is within easy reach, or you could take a variety of walks through forests and meadows such as the Mädchenwiese (Maiden's meadow). By express train, Feldkirch is about 35 minutes from Bregenz. It has a riding school, and its winter amenities include a skating rink and ski lift.

Rankweil, where the Montforts also had a castle, is a market town with a flourishing textile industry and today remains a place of pilgrimage. The Church of Our Lady is the chief place of worship, and is built into a steep rock which, in the fourteenth century, formed part of the walls of the former Montfort castle. The fortifications still exist, with the old court of the castle now a cemetery. The Gnadenkapelle, or Chapel of Miracles, is noted for its statue of the Virgin, carved in the fifteenth century and an object of worship for many pilgrims who crowd into the church each year.

While there are several churches in the Vorarlberg dating from the ninth and tenth centuries, St Peter's can claim to have been founded by two Merovingian kings, Dagobert and Siegebert in the seventh century. The road from Feldkirch runs into the Ill valley, which sounds off-putting, but is in fact delightful, and brings you to Bludenz, the fourth largest town of the province. Bludenz proves an ideal base for taking in some nearby Alpine regions. The town has a thriving textile industry and is also a chocolate producer. Most visitors do not stay long in Bludenz, preferring the outlying regions of the five valleys, the Brandnertal, Lünersee with its forest of electricity pylons, Klostertal, Montafon and Grosseswalsertal, of which Bludenz forms the junction.

The Grosseswalsertal, or Great Walser valley was settled by the people of the Valais who colonised the Hochtannberg, the 5500ft (1676m) mountain of the Bregenzer Ache, during the Middle Ages, and their descendants still live in wooden chalets similar in style to those of the Rhineland. The Great Walser valley is easy to reach by rail or bus and the mountain villages are great bases for climbers. Even if you don't climb, the ride up the steep gradient is fun and the views stunning.

Easily accessible from Bludenz is the Montafon, the most popular of the Vorarlberg's valleys. It is at Montafon that we again encounter the enterprising Fuggers of Augsberg who took charge of the silver mines at Silbertal, but who were forced to abandon them in the late sixteenth century when the silver deposits were exhausted. Like the Grosseswalsertal, the Montafon is well known to climbers and those with a passion for Alpine scenery. Gaschurn is popular with winter sports enthusiasts, but even if you don't ski you can enjoy it, for the atmosphere is that of a truly authentic mountain area without the worst trappings of tourism. Gaschurn lies between St Gallenkirch and Partenen on a hill above the river Ill. The Silvretta-Nova ski area is ideal for all standards of skiers. Ski parties are guided over the 10,000ft (3050m) peaks of the Silvretta glacier and sleep out in ski huts on the mountainside. Don't overestimate your skiing ability, however, for the terrain is best left to the experts. If you have any doubts stick to trout fishing in the mountain streams.

From Bludenz a fast train will take you back to Bregenz in an hour. If you are staying in town there is a variety of accommodation to choose from, from a 600 year old Gasthof, to traditional, or modern hotels. Should you be in Bludenz during Fasching you will find the town lively with processions, and just after Lent, two ancient traditions which date back to pagan times – the Funkenbrennen, or burning of bonfires (on Midsummer's Day throughout Austria the burning of fires, especially in the mountains, is customary) and Scheibenschlagen, the witches trial – are lively occasions. Spring and summer are the times for brass bands and folkloric displays and you can often encounter religious processions.

Brand, lying at an altitude of over 3000ft (915m) in the Brandnertal was settled by the Valaisians just as was the Hochtannberg and the Kleinwalsertal. These days it is a pleasant mountain resort which doubles as a winter sports centre and health resort set in a wide, open valley over which towers the Schesaplana mountain range. Climbers can take a bus from Bludenz and go to the mountain climbing base of Rhatikon. There they can stay in a hunting tavern or hotel and dance in the evenings in bar cafés. Brand is set in its valley close to the Swiss border and is an ideal ski resort for the beginner and intermediate skier. *Après ski* is typically Austrian – lighthearted and informal, with a real 'gemütlich' ambience. *Thés dansant* and delightful taverns are the singles bars of the slopes.

In comparison, the Kleinwalsertal, comprising a 38 square mile (98sq. km) region, is a complete curiosity, for although it is Austrian, albeit separated from the rest of the country by the Allgau Alps, it is to all intents and purposes a German community. Even the Austrians themselves consider it so. The people of the Kleinwalsertal, however, are a tough breed, clinging to their customs and traditions, despite great technical advances in the rest of the province. The building of a highway in 1930 established better communications, but the people of the Kleinwalsertal, who have enjoyed a special status since 1891, still look, from an economic standpoint, towards Germany rather than Austria. Whereas in earlier days they made their living from farming, they can now look to the developing tourist industry. They frequently use deutschmarks instead of schillings and their postal vans are German, while they buy Austrian stamps paid for in Germany currency. No wonder the Walsers are a puzzle to the uninitiated! But even the Kleinwalsertalers cannot ignore technical advances. About a mile away from Gaschurn, at Partenen, lies one of the biggest power plants of the Vorarlberg; another is situated on an artificial lake, and a third at Latschu, all of them constructed before the Second World War, and later extended.

During the past decade the ski areas of the Vorarlberg have gained in popularity. Previously the Vorarlberg was the province least frequented by tourists, but with the increasing popularity of resorts like Zürs and Lech, winter sports have taken off in the Vorarlberg. The Arlberg massif is reached from Bludenz by way of the Klostertal valley. If you are arriving by train, you get off at Langen for the Vorarlberg side of the Arlberg.

Stuben is the town where the ski pioneer Hannes Schneider was born. It is not as fashionable as Zürs and Lech, but does attract a great number of skiers who can ski there from December until April. Hotel accommodation though is limited, but you can usually find pensions with vacancies. The Flexenpass road, open all winter, runs directly to Zürs and Lech. When you drive along this magnificent piece of Alpine engineering you realise what a difference such mountain passes have made to travelling in the Alps. The road winds up steep mountain cliffs, part of it covered, part open when you catch a dazzling glimpse of Alpine sunlight before plunging back into a tunnel. Higher up the road, the immense barricades you can see were constructed as protection against avalanches.

While Zürs' treeless slopes may not be to everyone's taste, together with Lech this ski resort has suddenly become ultra chic, and has a strong following in Europe. The first modern ski town was installed at Zürs and today it is a resort full of hotels, enough *après ski* to interest the non skiers, and is fast moving up in the popularity polls. At Zürs ski lifts transport you to the 8000ft (2400m) high Trittkopf or lesser Seekopf at over 7000ft (2133m) from where you can ski some of the best downhill runs in Austria.

To reach Zürs take a bus from Langen or St Anton. Hotels in Zürs open from December to the end of April and from June to September. By comparison with other Vorarlberg hotels you will find those in Zürs, especially at peak periods, somewhat expensive, and they will probably become more so as Zürs' popularity soars still further. It is essential to book in advance for the winter season if you want to stay in the hotel of your choice. Every hotel has its inducements, from fireplaces in some of the rooms to smart cocktail bars, and dancing. There are Gasthöfe and pensions too. Zürs' ski school has 40 instructors. You can go up and down the mountains until the last ski lift is abandoned, skate, toboggan or take a sleigh ride.

The upper valley of the Lech runs between the Vorarlberg and Tirol, but the ski resort of Lech is firmly on Vorarlberg soil. Lech, situated at 4800ft (1463m), can trace its earliest tourist development back to the building of the Flexenpass in 1896. Emigrants from the Valais also descended on Lech during their infiltration of the Vorarlberg, and the church is a reminder of their fourteenth-century colonisation. In the ski fields the installations of the Rüfikopf cable car linked Lech to Zürs, giving even better skiing possibilities. While Zürs is higher, Lech has the advantage of being the prettier village, although it does not quite have the cachet of Zürs. Lech has great snow levels and the extensive ski lift system makes it possible to ski both at Zürs and Stuben. A bus connects St Anton and St Christoph in the Tirol, and it is said that if you stay a month in Lech you will still have plenty of pistes to try out.

Lech has three cable cars, 11 ski lifts and two ski schools, in addition to the usual winter sports facilities. Keen anglers can try their hand at catching trout in the stream. Tennis is also popular. During February there are Fasching balls and ski processions. Summer is the season for brass bands and for getting the folk costume out of mothballs.

Hotels in Lech are almost as expensive as those in Zürs. Rates are at their highest during the peak periods of Christmas, February, March and early April. The Post Hotel has been a long time favourite with the *cognoscenti*.

From Lech the road goes on to Warth, another pretty mountain village, where the road splits, running in one direction to the Hochtannberg and the winter sports resort of Schröken with its population of 250. Mountains reaching the everlasting snow level, such as the 8320ft (2535m) Widderstein, give the village a majestic air. Swiss immigrants from the Valais who had settled the Hochtannberg must have felt immediately at home in such surroundings. From Schröken, you can walk right into the Arlberg region and across the Alpine meadows, blooming in spring with edelweiss and gentians, to Körbersee. If you take the opposite direction from Warth am Arlberg, the road leads to Reutte, the administrative capital of Ausserfern. You are now in the Tirol.

For many years the Vorarlberg was unknown to travellers. While they spent time in the ski centres of the Tirol, revelled in the baroque architecture of Vienna, and the music festivals of Salzburg, few strayed into the most westerly of Austria's nine federal provinces. The Vorarlberg remained unexplored. It was dubbed 'unknown Austria', and few troubled themselves to discover what lay behind the tag. The Kleinwalsertal with its inhabitants of Swiss origin, its German customs, and currency which came under the Habsburg sovereignty during the mid-fifteenth century, and which clung, despite changes in the province, to its traditions, was no more than a curiosity. Today the Kleinwalsertal is visited by tourists both in summer and winter and the winter sports areas of Zurs and Lech now vie with Kitzbühel, the once outright ski resort leader.

Prices are lower in the Vorarlberg. Hotels and restaurants are varied, from traditional taverns to modern establishments, which are geared to cater to the increasing tourist trade. The Gemütlichkeit encountered in the Vorarlberg, the informality and fun-loving approach to life is also the key to Austria itself. The province relies unashamedly on tourism these days, but it makes the visitor welcome and does not resent his presence.

Epilogue

With scores of festivals, fêtes and carnivals in Austrian towns and villages, it is small wonder that most tourists find so much to do. The Austrians have agreed on one thing at least, and that is solidarity in the face of tourism. While all Austrians may not approve of the tourist invasion, they have the sound commonsense not to show it. It may be true that in Vienna everyone is against everyone else, but there is one sure way of getting Austrians together and that is for a foreigner to insult Austria or the Austrians, for then they will be collectively up in arms.

In the meantime they are ready to offer visitors a spectacular landscape, arts, music and a substantial slice of history. Even though each of the nine federal provinces may consider itself different, with its own ideas about everyone and everything, the one thing they share is Gemütlichkeit. When an Austrian says 'Wilkommen' he means it. The secret of Austria is that while the traveller *is* in a foreign country he never actually *feels* like a foreigner.

INDEX